Alcohol
Information
for Teens

**TEEN
HEALTH
SERIES**

First Edition

Alcohol Information for Teens

Health Tips about Alcohol and Alcoholism

*Including Facts about Underage Drinking,
Preventing Teen Alcohol Use, Alcohol's Effects
on the Brain and the Body, Alcohol Abuse Treatment,
Help for Children of Alcoholics, and More*

◆

Edited by Joyce Brennfleck Shannon

Omnigraphics

615 Griswold Street • Detroit, MI 48226

Bibliographic Note

Because this page cannot legibly accommodate all the copyright notices, the Bibliographic Note portion of the Preface constitutes an extension of the copyright notice.

Edited by Joyce Brennfleck Shannon

Teen Health Series

Karen Bellenir, *Managing Editor*
David A. Cooke, M.D., *Medical Consultant*
Elizabeth Barbour, *Permissions Associate*
Dawn Matthews, *Verification Assistant*
Laura Pleva Nielsen, *Index Editor*
EdIndex, Services for Publishers, *Indexers*

* * *

Omnigraphics, Inc.

Matthew P. Barbour, *Senior Vice President*
Kay Gill, *Vice President—Directories*
Kevin Hayes, *Operations Manager*
Leif Gruenberg, *Development Manager*
David P. Bianco, *Marketing Director*

* * *

Peter E. Ruffner, *Publisher*

Frederick G. Ruffner, Jr., *Chairman*

Copyright © 2005 Omnigraphics, Inc.

ISBN 0-7808-0741-3

Library of Congress Cataloging-in-Publication Data

Alcohol information for teens : health tips about alcohol and alcoholism : including facts about underage drinking, preventing teen alcohol use, alcohol's effects on the brain and the body, alcohol abuse treatment, help for children of alcoholics, and more / edited by Joyce Brennfleck Shannon.
   p. cm. -- (Teen health series)
   Includes index.
   ISBN 0-7808-0741-3 (hardcover : alk. paper)
   1. Teenagers--Alcohol use--Prevention--Juvenile literature. 2. Alcoholism--Juvenile literature. 3. Alcohol--Health aspects--Juvenile literature. 4. Alcohol--Physiological effect--Juvenile literature. 5. Children of alcoholics--Juvenile literature. I. Shannon, Joyce Brennfleck. II. Series.
   HV5135.A412 2005
   616.86'1'00835--dc22
                                                    2004026518

Table of Contents

Preface

About This Book

The use of alcohol contributes to the leading causes of death among teens—car crashes, murder, and suicide. In fact, alcohol use is a factor in the deaths of more young people than all illegal drugs combined. Despite this, underage alcohol use seems to be increasing. The *2002 National Survey on Drug Use and Health: National Findings* show that alcohol use among adolescents doubled from 2.2 million in 1990 to 4.1 million in 2000 even though all states have had a legal drinking age of 21 since 1988. Current statistics show that 82% of teens have used alcohol by 12th grade. Peer pressure, family relationships, and stress are key factors that impact the decision to drink alcohol, and many teens may believe that alcohol consumption is a normal part of becoming an adult. The reality, however, is that any alcohol use by teens can have negative consequences.

Alcohol Information For Teens provides information about alcohol and the effects it has on adolescents. It describes the underage drinking epidemic, strategies to prevent underage alcohol use, and alcohol's physical, mental, and social impact on teens. It offers information about finding alcohol abuse treatment and includes help for teens who are children of alcoholics. Directories of resources, support groups, and other organizations are provided for readers who need more information.

How To Use This Book

This book is divided into parts and chapters. Parts focus on broad areas of interest; chapters are devoted to single topics within a part.

Part I: Basic Information About Alcohol presents important facts about alcohol and alcoholism. It also sets straight many of the common myths which can lead teens to participate in underage drinking.

Part II: Preventing Teen Alcohol Use encourages teens to make good choices and explains the minimum legal drinking age, zero tolerance, and the dangers of combining alcohol with driving. Tips for handling peer pressure, having alcohol-free parties, and reducing teen access to alcohol are included.

Part III: Underage Drinking examines the related epidemic and how alcohol affects teens' lives. It presents factors that affect teen drinking, including stress and other mental health issues, gender, and alcohol advertising that targets teens.

Part IV: Alcohol's Effects On The Body describes the physical consequences of underage alcohol use. Topics include long-term health consequences, brain and liver damage, and alcohol intoxication and poisoning. This part concludes with information about fetal alcohol syndrome and other risks associated with drinking alcohol during pregnancy.

Part V: Alcohol's Influence On Behavior And Mental Health describes the problems that accompany underage drinking and its links to risky sexual behavior, assault, violence, suicide, and depression. Information is also provided about drug and alcohol interactions and the dangers associated with heavy drinking and binge drinking.

Part VI: Overcoming Alcohol Dependency discusses the topics of finding treatment and breaking alcohol dependency. Tips are also included for people who would like to help a friend face a problem with alcohol.

Part VII: Children Of Alcoholics offers encouragement for teens who have an alcoholic parent. It provides information which will help teens cope and make healthy choices for themselves.

Part VIII: If You Need More Information includes directories of national organizations able to provide information about alcohol, additional reading, and support group contacts.

Bibliographic Note

This volume contains documents and excerpts from publications issued by the following government agencies: Addiction Technology Transfer Center National Office (ATTC); Department of Transportation of National Highway Traffic Safety Administration (DOT–NHTSA); Leadership to Keep Children Alcohol Free; National Center on Birth Defects and Developmental Disabilities (NCBDDD); National Clearinghouse for Alcohol and Drug Information (NCADI); National Institute on Alcohol Abuse and Alcoholism (NIAAA); National Institute on Drug Abuse (NIDA); National Institutes of Health (NIH); NIH Osteoporosis and Related Bone Diseases– National Resource Center; National Women's Health Information Center (NWHIC); National Youth Anti-Drug Media Campaign; Substance Abuse and Mental Health Services Administration (SAMHSA); SAMHSA Center for Substance Abuse Treatment (CSAT); SAMHSA Office of Applied Studies (OAS); and the U.S. Department of Health and Human Services (HHS).

In addition, this volume contains copyrighted documents and articles produced by the following organizations: Al-Anon Family Group Headquarters; American Academy of Family Physicians; American Liver Foundation; Center for Science in the Public Interest; Center on Alcohol Marketing and Youth; Christian Science Publishing Society; Do It Now Foundation; Duke University Medical Center; Indiana Prevention Resource Center at Indiana University; Insurance Institute for Highway Safety, Highway Loss Data Institute; Kaiser Family Foundation; Mothers Against Drunk Driving (MADD); National Association for Children of Alcoholics; National Center on Addiction and Substance Abuse at Columbia University (CASA); National Commission Against Drunk Driving; National Council on Alcoholism and Drug Dependence; Nemours Foundation; Pacific Institute for Research and Evaluation; and the Washington Regional Alcohol Program.

Full citation information is provided on the first page of each chapter. Every effort has been made to secure all necessary rights to reprint the copyrighted material. If any omissions have been made, please contact Omnigraphics to make corrections for future editions.

Acknowledgements

In addition to the organizations listed above, special thanks are due to permissions associate Elizabeth Barbour and to managing editor Karen Bellenir.

About the *Teen Health Series*

At the request of librarians serving today's young adults, the *Teen Health Series* was developed as a specially focused set of volumes within Omnigraphics' *Health Reference Series*. Each volume deals comprehensively with a topic selected according to the needs and interests of people in middle school and high school.

Teens seeking preventive guidance, information about disease warning signs, medical statistics, and risk factors for health problems will find answers to their questions in the *Teen Health Series*. The *Series*, however, is not intended to serve as a tool for diagnosing illness, in prescribing treatments, or as a substitute for the physician/patient relationship. All people concerned about medical symptoms or the possibility of disease are encouraged to seek professional care from an appropriate health care provider.

If there is a topic you would like to see addressed in a future volume of the *Teen Health Series*, please write to:

Editor
Teen Health Series
Omnigraphics, Inc.
615 Griswold Street
Detroit, MI 48226

Locating Information within the *Teen Health Series*

The *Teen Health Series* contains a wealth of information about a wide variety of medical topics. As the *Series* continues to grow in size and scope, locating the precise information needed by a specific student may become more challenging. To address this concern, information about books within the *Teen Health Series* is included in *A Contents Guide to the Health Reference Series*. The *Contents Guide* presents an extensive list of more than 10,000 diseases, treatments, and other topics of general interest compiled from the Tables of Contents and major index headings from the books of the *Teen Health Series* and *Health Reference Series*. To access *A Contents Guide to the Health Reference Series*, visit www.healthreferenceseries.com.

Our Advisory Board

We would like to thank the following advisory board members for providing guidance to the development of this *Series*:

Dr. Lynda Baker, Associate Professor of Library and Information Science, Wayne State University, Detroit, MI

Nancy Bulgarelli, William Beaumont Hospital Library, Royal Oak, MI

Karen Imarisio, Bloomfield Township Public Library, Bloomfield Township, MI

Karen Morgan, Mardigian Library, University of Michigan-Dearborn, Dearborn, MI

Rosemary Orlando, St. Clair Shores Public Library, St. Clair Shores, MI

Medical Consultant

Medical consultation services are provided to the *Teen Health Series* editors by David A. Cooke, M.D. Dr. Cooke is a graduate of Brandeis University, and he received his M.D. degree from the University of Michigan. He completed residency training at the University of Wisconsin Hospital and Clinics. He is board-certified in internal medicine. Dr. Cooke currently works as part of the University of Michigan Health System and practices in Brighton, MI. In his free time, he enjoys writing, science fiction, and spending time with his family.

Part One

Basic Information About Alcohol

Chapter 1

Facts And Myths About Alcohol

Just about everyone knows that the legal drinking age throughout the United States is 21. But did you know that the average American has his or her first drink around age 14? According to the National Center on Addiction and Substance Abuse, almost 80% of high school students have tried alcohol. In an average month, about 9 million American teens drink alcohol.

Teens who drink put themselves at risk for many problems—problems with the law, at school, and with their parents just to name a few. Deciding whether to drink is a personal decision that we each eventually have to make. This article provides the facts about alcohol and teens, including how alcohol affects your body, so you can make an educated choice.

What Is Alcohol?

Alcohol is created when fruits, vegetables, or grains are fermented, that is, when a process using yeast or bacteria causes the sugars in the original food product to change chemically into alcohol. Fermentation is used to produce many necessary items, such as cheeses, penicillin and other medications,

About This Chapter: This information was provided by TeensHealth, one of the largest resources online for medically reviewed health information written for parents, kids, and teens. For more articles like this one, visit www.TeensHealth.org or www.KidsHealth.org. © 2001 The Nemours Center for Children's Health Media, a division of The Nemours Foundation.

B-complex vitamins, and citric acid. Alcohol has different forms and can be a useful product; it can be used as a cleaner, an antiseptic, or a sedative.

So if alcohol is a natural product, why do teens need to be concerned about drinking it? When people drink, alcohol is absorbed into their blood-stream. From there, it affects the central nervous system (the brain and spinal cord), which controls virtually all body functions. Alcohol is a depressant, which means it slows the function of the central nervous system. That's why drinking small amounts of alcohol reduces anxiety. Alcohol actually blocks some of the messages trying to get to the brain. This alters your perceptions, your emotions, and even your movements, vision, and hearing.

More alcohol causes greater changes in the brain, resulting in intoxication. People who have overused alcohol may stagger, lose their coordination, and slur their speech. They will probably be confused and disoriented. Intoxication can make people very friendly and talkative or very aggressive and angry. Reaction times are slowed dramatically. People who are intoxicated may think they're moving properly, when they're not. They may act totally out of character.

When large amounts of alcohol are consumed in a short period of time, alcohol poisoning can result. Alcohol poisoning is very dangerous. Violent vomiting is usually the first symptom, as the body tries to rid itself of the alcohol. Extreme sleepiness, unconsciousness, difficulty breathing, dangerously low blood sugar, seizures, and even death may result.

Why Do Teens Drink?

For starters, people drink and use other drugs to feel good. Experimentation with alcohol during the teen years is common. Some reasons that teens use alcohol and other drugs are:

- curiosity
- it feels good
- to reduce stress and relax
- to fit in
- to feel older

From a very young age, kids are bombarded with advertising messages depicting beautiful, hip young adults enjoying life—and alcohol. This glamorous portrayal of alcohol may not be geared toward teens and kids, but it can still affect them. Plus, many parents and other adults use alcohol socially, having beer or wine with dinner, for example. In this setting, alcohol seems harmless enough, so many teens may think, "Why not?"

Why Shouldn't I Drink?

Even though it is illegal to drink alcohol in the United States until you are 21, most teens can get access to alcohol, or will at least be exposed to it, or have friends who drink. It is therefore up to you to make a decision whether to drink.

Deciding to drink can have many harmful consequences. Some consequences show up right away, and others build up over long periods of time. Consider that the average teen first tries alcohol around age 13. This is long before the body or mind is ready to handle a powerful drug like alcohol. And the earlier kids start drinking, the more likely they will be to develop a problem with alcohol or drugs later in life.

Many teens think that drinking alcohol will help them to relax and feel cool. Actually, drinking often makes people do stupid things. You may end up feeling embarrassed. Drinking also gives you bad breath, and having a hangover is the pits. It's sort of like having the flu: pounding headache, intense thirst, nausea, extreme sensitivity to light and noise, blurry vision, shakiness, exhaustion, and more. Ugh!

Drinking can really damage your ability to perform well at school and sports. Many parents disapprove of their teen's drinking and punishment often results. Teens who drink are more likely to be sexually active and to have unsafe, unprotected sex. Resulting pregnancies and sexually transmitted diseases can change—or even end—lives.

Some teens drink because they think it will help them escape from other problems. Although this may seem like a good idea, drinking always leads to even bigger problems. Teens who drink are more likely to get into fights and commit other crimes. This increases your chance of having legal problems or going to prison. In fact, research shows that 32% of teens under 18 who are in long-term juvenile detention centers were under the influence of alcohol at the time of their crime and/or arrest.

Teens who drink may get seriously hurt or even die. Over 38% of all drowning deaths are alcohol-related. Use of alcohol greatly increases the chance that a teen will be involved in a car accident, homicide, or suicide. If you do choose to drink, don't drink and drive or let your friends drink and drive. According to Mothers Against Drunk Driving (MADD), on one of the most popular prom nights in 1999, as many as 62% of the traffic fatalities were alcohol-related.

Long-term alcohol use can have extremely serious health consequences. Liver damage is a widely known consequence of alcohol abuse. Years of drinking can also damage the pancreas, heart, and brain. Heavy drinking can lead to malnutrition (if alcohol is used as a substitute for food) or obesity (if regular or binge eating is combined with the high calorie content of alcoholic beverages).

How Can I Avoid Drinking?

Let's face it: if all your friends drink, it may be hard for you to say "no thanks." Not doing what many others do can be hard, especially for teens whose friends are really important to them. No one wants to risk feeling rejected or different.

If saying no to alcohol makes you feel uncomfortable, one effective strategy is to blame your parents or another adult for your refusal. Saying, "My parents are coming to pick me up soon," or "I already got in major trouble for drinking once, I can't do it again," can make saying no a little bit easier.

You can also make sure that you and your friends have plans to do something besides just hanging out in someone's basement drinking beer. Plan a trip to the movies, the mall, a concert, or a sports event—anything that gets you out of the house and keeps you active and entertained. You might also organize your friends into a volleyball, bowling, or softball team—any activity that gets you moving.

Myths About Alcohol For Teens

✔ **Quick Tip**

It's time to confront some of the most whacked out lies about alcohol. You've probably heard them all. So, why waste our time trying to de-bunk a bunch of harmless myths? Because they can be pretty fierce.

You may want to say no to your friends, but it's tough. And all these myths are just out there. You have heard all kinds of stuff, but this is the real story. And the next time some loser tries these lines on you, you'll know your stuff.

Myth: Alcohol gives you energy.

Nope. It's a depressant. It slows down your ability to think, speak, and move and all that other stuff you like to do.

Myth: Switching between beer, wine, and liquor will make you more drunk than sticking to one type of alcohol.

Whatever! Your blood alcohol content (BAC—the percent of alcohol in your blood) is what determines how drunk you are. Not the flavors you selected. Alcohol is alcohol.

Myth: You'll get drunk a lot quicker with hard liquor than with a beer or wine cooler.

Did we mention that alcohol is alcohol?

Myth: Everybody reacts the same to alcohol.

Not hardly. There are dozens of factors that affect reactions to alcohol—body weight, time of day, how you feel mentally, body chemistry, your expectations, and the list goes on and on.

Myth: A cold shower or a cup of coffee will sober someone up.

Not on your life. Nothing sobers you up but time. With coffee, you're simply a wide-awake drunk!

continued on next page...

...continued from previous page

Myth: It's just beer. It can't permanently damage you.

Large amounts of alcohol can do major damage to your digestive system. You can hurt your heart, liver, stomach, and several other critical organs as well as losing years from your life.

Myth: It's none of my business if a friend is drinking too much.

If you are a real friend, it is your business. You can't make someone change, but you can be honest. Maybe they'll listen. You might even talk them into getting help.

Myth: The worst thing that can happen is a raging hangover.

Sorry. If you drink enough alcohol, fast enough, you can get an amount in your body that can kill you in only a few hours.

Myth: Drugs are a bigger problem than alcohol.

Alcohol kills 6½ times the number of people killed by cocaine, heroin, and every other illegal drug combined. Ten million Americans are addicted to alcohol. Alcohol is the #1 drug problem of today's youth.

Myth: Alcohol makes you sexier.

The more you drink, the less you think. Alcohol may loosen you up and make someone more interested in sex, but it interferes with the body's ability to perform. And then there's pregnancy, AIDS, sexual assault, car crashes, and worse to worry about. Not sexy at all.

Myth: People who drink too much only hurt themselves.

Every person who drinks has a mother, grandfather, sister, aunt, best friend, boyfriend, or girlfriend who worries about them. Each of the 12 million problem drinkers in this country affects four other people.

Where Can I Get Help?

When a teen realizes that she has a drinking problem, she needs to get help as soon as possible. Contacting a caring adolescent doctor, school guidance counselor, or other trusted adult for advice is usually a good first step. They can refer students to a drug and alcohol counselor for evaluation and treatment. In some states, this treatment is completely confidential. After assessing a teen's problem, a counselor may recommend a brief stay in rehab or outpatient treatment. In recovery, a teen's physical and psychological dependence on alcohol will gradually be overcome.

What Can I Do If I'm Concerned About Someone Else's Drinking?

Many teens live in homes where a parent or other family member drinks too much. This may make you angry, scared, and depressed. It's important to realize that many people can't control their drinking without help. This doesn't mean that they love or care about you any less. Alcoholism does not make people bad; it just means that they have an illness that needs to be treated.

Here are some common signs that a person has a problem with alcohol:

- using alcohol to escape problems

- major changes in personality when drinking

- high tolerance level for alcohol (he or she needs to drink a lot more to get wasted)

- blackouts (not remembering what happened when drinking)

- problems at work or school because of drinking (like missing work or performing poorly)

- inability to control drinking (can't set limits and stick to them)

☞ **Remember!!**
You can enjoy your teen years without alcohol. And alcohol can take a lot of the enjoyment out of your teen years and your life to come.

People with drinking problems can't stop drinking until they are ready to admit they have a problem and get help. This can leave family members and loved ones feeling helpless. The good news is there are many places to turn for help. An adult, whom you trust, such as your guidance counselor, can refer you to a professional or group who can help.

If you have a friend whose drinking concerns you, make sure she is safe. Don't let anyone drink and drive—ever! If you can, try to keep friends who have been drinking from doing anything dangerous, such as trying to walk home at night alone or starting a fight.

Try to remember all the fun stuff you can do with your time instead of drinking. You can play sports, go out with your friends, learn new hobbies, work to earn extra spending money, go shopping, see movies, and dance, just to name a few.

Chapter 2

Alcohol: What You Don't Know Can Harm You

Risks Of Alcohol Use

Alcohol use is illegal under the age of 21 and is very risky business for young people. Did you know that even moderate drinking, under certain circumstances, can be risky? If you drink at more than moderate levels, you may be putting yourself at risk for serious problems with your health as well as problems with family, friends, and coworkers. This chapter explains some of the problems that can be caused by drinking that you may not have considered.

Drinking And Driving

It may surprise you to learn that you don't need to drink much alcohol before your driving ability is affected. For example, certain driving skills can be impaired by blood alcohol concentrations (BAC) as low as 0.02 percent. (The BAC refers to the amount of alcohol in the blood.) A 160-pound man will have a BAC of about 0.04 percent 1 hour after drinking two 12-ounce

About This Chapter: Information in this chapter is from "Alcohol: What You Don't Know Can Harm You," National Institute on Alcohol Abuse and Alcoholism (NIAAA), NIH Publication No. 99-4323. revised 2002. Additional text under the heading "High Potency Alcoholic Beverages: Know The Difference," is reprinted with permission from "FactLine on High Potency Alcoholic Beverages" by the Indiana Prevention Resource Center at Indiana University, http://www.iprc.indiana.edu. © Copyright 2004 The Trustees of Indiana University. All rights reserved.

beers or two other standard drinks on an empty stomach. And the more alcohol you drink, the more impaired your driving skills will be. Although all States have set the BAC limit for adults who drive after drinking at 0.08 percent, driving skills are affected at much lower levels.

Interactions With Medications

Drinking alcohol while taking certain medications can cause problems. In fact, there are more than 150 medications that should not be mixed with alcohol. For example, if you are taking antihistamines for a cold or allergy and drink alcohol, the alcohol will increase the drowsiness that the medicine alone can cause, making driving or operating machinery even more dangerous. And if you are taking large doses of the painkiller acetaminophen (Tylenol®) and drinking alcohol, you are risking serious liver damage.

Social And Legal Problems

The more heavily you drink, the greater the potential for problems at home, at school, at work, with friends, and even with strangers. These problems may include:

- Arguments with or separation from family members;

- Strained relationships with peers and coworkers;

- Absence from or lateness to school or work with increasing frequency;

- Loss of employment due to decreased productivity; and

- Committing or being the victim of violence.

♣ **It's A Fact!!**

What Is A Drink?

A standard drink is:

- One 12-ounce bottle of beer* or wine cooler

- One 5-ounce glass of wine

- 1.5 ounces of 80-proof distilled spirits

*Different beers have different alcohol content. Malt liquor has higher alcohol content than most other brewed beverages.

Alcohol-Related Birth Defects

Drinking alcohol while you are pregnant can cause a range of birth defects, and children exposed to alcohol before birth can have lifelong learning and behavioral problems. The most serious problem that can be caused by drinking during pregnancy is fetal alcohol syndrome (FAS). Children born with FAS have severe physical, mental, and behavioral problems. Because scientists do not know exactly how much alcohol it takes to cause alcohol-related birth defects, it is best not to drink any alcohol during this time.

Long-Term Health Problems

Some alcohol-related problems can occur after drinking over a relatively short period of time. But other problems—such as liver disease, heart disease, certain forms of cancer, and pancreatitis—often develop more gradually and may become evident only after many years of heavy drinking. Women may develop alcohol-related health problems sooner than men, and from drinking less alcohol than men. Because alcohol affects nearly every organ in the body, long-term heavy drinking increases the risk for many serious health problems.

Alcohol-Related Liver Disease

More than 2 million Americans suffer from alcohol-related liver disease. Some drinkers develop alcoholic hepatitis, or inflammation of the liver, as a result of heavy drinking over a long period of time. Its symptoms include fever, jaundice (abnormal yellowing of the skin, eyeballs, and urine), and abdominal pain. Alcoholic hepatitis can cause death if drinking continues. If drinking stops, the condition may be reversible.

About 10 to 20 percent of heavy drinkers develop alcoholic cirrhosis, or scarring of the liver. People with cirrhosis should not drink alcohol. Although treatment for the complications of cirrhosis is available, a liver transplant may be needed for someone with life-threatening cirrhosis. Alcoholic cirrhosis can cause death if drinking continues. Cirrhosis is not reversible, but if a person with cirrhosis stops drinking, the chances of survival improve considerably. People with cirrhosis often feel better, and liver function may improve, after they stop drinking.

About 4 million Americans are infected with hepatitis C virus (HCV), which can cause liver cirrhosis and liver cancer. Some heavy drinkers also have HCV infection. As a result, their livers may be damaged not only by alcohol but by HCV-related problems as well. People with HCV infection are more susceptible to alcohol-related liver damage and should think carefully about the risks when considering whether to drink alcohol.

Heart Disease

Moderate drinking can have beneficial effects on the heart, especially among those at greatest risk for heart attacks, such as men over the age of 45 and women after menopause. However, heavy drinking over a long period of time increases the risk for heart disease, high blood pressure, and some kinds of stroke.

Cancer

Long-term heavy drinking increases the risk of certain forms of cancer, especially cancer of the esophagus, mouth, throat, and larynx (voice box). Research suggests that, in some women, as little as one drink per day can slightly raise the risk of breast cancer. Drinking may also increase the risk for developing cancer of the colon and rectum.

Pancreatitis

The pancreas helps regulate the body's blood sugar levels by producing insulin. The pancreas also has a role in digesting the food we eat. Long-term heavy drinking can lead to pancreatitis, or inflammation of the pancreas. Acute pancreatitis can cause severe abdominal pain and can be fatal. Chronic pancreatitis is associated with chronic pain, diarrhea, and weight loss.

If you or someone you know has been drinking heavily, there is a risk of developing serious health problems. Because some of these health problems can be treated, it is important to see a doctor for help.

High Potency Alcoholic Beverages: Know The Difference

Most people who drink alcoholic beverages have learned to estimate their level of intoxication by counting drinks. Years of education and public service announcements have taught them that average-sized servings of beer, wine, and distilled spirits all have about the same amount of alcohol—roughly one-half ounce of 100% pure, or absolute alcohol. Drinkers have been told that they can reliably predict their level of intoxication using a formula or blood alcohol chart that calculates blood alcohol concentration (BAC) from the number of drinks consumed, body weight, and the amount of time that has passed since the first drink. The dose of alcohol in a typical 12 ounce can of beer is approximately equal to the dose of alcohol in a 4 to 5 ounce serving of wine, or in a shot of whiskey. This average-sized dose of alcohol is equal to one-half ounce of absolute alcohol, and is sometimes called a drink equivalent.

♣ It's A Fact!!

Alcohol is a powerful, mood-altering drug. Alcohol affects the mind and body in often unpredictable ways. Teens lack the judgment and coping skills to handle alcohol wisely. As a result:

- Alcohol-related traffic accidents are a major cause of death and disability among teens. Alcohol use also is linked with youthful deaths by drowning, fire, suicide, and homicide.

- Teens who use alcohol are more likely to become sexually active at earlier ages, to have sexual intercourse more often, and to have unprotected sex than teens who do not drink.

- Young people who drink are more likely than others to be victims of violent crime, including rape, aggravated assault, and robbery.

- Teens who drink are more likely to have problems with school work and school conduct.

- An individual who begins drinking as a young teen is four times more likely to develop alcohol dependence than someone who waits until adulthood to use alcohol.

Source: "Make a Difference—Talk to Your Child about Alcohol," National Institute on Alcohol Abuse and Alcoholism, NIH Publication No. 00-4314, reviewed 2002.

Problems can occur when people rely upon these formulas and charts when drinking beverages of unusually or unexpectedly high potency, particularly if they are unaware of the differences. A 12 oz. can of malt liquor appears very similar to beer, but has about twice beer's potency. An unsuspecting drinker who consumes three cans of malt liquor may be unaware that he or she has consumed the equivalent of a six-pack of beer. Compounding the problem is an archaic rule against potency comparisons in advertising that results in most beer and beer-like products being sold without the alcohol content on the label!

Most natural wine products have about 8% to 12% alcohol by volume, since the yeasts that are used in the fermentation process are killed by higher alcohol concentrations. However, fortified wines have alcohol added to increase their potency, which can be up to 20% by volume or more. Many fortified wine products are deliberately sold at the highest potency—they are the low-cost alcoholic beverages favored by many low-income and skid-row alcoholics. Table 2.2 shows some typical servings of alcoholic beverages that contain more than just a single drink equivalent.

Examples Of High Potency Alcoholic Beverages

- Fortified wines (most low cost brands are sold at nor near 20% alcohol by volume)

- Wine coolers (most are about 6% alcohol by volume, 1.5 times more potent than typical beer)

> **♣ It's A Fact!!**
> Most beer and beer-like products are sold without the alcohol content on the label!

- Specialty wine coolers, such as Cisco (up to 20% alcohol by volume)

- Malt liquors (up to 8% alcohol by volume, nearly twice the potency of typical American beer)

- Neutral grain spirits, such as Everclear (95% alcohol by volume)

- High proof liquors, such as 151 Rum (75.5% alcohol by volume, about twice the potency of other rums)

Table 2.1. Examples of Drink Equivalence

Drink	Absolute Alcohol Equivalent
12 ounces of 4% beer	0.48 ounces of absolute alcohol
5 ounces of 10% wine	0.50 ounces of absolute alcohol
1.25 ounces of 40% vodka (80 proof)	0.50 ounces of absolute alcohol
1.25 ounces of 43% whiskey (86 proof)	0.52 ounces of absolute alcohol

Note: All of the above servings have approximately 0.50 ounces of absolute alcohol

Table 2.2. Typical Servings Of Alcoholic Beverages That Contain More Than Just A Single Drink Equivalent

Dose of alcoholic beverage	Amount of absolute alcohol	Number of drink equivalents
40 ounce bottle of 8% malt liquor	3.2 oz.	6.4 drink equivalents
1.25 ounce shot of 151 proof rum	0.94 oz.	1.9 drink equivalents
12.5 ounce bottle of 20% fortified wine cooler	2.5 oz.	5.0 drink equivalents

Fortified Wines

Fortified wines are wines that have had additional alcohol added to raise their alcohol content. During fermentation, yeasts turn sugars into alcohol; when the alcohol content reaches about 8% to 12%, the yeasts are killed by the alcohol, so naturally-produced wines have maximum alcohol contents about 8% to 12%. Originally, fortified wines were made by adding brandy (distilled wine) to raise the alcohol content, so that the wines would not spoil during shipping. The higher alcohol contents killed off bacteria and other organisms. Port and sherry wines are examples of high-quality fortified wines.

Alcopops Quiz   ♣ It's A Fact!!

1. An alcopop is…
a. A lollipop that may come in a variety of liquor flavors.
b. A sweet, malt-based drink, resembling lemonade, fruit punch, or soda.
c. A nickname for popular alcoholic rock stars.

2. Which of these is not considered an alcopop?
a. Mike's Hard Lemonade
b. Hooper's Hooch
c. Coors Light
d. Smirnoff Ice

3. Which of the following is a reason why teens try alcopops?
a. They like the disguised taste of alcohol.
b. They are easy to get.
c. They are offered at parties.
d. All of the above.

4. What percentage of teens agrees that drinking alcopops make it more likely that teenagers will try other alcoholic beverages?
a. 54%
b. 75%
c. 83%
d. 90%

5. On average, young people begin to drink at what age?
a. 10
b. 13
c. 17
d. 20

6. In the 1990s, what percentage of girls began to drink between the ages of 10–14?
a. 7%
b. 12%
c. 23%
d. 31%

7. Which of the following kills more teenagers?

a. Heroin
b. Cocaine
c. Alcohol
d. Marijuana

8. Alcohol is a(n) ___.

a. Stimulant
b. Depressant
c. Sleep aid
d. Appetite suppressant

9. Who or which of the following agree with the notion that liquor and beer companies target young people with their advertising and that this contributes to underage drinking?

a. Teens
b. Liquor and beer companies
c. Adults
d. Both teens and adults

10. Which of the following are possible ways to help keep alcopops out of the hands of underage drinkers?

a. Label them with clear indications of alcohol content and quote, "This Is Not A Soft Drink."

b. Enact policies to ensure that alcopops are separated from non-alcoholic beverages on store shelves or in store coolers.

c. Put restrictions on youth-oriented images in the design of labeling and advertising of alcopops.

d. All of the above.

Answers:

1. b; 2. c; 3. d; 4. d; 5. b; 6. d; 7. c; 8. b; 9. d; 10. d

Source: "Cool or Clueless? Alcopops Quiz," Girl Power, U.S. Department of Health and Human Services (HHS), 2002, available at http://www.girlpower .gov/adultswhocare/cool/alcopops.asp.

Low priced fortified wines often are produced by adding grain alcohol to low grade wine. They produce a high-potency product that often sells, in screw-top bottles, for between $1 and $2 per 375 ml bottle (about 12.5 ounces). This makes them a favorite of low income alcoholics and of youth, since they produce more intoxication for fewer dollars than just about any other type of alcoholic beverage. A number of cities have developed programs to remove cheap fortified wines from inner city stores, as a means of controlling skid-row alcoholics.

In many states, fortified wines are effectively limited to a maximum of 20% alcohol content by volume, through the operation of tax and licensing laws. Indiana law defined wine as a beverage "that does not contain 21% or more alcohol." This means that if it carries a higher alcohol content it cannot be sold in grocery or convenience stores (which can sell only beer and wine) and it would be taxed at the much higher distilled spirits rates. The federal tax also jumps up for wines with alcohol content above 20%.

Some of the common brands of cheap fortified wines have become pop-culture symbols, memorialized in verse, slang, and song:

- **Night Train "Express"** (the pocket rocket): Sold in 375 ml bottle, this apple flavored wine is popular with both street alcoholics and teenagers. "I'm on the Night Train (I love that stuff), I'm on the Night Train (I can never get enough)."—Guns 'n Roses

- **MD20/20** (Mad Dog): Mogen David Wineries developed this product several decades ago, and it has been a favorite of high school and college students ever since. College students recognize its above average potency and use it as a quick drunk. It is produced in several flavors that resemble soda pop, including: "pink grapefruit," "wild berry," "Hawaiian blue," and "lightning creek," which make it more palatable to the tastes of new drinkers.

- **Thunderbird** ("An American Classic"): Thunderbird was introduced immediately after the repeal of prohibition, by Ernest and Julio Gallo, as a means of gaining market share and becoming the "Campbell Soup company of the wine industry." It is a favorite seller in inner-city, skid-row retail outlets.

- **Richard's Wild Irish Rose:** Another favorite seller in inner-city outlets and other places serving a low-income alcoholic clientele, Wild Irish Rose was immortalized in song by Neil Diamond. Diamond wrote *Cracklin' Rosie* to describe the relationship of an alcoholic to his wine, after a trip to an Indian reservation in Canada in 1970, where he saw the damage caused by cheap fortified wine sold to low income alcoholics. On the reservation, there were many more men than women, so on Saturday nights, those men left without a date made the wine their "woman for the night."

Wine Coolers And Wine Foolers

Wine coolers are mixtures of wine and fruit juice, based upon the "Sangria" punches that were popular in Europe and in the 1960s and 1970s in California. These pre-mixed punches range in potency from 5% to 8%, with most being about 6% alcohol by volume. This is about 1.5 times more potent than beer. Since both are sold in approximately the same size bottles [beer usually is sold in 12 ounce bottles, wine coolers may be 12 ounce or 375 ml (about 12.5 ounce bottles)], many drinkers presume that they are equally potent. The typical wine cooler is one and one-half times as potent as the typical American beer.

During the late 1980s, fortified wine coolers were introduced. These products contained about 20% alcohol by volume, and were blamed for several alcohol overdose deaths of children. Banning Cisco, one of the fortified wine coolers, became popular during the early 1990s, because it was packaged deceptively similar to normal wine coolers, and sold in the same beverage cases in convenience stores. Its very sweet flavorings made it a favorite target of young adolescent shoplifters, who failed to recognize its potency. Former U.S. Surgeon General Antonio Novello called them "wine foolers"—innocent bottles of a concoction of wine and sugared fruit juices that looked like a regular wine cooler, but packed more than three times the punch. One 375 ml bottle contained the alcohol equivalent of five beers—a 750 ml bottle was the equivalent of ten beers.

Malt Liquors

The rise in popularity of gangsta rap music and the gangsta culture has been accompanied by an increase in the popularity of malt liquors. Malt liquors are beer-like beverages that range in potency from about 6% to 8% alcohol by volume, compared with American beer's usual 4% to 4.5%.

Often sold in and consumed directly from 40 oz. bottles, malt liquor packs an extra punch. At about eight percent alcohol by volume, one 40 oz. bottle of Old English 800, a popular brand with young urban black males, has about the same amount of alcohol as six 12 oz. cans of Budweiser. A subculture of malt liquor drinkers who consume directly from 40 oz. bottles wrapped in plain brown bags has become a regular fixture on many big-city street corners.

Although much of the marketing of malt liquor products is directed at African-American audiences, use of rap singers such as "Ice Cube," "Snoop Doggy Dog," and the "Geto Boys" in malt liquor advertising and promotion has increased interest in and use of malt liquor by upscale college students. Urban blacks, however, make up almost 75% of the malt liquor market.

Neutral Grain Spirits And High Proof Liquors

During distillation, water is removed from the alcohol that was produced by the fermentation process to increase its potency. What started as a fermented liquid with an alcohol content of about 10% by volume becomes a distilled spirit with an alcohol content of 40% to 50% (80 proof to 100 proof) or more. In the United States, most distilled spirits have an alcohol content of 40% to 50%. Blood alcohol charts assume this potency when describing the number of drinks needed to reach a given BAC. However, some distilled spirits have more water removed and reach potencies of 60%, 75%, or even 95%.

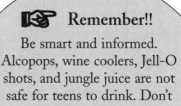

☞ Remember!!

Be smart and informed. Alcopops, wine coolers, Jell-O shots, and jungle juice are not safe for teens to drink. Don't be fooled.

Neutral Grain Spirits Or Grain Alcohol

If nearly all of the water is removed from the fermented liquid, all that is left is the alcohol. Due to alcohol's natural attraction to water, it is very difficult to get all of the water out (which creates "scientific alcohol"), but it is relatively easy to get the alcohol content to 190 or 195 proof (95% or 97.5% alcohol by volume). Neutral grain spirits are nearly pure alcohol. Originally used as an ingredient in other alcoholic beverages or medicine, neutral grain spirits are sold in some states as a high potency beverage in its own right. It is odorless and tasteless, but extremely potent. Since taste is not an object, production costs are very low, and most of the beverage cost is tax.

Everclear is a popular brand of neutral grain spirits. In most states where it is sold, Everclear is sold at 190 proof. Some states require lower potency, such as 155 proof. Everclear is a popular ingredient in some high-potency drinks popular with college students as a means of rapidly increasing BAC. Everclear is an ingredient in such college-student favorites as "Jell-O Shots" and punches such as: Tyson Punch (Everclear, Mellow Yellow, Kool Aid, Orange Juice, Sprite), Purple Jesus (Everclear and purple Kool-Aid), Jungle Juice (Everclear and any Kool-Aid), Smurf Piss (Everclear, Blue Kool-Aid and Mountain Dew), and Romulan Ale (Everclear, Vodka, Blue Curacao, Orange Flower Water).

High Proof Liquors

This category includes distilled spirits products that are sold at more than 100 proof (50% alcohol by volume). Products such as Bacardi 151, a 151 proof rum, and whiskeys sold at 120 and 150 proof, are popular ingredients in college student recipes, such as "Hop, Skip, and Go Naked," "Skylab Fallout," and the "Zombie." Since alcohol more than 100 proof will ignite and burn, these high proof liquors are used in many flaming drinks.

Chapter 3

Blood Alcohol Concentration (BAC)

Facts About Blood Alcohol Concentration

The amount of alcohol in a person's body is measured by the weight of the alcohol in a certain volume of blood. This is called the blood alcohol concentration (BAC). Because the volume of blood varies with the size of a person, BAC establishes an objective measure to determine levels of impairment.

The measurement is based on grams per deciliter (g/dl), and in all states a person is considered legally intoxicated if his or her BAC is .08 g/dl or greater; that is, alcohol makes up eight-hundredths of one percent of the person's blood.

A driver's BAC can be measured by testing the blood, breath, urine, or saliva. Breath testing is the primary method used by law enforcement agencies. Preliminary breath testing can be performed easily during a roadside stop using a hand-held device carried by law enforcement officers. It is non-invasive and can even be performed while the person is still in his or her vehicle.

About This Chapter: This text is excerpted from "Setting Limits, Saving Lives," U.S. Department of Transportation, DOT HS 809 241, April 2001. Additional text under its own heading is from "All U.S. States Now Have .08 BAC Laws, With Passage of Legislation in Delaware," DOT, News Release, National Highway Traffic Safety Administration, Friday, July 2, 2004.

Evidentiary breath testing equipment is evaluated for precision and accuracy by National Highway Traffic Safety Administration (NHTSA). Test instruments approved by NHTSA as conforming to specifications are accurate within plus or minus .005 of the true BAC value.

> **✔ Quick Tip**
>
> 1 drink equals .54 ounces of alcohol. This is the approximate amount found in: one shot of distilled spirits, or one can of beer, or one glass of wine.

The Effect Of Alcohol On Ability

With each drink consumed, a person's blood alcohol content increases. Although the outward appearances vary, virtually all drivers are substantially impaired at .08 BAC. Laboratory and on-road research shows that the vast majority of drivers, even experienced drinkers, are significantly impaired at .08 with regard to critical driving tasks such as braking, steering, lane changing, judgment, and divided attention. In a recent study of 168 drivers, every one was significantly impaired with regard to at least one measure of driving performance at .08 BAC. The majority of drivers (60–94%) were impaired at .08 BAC in any one given measure. This is regardless of age, gender, or driving experience.

> **♣ It's A Fact!!**
>
> In 2002, 41 percent of the motor vehicle deaths were alcohol-related. This translates to an average of one alcohol-related fatality every 30 minutes.
>
> Source: "Laws," *Traffic Safety Facts*, Volume 2, Number 1, March 2004, National Highway Traffic Safety Administration.

All U.S. States Have .08 BAC Laws

On the eve of the busy July 4, 2004 weekend, U.S. Transportation Secretary Norman Y. Mineta commended Delaware for lowering the state's legal threshold for impaired driving to a .08 blood alcohol concentration (BAC). Once signed into law by Gov. Ruth Ann Minner, Delaware

Table 3.1. BAC And Areas Of Impairment

BAC	Impairment
.01	divided attention, choice reaction time, visual function
.02	tracking and steering
.03	eye movement control, standing steadiness, emergency responses
.04	coordination
.05–.06	information processing judgment
.07–.08	concentrated attention, speed control

The risk of being in a motor vehicle crash also increases as the BAC level rises. The risk of being in a crash rises gradually with each BAC level, but then rises very rapidly after a driver reaches or exceeds .08 BAC compared to drivers with no alcohol in their system. A recent NHTSA study indicates that between .08 and .10 BAC, the relative risk of a fatal single vehicle crash varied between 11% (drivers 35 and older) and 52% (male drivers age 16–20).

will become the final state in the country to adopt the .08 BAC legal standard. The District of Columbia and Puerto Rico also have adopted .08.

"We now have a law of the land. The message is clear: nationwide, there is no room on our roads for drinking and driving," said U.S. Secretary of Transportation Norman Y. Mineta. "Tougher laws mean safer roads and more lives saved." According to preliminary estimates, 40 percent—17,401—of 43,220 highway deaths in 2003 were alcohol-related.

With police agencies nationwide stepping up enforcement over the July 4 holiday weekend, National Highway Traffic Safety Administration (NHTSA) Administrator Jeffrey Runge, M.D., warned about the consequences of drinking and driving. "If you drive impaired, it can ruin your life," said Dr. Runge. "It's just not worth the risk of being arrested, or worse, harming someone else."

When Congress adopted the Transportation Equity Act for the 21st Century (TEA-21) in 1998, it provided $500 million in incentives to states adopting .08 BAC laws. With Delaware's approval, all states have met the requirements for those incentive grants.

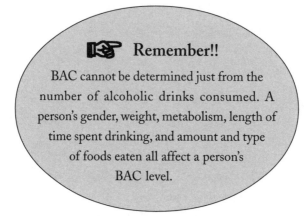

☞ Remember!!

BAC cannot be determined just from the number of alcoholic drinks consumed. A person's gender, weight, metabolism, length of time spent drinking, and amount and type of foods eaten all affect a person's BAC level.

Chapter 4

Alcoholism:
Facts And Frequently Asked Questions

Getting The Facts

What is alcoholism?

Alcoholism, also known as alcohol dependence, is a disease that includes four symptoms:

- **Craving**: A strong need, or compulsion, to drink.

- **Loss of control**: The inability to limit one's drinking on any given occasion.

- **Physical dependence**: Withdrawal symptoms, such as nausea, sweating, shakiness, and anxiety occur when alcohol use is stopped after a period of heavy drinking.

- **Tolerance**: The need to drink greater amounts of alcohol in order to get high.

People who are not alcoholic sometimes do not understand why an alcoholic can't just use a little willpower to stop drinking. However, alcoholism

About This Chapter: Information in this chapter is from "Alcoholism: Getting the Facts," updated May 2002; and under its own heading "Frequently Asked Questions–Alcohol," updated 2003. Both documents are from the National Institute on Alcohol Abuse and Alcoholism (NIAAA).

has little to do with willpower. Alcoholics are in the grip of a powerful craving, or uncontrollable need, for alcohol that overrides their ability to stop drinking. This need can be as strong as the need for food or water.

Although some people are able to recover from alcoholism without help, the majority of alcoholics need assistance. With treatment and support, many individuals are able to stop drinking and rebuild their lives.

What is alcohol abuse?

Alcohol abuse differs from alcoholism in that it does not include an extremely strong craving for alcohol, loss of control over drinking, or physical dependence. Alcohol abuse is defined as a pattern of drinking which results in one or more of the following situations within a 12-month period:

- Failure to fulfill major work, school, or home responsibilities;

- Drinking in situations that are physically dangerous, such as while driving a car or operating machinery;

- Having recurring alcohol-related legal problems, such as being arrested for driving under the influence of alcohol or for physically hurting someone while drunk; and

♣ It's A Fact!!

Recent research reports that 50 to 60 percent of the risk for alcoholism is genetically determined, for both men and women. Genes alone do not preordain that someone will be alcoholic; features in the environment along with gene environment interactions account for the remainder of the risk. Research suggests that many genes play a role in shaping alcoholism risk. It is considered genetically complex, distinguishing it from genetic diseases, such as cystic fibrosis, that result primarily from the action of one or two copies of a single gene and in which the environment plays a much smaller role, if any.

Source: "The Genetics of Alcoholism," *Alcohol Alert*, No. 60, July 2003, National Institute on Alcohol Abuse and Alcoholism.

- Continued drinking despite having ongoing relationship problems that are caused or worsened by the drinking.

Although alcohol abuse is basically different from alcoholism, many effects of alcohol abuse are also experienced by alcoholics.

Alcoholism Treatment

The type of treatment a person receives depends on the severity of their alcoholism and the resources that are available in their community. Treatment may include detoxification (the process of safely getting alcohol out of the body); taking doctor-prescribed medications, such as disulfiram (Antabuse®) or naltrexone (ReVia™) to help prevent a return (or relapse) to drinking once drinking has stopped; and individual and/or group counseling. There are promising types of counseling that teach alcoholics to identify situations and feelings that trigger the urge to drink and to find new ways to cope that do not include alcohol use. These treatments are often provided on an outpatient basis.

Because the support of family members is important to the recovery process, many programs also offer brief counseling and family therapy as part of the treatment process. Programs may also link individuals with vital community resources, such as legal assistance, job training, childcare, and parenting classes.

Alcoholics Anonymous

Virtually all alcoholism treatment programs also include Alcoholics Anonymous (AA) meetings. AA describes itself as a worldwide fellowship of men and women who help each other to stay sober. Although AA is generally recognized as an effective mutual help program for recovering alcoholics, not everyone responds to AA's style or message, and other recovery approaches are available. Even people who are helped by AA usually find that AA works best in combination with other forms of treatment, including counseling and medical care.

Can alcoholism be cured?

Although alcoholism can be treated, a cure is not yet available. In other words, even if an alcoholic has been sober for a long time and has regained health, he or she remains susceptible to relapse and must continue to avoid all alcoholic beverages. Cutting down on drinking doesn't work; cutting out alcohol is necessary for a successful recovery.

However, even individuals who are determined to stay sober may suffer one or several slips, or relapses, before achieving long-term sobriety. Relapses are very common and do not mean that a person has failed or cannot recover from alcoholism. Keep in mind, too, that every day that a recovering alcoholic has stayed sober prior to a relapse is extremely valuable time, both to the individual and to his or her family. If a relapse occurs, it is very important to try to stop drinking once again and to get whatever additional support you need to abstain from drinking.

Frequently Asked Questions

Is alcoholism a disease?

Yes, alcoholism is a disease. The craving that an alcoholic feels for alcohol can be as strong as the need for food or water. An alcoholic will continue to drink despite serious family, health, or legal problems.

Like many other diseases, alcoholism is chronic, meaning that it lasts a person's lifetime; it usually follows a predictable course; and it has symptoms. The risk for developing alcoholism is influenced both by a person's genes and by his or her lifestyle.

Does alcoholism treatment work?

Alcoholism treatment works for many people. But just like any chronic disease, there are varying levels of success when it comes to treatment. Some people stop drinking and remain sober. Others have long periods of sobriety with bouts of relapse. And still others cannot stop drinking for any length of time. With treatment, one thing is clear, however: the longer a person abstains from alcohol, the more likely he or she will be able to stay sober.

Do you have to be an alcoholic to experience problems?

No. Alcoholism is only one type of an alcohol problem. Alcohol abuse can be just as harmful. A person can abuse alcohol without actually being an alcoholic—that is, he or she may drink too much and too often but still not be dependent on alcohol. Some of the problems linked to alcohol abuse include underage drinking; not being able to meet work, school, or family

♣ **It's A Fact!!**

What are the signs of a drinking problem?

- Have you ever felt you should cut down on your drinking?

- Have people annoyed you by criticizing your drinking?

- Have you ever felt bad or guilty about your drinking?

- Have you ever had a drink first thing in the morning (as an eye opener) to steady your nerves or get rid of a hangover?

One yes answer suggests a possible alcohol problem. If you answered yes to more than one question, it is highly likely that a problem exists. In either case, it is important that you see your doctor or other health care provider right away to discuss your answers to these questions. He or she can help you determine whether you have a drinking problem, and if so, recommend the best course of action.

Even if you answered no to all of the above questions, if you encounter drinking-related problems with your job, relationships, health, or the law, you should seek professional help. The effects of alcohol abuse can be extremely serious—even fatal—both to you and to others.

responsibilities; drunk-driving arrests and car crashes; and drinking-related medical conditions. Under some circumstances, even social or moderate drinking is dangerous—for example, when driving, during pregnancy, or when taking certain medications.

Are specific groups of people more likely to have problems?

Alcohol abuse and alcoholism cut across gender, race, and nationality. Nearly 14 million people in the United States—1 in every 13 adults—abuse alcohol or are alcoholic. In general, though, more men than women are alcohol dependent or have alcohol problems. And alcohol problems are highest among young adults ages 18–29 and lowest among adults ages 65 and older. We also know that people who start drinking at an early age—for example, at age 14 or younger—greatly increase the chance that they will develop alcohol problems at some point in their lives.

Can a problem drinker simply cut down?

It depends. If that person has been diagnosed as an alcoholic, the answer is no. Alcoholics who try to cut down on drinking rarely succeed. Cutting out alcohol—that is, abstaining—is usually the best course for recovery. People who are not alcohol dependent but who have experienced alcohol-related problems may be able to limit the amount they drink. If they can't stay within those limits, they need to stop drinking altogether.

✔ Quick Tip

How To Help An Alcoholic

Helping someone who is an alcoholic can be a challenge. An alcoholic can't be forced to get help except under certain circumstances, such as a violent incident that results in court-ordered treatment or medical emergency. But you don't have to wait for someone to hit rock bottom to act. Many alcoholism treatment specialists suggest the following steps to help an alcoholic get treatment:

Stop all cover ups. Family members often make excuses to others or try to protect the alcoholic from the results of his or her drinking. It is important to stop covering for the alcoholic so that he or she experiences the full consequences of drinking.

Time your intervention. The best time to talk to the drinker is shortly after an alcohol-related problem has occurred—like a serious family argument or an accident. Choose a time when he or she is sober, both of you are fairly calm, and you have a chance to talk in private.

Be specific. Tell the family member that you are worried about his or her drinking. Use examples of the ways in which the drinking has caused problems, including the most recent incident.

State the results. Explain to the drinker what you will do if he or she doesn't go for help—not to punish the drinker, but to protect yourself from his or her problems. What you say may range from refusing to go with the person to any social activity where alcohol will be served, to moving out of the house. Do not make any threats you are not prepared to carry out.

What is a safe level of drinking?

For most adults over 21, moderate alcohol use—up to two drinks per day for men and one drink per day for women and older people—causes few if any problems. (One drink equals one 12-ounce bottle of beer or wine cooler, one 5-ounce glass of wine, or 1.5 ounces of 80-proof distilled spirits.) However, certain people should not drink at all including:

- People younger than age 21

- People who plan to drive or engage in other activities that require alertness and skill (such as using high-speed machinery)

Get help. Gather information in advance about treatment options in your community. If the person is willing to get help, call immediately for an appointment with a treatment counselor. Offer to go with the family member on the first visit to a treatment program and/or an Alcoholics Anonymous meeting.

Call on a friend. If the family member still refuses to get help, ask a friend to talk with him or her using the steps just described. A friend who is a recovering alcoholic may be particularly persuasive, but any person who is caring and nonjudgmental may help. The intervention of more than one person, more than one time, is often necessary to coax an alcoholic to seek help.

Find strength in numbers. With the help of a health care professional, some families join with other relatives and friends to confront an alcoholic as a group. This approach should only be tried under the guidance of a health care professional who is experienced in this kind of group intervention.

Get support. It is important to remember that you are not alone. Support groups offered in most communities include Al-Anon, which holds regular meetings for spouses and other significant adults in an alcoholic's life, and Alateen, which is geared to children of alcoholics. These groups help family members understand that they are not responsible for an alcoholic's drinking and that they need to take steps to take care of themselves, regardless of whether the alcoholic family member chooses to get help.

You can call the National Drug and Alcohol Treatment Referral Routing Service (Center for Substance Abuse Treatment) at 1-800-662-HELP (4357) for information about treatment programs in your local community and to speak to someone about an alcohol problem.

- People taking certain over-the-counter or prescription medications
- People with medical conditions that can be made worse by drinking
- Women who are pregnant or trying to become pregnant
- Recovering alcoholics

Is it safe to drink during pregnancy?

No, drinking during pregnancy is dangerous. Alcohol can have a number of harmful effects on the baby. The baby can be born mentally retarded or with learning and behavioral problems that last a lifetime. We don't know exactly how much alcohol is required to cause these problems. We do know, however, that these alcohol-related birth defects are 100-percent preventable, simply by not drinking alcohol during pregnancy. The safest course for women who are pregnant or trying to become pregnant is not to drink alcohol at all.

Does alcohol affect older people differently?

Alcohol's effects do vary with age. Slower reaction times, problems with hearing and seeing, and a lower tolerance to alcohol's effects put older people at higher risk for falls, car crashes, and other types of injuries that may result from drinking.

Older people also tend to take more medicines than younger people. Mixing alcohol with over-the-counter or prescription medications can be very dangerous, even fatal. More than 150 medications interact harmfully with alcohol. In addition, alcohol can make many of the medical conditions common in older people, including high blood pressure and ulcers, more serious. Physical changes associated with aging can make older people feel high even after drinking only small amounts of alcohol. So even if there is no medical reason to avoid alcohol, older men and women should limit themselves to one drink per day.

Does alcohol affect women differently?

Yes, alcohol affects women differently than men. Women become more impaired than men do after drinking the same amount of alcohol, even when differences in body weight are taken into account. This is because women's bodies have less water than men's bodies. Because alcohol mixes with body water, a given amount of alcohol becomes more highly concentrated in a woman's body than in a man's. In other words, it would be like dropping the same amount of alcohol into a much smaller pail of water. That is why the recommended drinking limit for women is lower than for men. In addition, chronic alcohol abuse takes a heavier physical toll on women than on men. Alcohol dependence and related medical problems such as brain, heart, and liver damage progress more rapidly in women than in men.

Is alcohol good for your heart?

Studies have shown that moderate drinkers—adult men who have two or less drinks per day and adult women who have one or less drinks per day—are less likely to die from one form of heart disease than are people who do not drink any alcohol or who drink more. It's believed that these smaller amounts of alcohol help protect against heart disease by changing the blood's chemistry, thus reducing the risk of blood clots in the heart's arteries.

☞ **Remember!!**

The best way for teens to avoid alcoholism is to never start drinking alcohol. If you already have an alcohol problem, tell someone and get help now.

However, if you are a nondrinker, you should not start drinking solely to benefit your heart. You can guard against heart disease by exercising and eating foods that are low in fat. And if you are pregnant, planning to become pregnant, have been diagnosed as alcoholic, or have another medical condition that could make alcohol use harmful, you should not drink.

If you can safely drink alcohol, are 21, and you choose to drink, do so in moderation. Heavy drinking can actually increase the risk of heart failure, stroke, and high blood pressure, as well as cause many other medical problems, such as liver cirrhosis.

When taking medications, must you stop drinking?

Possibly. More than 150 medications interact harmfully with alcohol. These interactions may result in increased risk of illness, injury, and even death. Alcohol's effects are heightened by medicines that depress the central nervous system, such as sleeping pills, antihistamines, antidepressants, anti-anxiety drugs, and some painkillers. In addition, medicines for certain disorders, including diabetes, high blood pressure, and heart disease, can have harmful interactions with alcohol. If you are taking any over-the-counter or prescription medications, ask your doctor or pharmacist if you can safely drink alcohol.

Part Two

Preventing Teen Alcohol Use

Chapter 5

Be In Charge Of Your Life, Say No To Alcohol

The Truth About Being A Teenage Girl

You are trying to be an individual, your own person. You're totally psyched one minute and in major trauma the next. It's definitely a tough time. Your parents want to protect you. Your friends want to influence you. You're still trying to decide what you want.

So many choices! And to top it off, there's all this pressure about alcohol. Sure, giving in to pressure is easier than taking a stand. This is the first time in your life that you get to make your own decisions, and be your own woman. And what's the first choice so many girls make? To fit in with the crowd.

Somewhere between the brain, heart, and mouth, a girl's individuality gets lost. Maybe it's swallowed with that first sip of beer. Be an individual. You don't need alcohol to be amazing.

Popularity Puzzle: It may look like you have to drink to be popular, but think about it. Drinking gives you bad breath, makes your face puffy and your stomach bloated, and gives you zits. How's that going to get you a date or make people like you? Not only that, alcohol is loaded with empty calories.

Body Stuff: Alcohol can seriously mess with your body. Too much alcohol can cause stomach ulcers. Girls can drink less than guys, over less time, and get more serious damage to their internal organs. Girls feel alcohol's effects differently from day to day because of their menstrual cycle.

✔ Quick Tip

Practice ahead what you will say if you are offered alcohol. "No, thanks," works.

Guys: Maybe you're shy and think alcohol will make you cool. Or think a good time means drinking. But alcohol robs you of your ability to think or react. When you can't think clearly, it's easier for a guy to force you to have sex. Lots of guys say if a girl is drunk, it's her fault if she gets raped. Did you know one study of teens showed that almost half had been drinking and/or using drugs before engaging in sex that resulted in an unintended pregnancy? Not to mention things like syphilis and AIDS.

Fab Friends: Your friends are totally lame if they pressure you to drink. It's illegal. It can make you sick. It can get you killed. Keep quarters in your pocket. If your ride is drinking, pick up a phone. Don't get in a car with someone who has been drinking. You've got way too much to accomplish in life.

Life In A Pressure Cooker: All the perfect models drinking in the alcohol ads are bogus. Drinking doesn't solve problems, whether you are a super model or not. It usually makes them worse. Girls have to work really hard to take control of their lives. Control is the first thing you lose when you drink. Be in charge of your life, take control, and say no to alcohol.

The Truth About Being A Teenage Guy

It doesn't matter where you live or how much money you have. Or even what color your skin is. Every guy goes through the same teenage junk. Technology may change the world, but for some things time stands still. This may blow your mind, but your dad (and even his dad before him) had to wade through the same problems to get to manhood.

You've got to act like a man. You've got to grow up. Make the right choices, whatever they are. Whatever you do, make sure all the girls think you're a stud. Make sure all the guys respect you. Not much to do. And in your spare time could you graduate from high school?

Alcohol is just one more thing. But here's your chance to be a man. Don't bother with alcohol. Take a stand. You'll be surprised what independence can do for your image. Very cool.

Hanging Out With The Guys: You want to chill with your friends. Chances are alcohol is going to be around at some point. Maybe at every point. Sure, it's easier to take a beer than a stand. But there's a lot riding on that drink. If they are real friends, they'll be cool with your choice.

Girls: You may want to loosen up. But alcohol is not liquid courage. You could end up making a fool of yourself and doing something you'll regret. You're eyesight's blurry. Your judgment is blurry too. Drinking doesn't turn you into a stud. Be yourself. If the girls don't respond, it's their loss.

Power Play: You want to be in control. But when you wake up in a strange place and don't remember how you got there, you're definitely not in control. Alcohol robs you of your ability to think. You don't know what you're doing. You could wind up with AIDS, in a car crash, or worse.

Buff Bod: You're looking good now. But alcohol can do major damage to your body. We're talking stomach problems, memory loss, sexual impotence, and liver damage to name a few. That's not even mentioning all the empty, gut-causing calories in alcohol. Ever heard of a beer belly? Not attractive!

Remember!!
Be in charge of your life, take control, and say no to alcohol.

Stressing Big Time: It's tough being your age. There's serious pressure to do the right thing. But it's your chance to be your own man. If you feel good about yourself, people will think you're okay. Don't be pressured into drinking. It doesn't solve your problems. It doesn't even postpone them. Drinking just makes new problems. And who wants more of those?

Chapter 6

The Minimum Legal Drinking Age

Responses To Arguments Against The Minimum Legal Drinking Age (MLDA)

Despite an abundance of research demonstrating the effectiveness of the age 21 MLDA in reducing youth drinking and alcohol-related problems, a few States are again considering lowering their legal age limits for drinking. Many issues and arguments heard decades ago are resurfacing, and many are similar to arguments college administrators hear against campus policies to discourage high-risk alcohol use.

Issue: "Establishing a legal drinking age of 21 is unconstitutional age discrimination."

Response: This question has been treated in detail in two court cases, one in Michigan, the other in Louisiana. In both instances, the courts upheld the constitutionality of the laws, based in part on the demonstrated value of age 21 laws in preventing traffic crashes.

About This Chapter: This information is from "How To Reduce High-Risk College Drinking: Use Proven Strategies, Fill Research Gaps: Appendix 3–Responses to Arguments Against the Minimum Legal Drinking Age," National Institute on Alcohol Abuse and Alcoholism (NIAAA), April 2002.

♣ It's A Fact!!

What's Magic About The Number 21?

Are you wondering what the deal is with the 21 minimum drinking age law? Sure, it's a law but it doesn't always feel like it. It's in all 50 states, but do people pay attention to it? You might question why the laws were written with 21 as the minimum drinking age, what's so special about that age, and how the law came to be. Here's a lowdown on the most relevant information.

A Walk Down Memory Lane

Some folks think 21 was pulled out of the air. But despite what you may think, there are some pretty good reasons that age 21 was selected.

Back in the late 1960s and early 70s a number of states lowered their drinking age from 21 to 18. In many of these states, research documented a significant increase in highway deaths of the teens affected by these laws. So, in the early 1980s a movement began to raise the drinking age back to 21. After the law changed back to 21, many of the states were monitored to check the difference in highway fatalities. Researchers found that teenage deaths in fatal car crashes dropped considerably—in some cases up to 28%—when the laws were moved back to 21.

Like it or not, it is clear that more young people were killed on the highways when the drinking age was 18. Back in 1982 when many of the states had minimum drinking ages of 18, 55% of all fatal crashes involving youth drivers involved alcohol. Since then, the alcohol-related traffic fatality rate has been cut in half! Research estimates that from 1975–2002 more than 21,000 lives have been saved. Hard to argue with that!

A Strain In The Brain

According to the book *Buzzed*, the use of alcohol by young people is especially frightening. We all hear about the dangers and consequences of underage drinking, but most of us know very little about how alcohol affects the brains of young people.

Buzzed says we should look at what we do know about young brains like the fact that they don't finish developing until a person is around 20 years old. And one of the last regions to mature is intimately involved with the ability to plan and make complex judgments. Young brains are built to acquire new memories and are "built to learn." *Buzzed* reports that, "It is no accident that people are educated in our society during their early years, when they have more capacity for memory and learning. However, with this added memory capacity may come additional risks associated with the use of alcohol." Apparently in studies using animals, young brains are vulnerable to dangerous effects of alcohol, especially in learning and memory function. If this is true of people, then young people who drink may be "powerfully impairing the brain functions on which they rely so heavily for learning." So, in case there wasn't enough pressure to perform at school, at your job, or just in life, alcohol can prevent your use of your own brain.

So in answer to the question "Why?" the 21 minimum age drinking laws were established to save your brain and your life.

Sources

- Kuhn, Cynthia, Swartzwelder, Scott, and Wilson, Wilkie. *Buzzed—The Straight Facts About the Most Used and Abused Drugs from Alcohol to Ecstasy.*

- *1997 Youth Fatal Car Crash and Alcohol Facts.* National Highway Traffic Safety Administration.

- *Youth Impaired Driving Issues Compendium.* Mothers Against Drunk Driving.

Issue: "If I'm old enough to go to war, I should be old enough to drink."

Response: Many rights have different ages of initiation. A person can obtain a hunting license at age 12, driver's license at age 16, vote and serve in the military at 18, serve in the U.S. House of Representatives at age 25 and in the U.S. Senate at age 30, and run for President at age 35. Other rights that are regulated include the sale and use of tobacco and legal consent for sexual intercourse and marriage. The minimum age for initiation is based on the specific behaviors involved and must take into account the dangers and benefits of that behavior at a given age. The age 21 policy for alcohol takes into account the fact that underage drinking is related to numerous serious health problems, including injuries and death resulting from car crashes, suicide, homicide, assault, drowning, and recreational injuries. In fact, the leading cause of death among teens is car crashes, and alcohol is involved in approximately one-third of these deaths.

Issue: "Europeans let their teens drink from an early age, yet they don't have the alcohol-related problems we do. What we need are fewer restrictions, not more."

Response: The idea that Europeans do not have alcohol-related problems is a myth. European youth may be at less risk of traffic crashes since youth drive less frequently in Europe than in the United States. However, European countries have similar or higher rates of other alcohol-related problems compared to those in the United States.

Issue: "Lower rates of alcohol-related crashes among 19- to 20-year-olds aren't related to the age 21 policy, but rather they're related to increased drinking-driving education efforts, tougher enforcement, and tougher drunk-driving penalties."

Response: When the age 21 restriction was initiated, alcohol-involved highway crashes declined immediately (i.e., starting the next month) among the 18- to 20-year-old population. Careful research has shown the decline was not due to DUI [driving under the influence] enforcement and tougher DUI penalties, but is a direct result of the legal drinking age. Studies have also shown that education alone is not effective in reducing youth drinking.

Achieving long-term reductions in youth drinking problems requires an environmental change so that alcohol is less accessible to teens.

Issue: "Making it illegal to drink until 21 just increases the desire for the 'forbidden fruit.' Then, when students turn 21, they'll drink even more."

Response: Actually, the opposite is true. Early legal access to alcohol is associated with higher rates of drinking as an adult.

Issue: "Who will pay for enforcement of these laws? The age 21 law is too expensive."

Response: We already pay large portions of our tax dollars for problems resulting from alcohol. For example, in Minnesota, cities use approximately one-third of their police budgets to deal with alcohol-related problems; the U.S. pays more than $10 billion annually just for the costs associated with drunk driving. The higher drinking age saves money by resulting in fewer alcohol-related health problems, fewer alcohol-related injuries, and less vandalism.

Issue: "We drank when we were young and we grew out of it. It's just a phase that all students go through."

Response: Unfortunately, many teens will not grow out of it. Studies indicate that youth who start drinking before they are 21 are more likely to drink heavily later in life. Those who do not drink until age 21 tend to drink less as adults. Teens who drink are also more likely to try other illegal drugs and to become victims of crime. If teen drinking is accepted as normal behavior, youth will continue to experience car crashes, other injuries, early unprotected sex, and other problems commonly associated with drinking.

☞ Remember!!
The minimum age drinking laws were established to save your brain and your life.

Issue: "If students can't get alcohol, they'll just switch to other, perhaps even more dangerous, drugs."

Response: Research shows that the opposite is true; teens who drink and/or smoke are more likely to move on to use other drugs. Preventing youth from using alcohol and tobacco reduces the chance that they will try other illegal drugs. Moreover, when the drinking age was raised to 21, and teen drinking declined, there was no evidence of a compensatory increase in other drug use.

Chapter 7

Deterring Alcohol-Impaired Drivers

What's the goal of alcohol-impaired driving laws?

State laws making it illegal to drive with high blood alcohol concentration (BAC) serve as the cornerstone of all efforts to reduce alcohol-impaired driving. Many people think the principal goal of such laws is to arrest and punish the drivers who put everyone else at risk. But arrest and punishment of offenders is a secondary objective. The most important objective is for the law to be a deterrent so that police find no alcohol-impaired drivers to arrest.

Why is deterrence so important and how can it be achieved?

Most impaired drivers are never stopped. Others are stopped, but police often miss signs of impairment. It has been estimated that close to 1,000 alcohol-impaired driving trips occur for every arrest. Because the police cannot catch all offenders, the success of alcohol-impaired driving laws depends on deterring potential offenders by creating the public perception that apprehension and punishment of offenders is likely. Research has shown that likelihood of apprehension is more important in deterring offenders than is the severity of punishment. The key to creating this perception is enforcement. Merely putting strong laws on the books is not enough. Enforcement efforts must be sustained and well publicized and create a realistic threat of apprehension.

✎ Weird Words

Deterrence: Making the punishment of an action such that people choose to avoid that behavior, for example, losing driving privileges if arrested with a BAC over .02.

Graduated Licensing: Restrictions applied to newly licensed drivers under age 18. These restrictions may affect time of day when the person may drive, and/or the length of time they must have a license before carrying minor passengers. Each state determines their license requirements.

Sobriety: Not having alcohol or drugs in your body.

How do laws define alcohol-impaired driving?

The first state laws prohibited driving while intoxicated or while under the influence of alcohol. In practical terms, this meant that only obviously impaired drivers—so-called drunks—were likely to be arrested, and even then it was difficult to obtain a conviction because no objective standard existed to prove intoxication. When the relationship between BAC and impairment of skills was established, it became possible to define offenses in terms of a BAC above a defined threshold.

Every state now uses BAC results to prosecute offenders. Initially, this was done through what are known as presumptive laws that establish a presumption of impairment at or above a specified BAC (defendants could try to rebut the presumption). All states and the District of Columbia have per se laws defining the offense as driving with a BAC above a proscribed limit, rather like a speed limit. Defendants can no longer try to prove they were not impaired, although they can challenge the validity of the BAC tests. As of July 2004, in all states a BAC of 0.08 or more creates a presumption that the person was driving while intoxicated.

What does blood alcohol concentration measure?

Blood alcohol concentration describes the concentration of alcohol in a person's blood expressed as weight per unit of volume. For example, at 0.10 percent BAC, there is a concentration of 100 mg of alcohol per 100 ml of blood. For most legal purposes, however, a blood sample is not necessary to determine a person's BAC. It can be measured much more simply by using sophisticated breath testing instruments.

♣ It's A Fact!!
Strict Graduated Driver Licensing Laws Associated With Less Teen Drinking And Driving

Young drivers in states with more restrictive driver-licensing laws had lower rates of heavy drinking and driving under the influence of alcohol than those in states with less restrictive laws. That is the finding in a new report that utilizes data analysis of 1999, 2000, and 2001 Substance Abuse and Mental Health Services Administration (SAMHSA) National Household Surveys.

While nationwide, one in ten drivers aged 15 to 17 reported driving under the influence of alcohol, the drinking and driving increased as the restrictiveness of graduated drivers license laws decreased. In the most restrictive states, 8.2 percent of 15–17 year old drivers reported driving under the influence of alcohol in the past year, while 11.5 percent of young drivers drove under the influence of alcohol in the least restrictive states.

The report, "Graduated Driver Licensing and Drinking among Young Drivers," released April 30, 2004 by SAMHSA, shows that while six percent of young drivers nationally were heavy drinkers, young drivers in states with the most restrictive graduated licensing laws had lower rates (5.4 Percent) of heavy drinking than did young drivers in states with the least restrictive licensing provisions (7.0 percent).

Source: SAMHSA News Release, April 30, 2004 available at http://www.samhsa .gov/news/newsreleases/040430nr_teenlicense.htm

♣ It's A Fact!!

Underage Drinking And Driving

Is alcohol a significant factor in teenage crashes?

Yes. Young drivers are less likely than adults to drive after drinking alcohol, but their crash risks are substantially higher when they do. This is especially true at low and moderate blood alcohol concentration (BAC) and is thought to result from teenagers' relative inexperience with drinking and driving and with combining these activities.[1]

In 2002, 25 percent of 16–20-year-old passenger vehicle drivers fatally injured in crashes had high blood alcohol concentration (0.08 percent or more). Teenage drivers with BAC in the 0.05–0.08 percent range are far more likely than sober teenage drivers to be killed in single-vehicle crashes—17 times more likely for males, 7 times more likely for females. At BAC of 0.08–0.10, risks are even higher, 52 times for males, 15 times for females.

What works to reduce drinking and driving among teenagers?

Minimum alcohol purchasing age laws work. For a long time, the legal age for purchasing alcohol was 21 years old in most of the United States. Then, in the 1960s and early 1970s, many states lowered their minimum purchasing ages to 18 or 19 years old. The Institute's research on the consequences of this action indicated an increase in the number of drivers younger than 21 involved in nighttime fatal crashes.[2]

As a result of this and other studies with similar findings, a number of states raised their minimum alcohol purchasing ages—in some states back to 21 years old and in other states to 19 or 20. Institute researchers evaluated this development in nine states in 1981, finding reductions in nighttime fatal crashes among young drivers. The average fatality reduction based on all nine states was 28 percent.[3] A subsequent study in 26 states that raised minimum legal alcohol purchasing ages during 1975–84 estimated a 13 percent reduction in nighttime driver fatal crash involvement.[4]

In 1984, 23 states had minimum alcohol purchasing ages of 21 years old, and federal legislation was enacted to withhold highway funds from the remaining 27 states if they did not follow suit. Since July 1988, all 50 states and the District of Columbia have required alcohol purchasers to be 21 years old.

How has the teenage drinking and driving problem changed over time?

Trends in alcohol involvement in fatal crashes can be monitored through the National Highway Traffic Safety Administration's Fatality Analysis Reporting System, a census of virtually all fatal crashes in the United States. During the 1980s, percentages of fatally injured drivers with high BAC (0.08 percent or more) declined among drivers of all ages. Reductions among young drivers were greatest, in part because of changing alcohol purchasing age laws. In 1982, fewer than half of the states had purchasing requirements for 21 year-olds, and 49 percent of all fatally injured drivers younger than 21 had high BAC. This statistic declined dramatically as states adopted older purchasing ages, and by 1995 it had declined to 24 percent, the biggest improvement for any age group. This decline ended in 1995.

What can be done to further reduce teenage drinking and driving?

In 1990–1991, Institute researchers found 19–20 year-olds could easily buy a six-pack of beer in Washington, DC and a New York City suburb.[5] But in two New York counties where police had recently cracked down on underage alcohol purchases, youths were less successful. In these studies, the underage purchasers were generally not even asked by sellers for proof of their age. In 1994 and 1995, Institute researchers surveyed high school and college students younger than age 21 in New York and Pennsylvania about alcohol use and purchase. Fifty-nine percent of college students and 28 percent of high school students in New York and 37 percent of college students and 14 percent of high school students in Pennsylvania reported they had used false identification to obtain alcohol.[6] Many communities are stepping up enforcement of alcohol purchasing age laws—clearly this is needed to make them more effective.

continued on next page...

...continued from previous page

Are the BAC thresholds for illegal driving per se lower for teenagers than for older drivers?

All 50 states and the District of Columbia have established lower blood alcohol thresholds that are illegal per se for drivers younger than 21. Federal legislation enacted in 1995 that allowed for the withholding of highway funds played a role in motivating states to pass such laws. Research indicates such policies reduce nighttime fatal crashes in this age group.[7]

References

1. Mayhew, D.R.; Donelson, A.C.; Beirness, D.J.; and Simpson, H.M. 1986. Youth, alcohol and relative risk of crash involvement. *Accident Analysis and Prevention* 18(4): 273-287.

2. Williams, A.F.; Rich, R.F.; Zador, P.L.; and Robertson, L.S. 1975. The legal minimum drinking age and fatal motor vehicle crashes. *Journal of Legal Studies* 4(1): 219-239.

3. Williams, A.F.; Zador, P.L.; Harris, S.S. and Karpf, R.S. 1983. The effect of raising the legal minimum drinking age on involvement in fatal crashes. *Journal of Legal Studies* 12: 169-179.

4. Du Mouchel, W.; Williams, A.F.; and Zador, P.L. 1987. Raising the alcohol purchase age: its effects on fatal motor vehicle crashes in twenty-six states. *Journal of Legal Studies* 16: 249-266.

5. Preusser, D.F. and Williams, A.F. 1992. Sales of alcohol to underage purchasers in three New York counties and Washington, D.C. *Journal of Public Health Policy* 13(3): 306-317.

6. Preusser, D.F.; Ferguson, S.A.; Williams, A.F.; and Farmer, C.M. 1997. Underage access to alcohol: sources of alcohol and use of false identification. *Proceedings of the 14th International Conference on Alcohol, Drugs and Traffic Safety*, 3: 1017-1025 (ed. C. Mercier-Guyon). Annecy, France: CERMT.

7. Hingson, R.; Heeren, T.; and Winter, M. 1994. Lower legal blood alcohol limits for young drivers. *Public Health Reports* 109:739-744.

How do BAC thresholds in the United States compare with those in other countries?

Alcohol-impaired driving is a serious problem throughout the industrialized world. BAC thresholds range from 0.08 percent in Austria, Canada, Great Britain, and Switzerland to 0.05 in Australia, France, and Germany, and 0.02 in Sweden. There are national differences in forensic testing and reporting procedures. In Britain, for example, a driver must have a reported BAC above 0.08 percent to be in violation of the law, but the reported BAC is reduced somewhat from what is actually measured to account for test variability. The net result is a BAC closer to 0.09 percent is needed in Great Britain for a violation, whereas a measured BAC of 0.08 is sufficient for arrest in the United States.

Who can be stopped for alcohol-impaired driving?

Although police cannot stop and test individual drivers without cause, they can investigate any driver who based on established criteria appears to be driving while impaired by alcohol. Most alcohol-impaired driving arrests are made by officers on routine patrol who discern signs of impairment after stopping a driver for an ordinary traffic violation. In some jurisdictions, specialized patrols work exclusively on alcohol-impaired driving enforcement. Plus, police can stop drivers at roadblocks known as sobriety checkpoints.

How do sobriety checkpoints work?

Police can use checkpoints to stop drivers at specified locations to identify impaired drivers. All drivers, or a predetermined proportion of them, are stopped based on rules that prevent police from arbitrarily selecting drivers to stop. Checkpoints are a very visible enforcement method intended to deter potential offenders as well as to catch violators. If checkpoints are set up frequently over long enough periods and are well publicized, they can establish a convincing threat in people's minds that impaired drivers will be apprehended—a key to general deterrence. A recent Institute study shows that 37 states and the District of Columbia conduct sobriety checkpoints—only 11 of these states set up checkpoints on a weekly basis, while 13 states and the District of Columbia conduct checkpoints once or twice a month.

♣ It's A Fact!!
Administrative License Suspension (ALS)

Hundreds of state laws targeting alcohol-impaired driving were enacted during the early 1980s, and among those shown to be the most effective are administrative license suspension (ALS) laws. Forty-two states and the District of Columbia have ALS laws.

How do ALS laws work?

ASL laws authorize police to confiscate the licenses of drivers who either fail or refuse to take a chemical test for alcohol. Drivers are given a notice of suspension, which in some states also serves as a temporary permit. Depending on the state, this permit may be valid for 7 to 90 days, during which time the suspension may be appealed. If there is no appeal, or if the appeal is not upheld, the license is suspended for a prescribed period of time. Suspensions vary from 2 days to a year for first-time offenders, but most commonly last 90 days. Longer suspensions are specified for repeat violators. It is important to note that ALS laws do not replace criminal prosecution handled separately through the courts.

How do ALS laws differ from traditional license suspension?

The administrative licensing action is triggered by failing or refusing to take a chemical test—not by conviction—so anyone arrested is immediately subject to suspension. People whose licenses are suspended have the right to a prompt administrative hearing to determine the validity of the arrest and any alcohol testing.

Is license suspension an effective sanction?

Although many offenders continue to drive after having their licenses suspended, this action has been shown by many well-designed studies to reduce crashes and repeated offenses compared with offenders whose licenses are not suspended. The reductions in violations and crashes associated with license suspension continue well beyond the suspension period.

Longer periods of license suspension may be expected to have stronger effects, while those of short duration may have very limited effects. The National Highway Traffic Safety Administration (NHTSA) recommends that ALS laws impose at least a 90-day suspension or a 30-day suspension followed by 60 days of restricted driving.

How effective are ALS laws?

An Institute study found ALS laws reduce the number of drivers involved in fatal crashes by about 9 percent during nighttime hours when alcohol is very likely to be involved. NHTSA reports that, among 17 states implementing ALS either alone or in combination with other laws, the median effect is a 6 percent decrease in crashes likely to be alcohol-related.

What's the advantage of ALS?

ALS laws, which apply to both first-time and multiple offenders, remove impaired drivers from the road quickly and virtually ensure that penalties will be applied. ALS laws allow a greater number of cases to be moved swiftly through the legal system and result in far more suspensions than do laws that require a criminal conviction. They reduce the incentive for offenders to delay their criminal cases to avoid suspension. They also reduce the likelihood of future alcohol-related violations and crashes. Despite success in all of these areas, ALS laws still affect only a very small fraction of offenders on the roads.

The success of laws against alcohol-impaired driving depends largely on deterrence, or keeping potential offenders off the roads in the first place. A 1996 study showed that about 3 out of every 100 drivers on U.S. roads on weekend nights had blood alcohol concentrations of 0.10 percent or greater.[1] With so many offenders, it is not possible to apprehend more than a relatively small proportion. A well-publicized and enforced ALS law increases public perception that punishment for alcohol-impaired driving is likely to occur and will be swiftly applied and appropriately severe—a perception that is necessary to deter potential offenders.

continued on next page...

...continued from previous page

Are ALS laws constitutional?

Yes. Courts have held that although licenses are taken prior to a hearing, due process is provided because ALS laws allow for prompt post-suspension hearings. Defendants have claimed that the double jeopardy clause of the U.S. Constitution prohibits the state from prosecuting an offender whose license has been suspended under ALS. But high courts in several states have found that a criminal prosecution following ALS doesn't violate the double jeopardy clause.

References

1. Voas, R.B.; Wells, J.K.; Lestina, D.; Williams, A.F.; and Greene, M. 1998. Drinking and driving in the United States: the 1996 national roadside survey. *Accident Analysis and Prevention* 30(2): 267-275.

2. Latchaw, J. 1986. *Overcoming problems and costs of administrative hearings* (DOT HS-806-921). Washington, DC: Department of Transportation.

3. Baker, S.P. and Robertson, L.S. 1975. How drivers prevented from driving would reach work: implications for penalties. *Accident Analysis and Prevention* 7: 45-48.

Source: "Q & A: Alcohol: Administrative License Suspension," Copyright © 2004 Insurance Institute for Highway Safety, Highway Loss Data Institute. Reprinted with permission. For additional information, visit http://www.iihs.org.

Are sobriety checkpoints constitutional?

The U.S. Supreme Court held in 1990 that properly conducted sobriety checkpoints are legal under the federal Constitution. Most state courts that have addressed the issue have upheld checkpoints, too, but some have interpreted state law to prohibit checkpoints.

How can passive alcohol sensors aid in enforcement?

Many people can effectively conceal the symptoms of impairment for short periods, but it is much more difficult to hide the information available from a passive alcohol sensor, which identifies alcohol in the exhaled breath near a driver's mouth. Passive alcohol sensors are screening devices that help an officer detect possible impaired drivers for further testing. Passive alcohol sensors are not intrusive, and therefore do not violate constitutional prohibitions against unreasonable search and seizure. A 1993 Institute study of sobriety checkpoints in Fairfax County, Virginia involved police using sensors who were able to detect more offenders compared with officers who did not use sensors. Police without sensors detected 55 percent of drivers whose BAC were at or above 0.10 percent. With sensors, police successfully detected 71 percent of the drivers with illegal BAC. Results of the Fairfax study parallel previous Institute evaluations.

Is license suspension an effective sanction?

Laws providing for the suspension or revocation of licenses have been shown to reduce the subsequent crash involvement of drivers convicted of alcohol offenses. Even after the suspension, the effects of this sanction last. Although it is known that many suspended drivers continue to drive, they tend to drive less and perhaps more carefully so as to avoid apprehension. License suspension also has led to a general reduction in fatal crashes in states where the threat of this sanction has been made more certain through laws that provide for administrative license suspension.

What is the effect of education and other treatment programs?

Research has shown these may have a small, positive effect on the subsequent behavior of alcohol-impaired drivers, but the effect is limited to first offenders and to those identified as non-problem drinkers. There is very little evidence treatment programs have any effect on multiple offenders or on problem drinkers. In addition, any positive effect has been limited to subsequent convictions for alcohol-impaired driving. No effect has been shown on subsequent crashes, whether alcohol-related or not.

♣ It's A Fact!!

What Is Zero Tolerance?

Zero Tolerance laws make it illegal for anyone under the legal drinking age to drive with blood alcohol levels above .00, .01, or .02 percent (depending on what state you live in). Any measurable amount of alcohol can result in a stiff penalty for anyone under 21 caught drinking and driving—you could lose your driver's license. Zero tolerance means zero chances for mistakes.

Source: "Zero Tolerance Means Zero Chances," National Highway Traffic Safety Administration, available at http://www.nhtsa.dot.gov/people/injury/alcohol/zero/page1/understand.html.

Have other countries done a better job controlling alcohol-impaired driving?

Australia has the most successful documented programs to reduce alcohol-impaired driving. All have in common highly visible and sustained, widespread, but not burdensome enforcement. The state of Victoria maintains an aggressive program of random breath testing of drivers. More than half of all licensed drivers each year are tested in this program. The percentage of drivers and motorcyclists with BAC above 0.05 killed in crashes dropped from 50 percent in 1977 to about 25 percent in 1995, indicating the deterrent result of the random breath testing. An Australian university study concluded the key to the random breath testing program's success is high visibility, rigorous enforcement sustained on a long-term basis, and good publicity.

Why don't we test all drivers and arrest those who don't pass a chemical test?

In Australia, police officers are allowed to administer a breath test to any driver, regardless of whether or not they have reason to believe the person has been drinking. In the United States, breath testing is considered a search and the U.S. Constitution prohibits those searches unless the police have some reasonable basis for suspecting that the driver may be impaired by alcohol. U.S. police can carry out sobriety checkpoints that briefly stop some or all drivers, if the checkpoint is done in accordance with strict guidelines to ensure that there is no discriminatory stopping and testing some people and not others. Again, the key is that the police must show they have a reasonable basis to administer the breath test to a driver. Depending on state law, police may be able to ask all drivers legally stopped to voluntarily consent to a breath test, but they cannot require a test without reasonable suspicion of an alcohol offense. Research has shown that well-publicized sobriety checkpoints, especially those that use passive alcohol sensors to detect the presence of alcohol in the exhaled breath of the driver, are effective in reducing alcohol-impaired driving.

Remember!!

There is no safe level of alcohol for drivers under 21.

Chapter 8

Handling Peer Pressure

Decision-Making Animals

We're decision-making animals, every one of us. From the moment we wake up and decide what kind of mood we're in, to the final choice we make whether or not to floss our teeth at night, we're all making decisions all the time. We decide whether to shoot hoops or watch TV after school (or watch hoops on TV), and whether to have vanilla, chocolate, or Strawberry-Pickle Parfait at the local 57 Flavors.

On the other hand—or foot (we decided to be different); we also make a lot of decisions that don't even seem like decisions. Example: Passing when mom tries to pawn off turnips as food. That isn't a decision we spend a lot of time thinking about. Most of us just pass the bowl as fast as we can.

Saying yes or no (or uh-huh or huh-huh) on the spur of the moment works pretty well most of the time. But big decisions need a little more attention. And choosing about drugs and alcohol is as big as decisions ever get. That's what this chapter is all about. In it, we'll discuss how to figure out what's right for you in making choices about drugs and alcohol. We'll also talk about peer pressure and discuss how you can say no—if and when you need to—in a way that gets heard and respected. That way, you won't have to be someone who says yes when you mean no, and spend the rest of your life in therapy, wondering why no one understands you and waiting for your 50-minute hour of therapy to be up. Sound worthwhile? You decide.

Peers And Pressures

The first thing we'll talk about is why people use drugs and alcohol in the first place. There are as many different answers to that question as there are burgers at McDonald's: about 16 bazillion—and still counting.

- Some people drink or do drugs to relax or forget their problems or have fun or fall asleep.

✔ Quick Tip
Making Decisions

How do you decide what you really want? Try considering your options at each of the five stages that go into every decision. Usually, we choose so fast that we don't realize just how detailed the process is. But when you think about it, there really are five parts to every decision:

- **Identify** the problem (Turnips! Yipes!)

- **Describe** possible solutions or alternatives (Feed 'em to the dog! Spit 'em out! Close your eyes and swallow...)

- **Evaluate** the ideas (The dog is outside! The napkin's too small! Just get it over with...)

- **Act** out a plan (Play dead! Barf.)

- **Learn** for the future (Find out beforehand what's for dinner and play sick if necessary...)

Didn't know you were that complicated? In case you didn't notice, the first letter of each step spells out IDEAL, and it is pretty much an ideal way to figure out what your options are in any situation—and predict possible consequences.

- Others do it because they think everybody else does—and they're afraid they'll look clueless or totally out of it if they don't.

- But if you peel away the first 16 bazillion layers of the onion away, you'll find that most people get into drugs or drinking in the first place because someone they know is into it.

The fancy word for the process is peer pressure. It means that we feel pressure (either from inside or outside ourselves) to be like other people. Peer pressure isn't a bad thing. It plays a big role in determining who we are and how we dress and talk and act. It's a main reason that kids in America dress and talk and act more or less alike, instead of looking and acting and talking like people in Lithuania or Katmandu.

Still, peer pressure can cause problems, too. Because, sometimes, people in groups act differently and do things they'd never do on their own. Why? Because we all lose at least some of our identity in a group. And the normal controls we put on our behavior can crumble before the need we all feel to fit in and be respected by others.

Peer pressure isn't always (or even usually) the obvious stuff they show in TV commercials. (Wanna try a joint? No? Wussamadda? Chicken?) More often, it's hard to even notice, much less resist. But if you want to pull your own strings in life, you need to be aware of it, know how it works, and learn how to make choices for yourself in spite of it.

Truth Or Consequences

Ever wonder why our society makes such a big deal out of drugs and alcohol—and spends so much time and money to talk you out of trying them? It's not that drugs and alcohol are bad and ducking them is good, although a lot of people believe that. Drugs are drugs. Period. Alcohol is alcohol. They're not good or bad. They're chemicals.

Think of it this way: Drugs and alcohol are like dynamite—it's not good or bad, either. Use a couple of sticks to clear away a boulder that's blocking a road to a jungle hospital, and it's good. Use it to blow up the hospital, and it's bad.

Drugs are like that. Some have real value, but any chemical that can change the way you think and feel is something you need to consider carefully. That's especially true because the effects of drugs and alcohol aren't external (like dying your hair green on St. Patrick's Day), but internal, and can cause real changes in the body and brain. Even though some drug effects feel cool for a while (or people wouldn't do them), they always wear off. Then the body—and-brain's owner—is back at Square One, dealing with the consequences.

> ☞ **Remember!!**
>
> Plan now how you will say no to drugs and alcohol.

What Consequences?

The same kind of stuff that follows in the wake of every choice we make. (If you choose chocolate, you can't have vanilla. Choose vanilla, and you can't have Strawberry-Pickle Parfait. Duh!) Drugs and alcohol have consequences too, and some of them aren't cool at all.

It isn't just hangovers or failing in school or getting arrested that you need to consider—although those are real consequences that can affect the quality of your life for a long time. There are other consequences, too, and we're just beginning to understand some of them—like the changes in brain chemistry that can follow periods of drug use. Because the fact is that all drugs change brain chemistry somehow—or they wouldn't work at all. Anything that powerful really ought to be treated with respect and taken a lot more seriously than some people take the choice to drink or do drugs.

A, B, or C—Made E-Z

The downside of drugs has nothing to do with good or bad, and everything to do with how they affect the quality of life—and the consequences they tend to leave behind. That's why it's smart to think about drinking and drugs before you start bumping up against hard choices in the real world. Because you know what happens if you put off thinking about important stuff. It keeps on being important and you get more likely to do some dumb, spur-of-the-moment thing (especially if your friends are doing it) than what's best for you.

Think things through, and if you come up with 16 bazillion and one reasons for not trying drugs and alcohol, remember that there are almost that many ways to say no, should the need ever arise. You can say:

- "Not tonight. I have to study."

- "No, thanks. I'm in training."

- "Nope, not for me!"

- "Hey! No way!"

- "Thanks, but no thanks."

- "Just leave me alone."

But of all the ways anyone ever devised for saying no to drugs and alcohol, we like one better than all the rest. We'll share it with you, in case you ever want to try it out yourself. Just say: I'm fine.

You really are, you know. You always have been. The trick is keeping you that way. But you're up to it, aren't you?

Chapter 9

Tips For Alcohol-Free Parties

Safe And Sober Event Planning

Why wait for your school or parents to organize activities for you and your friends? Show adults that you are responsible and take the lead yourself. Organizing a substance-free party is a great idea, one that you shouldn't have a hard time selling to your friends, parents, or teachers. Here are a few tips on getting started:

- **Start Early**—Get a jump on the planning as soon as possible in the school year. Gather a small, but diverse group of student planners to help you work out the details. It's best to include at least one or two members from key support groups—teachers, parents, law enforcement, and even local businesses that can help you plan and assist with resources.

- **Develop a Plan**—Make an agenda for the first meeting. Include topics to figure out how many committees you may need and who will participate, how much money you will need to raise through donations, fundraisers, and ticket sales and how to spread the word.

- **Choose a Chairperson**—This should be someone who has the time and expertise to take the lead in planning the party. It may be a good

About This Chapter: Text in this chapter is excerpted from "Make Your Parties Rock—Substance Free: A Guide to Safe and Sober Event Planning," U.S. Department of Transportation, National Highway Safety Traffic Administration, 2002.

idea to enlist class leaders or your student government. Chairing is a big job and it's not always easy. The good news is that it's also rewarding. Just think of all of the new people you'll meet! Plus, you'll be playing a role in saving lives, which is more important than all of the headaches that come from being the boss.

- **Set the Hours**—Decide when the party will begin and end. It is important that your party lasts late into the night. Often when events end while people still want to party, a few might be tempted to continue celebrating in ways that are not safe.

What Should We Do?

Once you have the basics in place, its time to focus on settings, themes, and activities. Get input from a large group of people. It's best to plan a lot of activities, especially those that keep you moving, like contests and dancing. The most successful parties provide intense natural stimulation on a variety of levels that make the artificial stimulation of alcohol and other drugs pale in comparison.

Settings

Each community has its own assets when it comes to choosing activities. So look at the special benefits that your area has to offer and get lots of input from your friends. In addition to being substance-free, the most memorable events bring everyone together for a common experience.

> ### ✔ Quick Tip
> ### How To Host A Teen Party
>
> - Agree on a guest list and don't admit party crashers.
>
> - Discuss ground rules with your parents before the party.
>
> - Plan the party with a responsible friend so you have support if problems arise.
>
> - Brainstorm fun activities for the party.
>
> - If a guest brings alcohol, ask him or her to leave.
>
> - Serve plenty of snacks and non-alcoholic drinks.
>
> - Ask your parents or chaperones to be visible and available.
>
> Source: Adapted from "Make a Difference: Talk to Your Child About Alcohol," National Institute on Alcohol Abuse and Alcoholism, reviewed May 2002.

The following are some successful settings, themes, and activities to help you get started with your own plans. Take advantage of the variety of places to gather friends together. Great party sites can be found in every community. With decorations and your friends, you can turn just about any place into the place to be. Here are a few low-cost ideas to get you started:

- Community clubhouses, YMCA/YWCA, Big Brothers/Big Sisters, Elks/Moose/Masonic lodges, Veterans lodges

- Campgrounds

- College campuses Student Union, The Green

- Natural areas (for example, river, lake, park, mountain)

- Local attractions (for example, amusement park, train, bowling alley, movie theater, river boat, convention center, ranch)

- Private homes with parental approval

- School facilities

- City parks and recreation centers

And remember, having a good time doesn't end with the school year. Keep the parties going over the summer. Invite new friends or people that you want to meet!

Involve others in your efforts by contacting student safety organizations such as SADD (Students Against Destructive Decisions), Key Club, or Student Government. These groups can provide ideas for your activities as well as tips on organization and development. Ask for a list of their members and invite them to join in the fun.

Activities

What is a party anyway? It's just an excuse for getting together with your friends to have fun. So think of all of the things you can do that don't involve drinking alcohol. It's not hard to turn anything into a party. Parties should include physical activities such as sports, sensory activities, emotional activities, or awards presentations which bring everyone together. Here are some ideas to get your thoughts going. Read through them and then see what else you can come up with.

✔ Quick Tip
Prom: Promise To Keep It Safe

Make sure prom night is a positive experience you'll always remember; don't drink alcohol or use any other substances that will compromise your ability to make good decisions.

- Discuss plans with your friends/date ahead of time. Know your agenda and communicate with your parents.

- Plan ahead what you will say or do if someone offers you alcohol or another illegal drug. Use phrases such as, "No thanks," "Are you kidding? I want to remember this night!" or "Actually, I'd rather have a soda. Do you have one?"

- Know your date before you go. If your date is a set-up, try to take a walk at a park or go for a smoothie before the big night. Both you and your parents will feel better about you staying out late with someone you know.

- Find out what your curfew is and share it with your date/friends before prom night. Discuss with your parents after-curfew possibilities (the party at your friend's house or early morning breakfast at your place).

- Ask a trusted adult to be near a phone and to be available prom night in case you need to call them, and carry enough change with you to make several phone calls.

- Take your, or borrow your parent's, cell phone and slip it into your purse or pocket.

Get To Your Destination Safely

- Keep an eye on your date/driver to make sure he/she doesn't drink any alcohol. Alcohol slows reaction time and impairs vision, clear thinking, judgment, and coordination.

- There are more drunk drivers on the roads during the weekend. Keep a close eye on oncoming drivers, as impaired drivers tend to drive toward lights.

- Know where you're going before prom night and have directions to those places.

- After your red light turns green, wait a second before pulling into the intersection, just to be safe.

- Drive on well lit roads, and carry a phone if possible. That way, if you get a flat tire, you're not stranded, waving down a cab with your silk tie or sequin purse.

- Beautiful girls are distracting enough—keep the radio volume turned low enough so your driver can concentrate on getting you to the fun. And don't forget your seat belt!

- Make sure the car has enough gas to get where you're going (besides, parents are definitely on to the "But we ran out of gas" excuse!).

- Remember—if you find yourself in an uncomfortable position, or if the driver isn't safe, have enough money with you to call a friend or a cab.

Ways To Have Fun Without Drinking

- Go to a late-night diner all dressed up and order fries and a milkshake; it'll hit the spot and you'll get tons of attention!

- Buy a bunch of one-use cameras, pass them around to your friends, and set a goal to use every last picture before the night is through!

- Have a "Cranium" or "Act One" party at someone's house; don't forget to have lots of sodas, chips, and dips. You'll be hungry after all that dancing!

- Host a karaoke party at your house, in a friend's barn, or at a local Elks or Rotary lodge.

- Visit an arcade with your date or with a group, and challenge each other to a game or two.

continued on next page...

...continued from previous page

- Ask your local YMCA if you can plan an after-prom basketball tournament. Bring your favorite CDs to play in the background.

- Go to a late night coffee house and relive the evening for hours!

- After prom, gather in a friend's house or backyard, take your shoes off, turn up the music, and really dance! Don't forget to notify neighbors and police of your special event, and don't let guests come and go.

Things You Can Do In Your Community

- Before prom, work with your local law enforcement agency to plan a compliance check to help the police identify area retail alcohol outlets that are illegally selling alcohol to people under 21.

- Work with school officials to organize an assembly that sends positive messages about abstaining from alcohol and other drugs and shows the possible consequences.

- Work with your school's prom committee to plan a fun and safe after-prom celebration.

- Prepare facts and statistics about alcohol consumption and consequences for use/abuse and make school announcements.

- Help your or your friends' little brother or sister say "no" to alcohol. See if your local elementary school knows about "Protecting You/Protecting Me", an alcohol prevention curriculum for grades 1–5.

- Call your local MADD chapter and ask how you can prevent underage drinking in your community.

Stats You Need To Know

- Contrary to what you may hear or see, most teens aren't drinking. 81% of adolescents age 12 to 17 have chosen not to drink in the past year. (SAMHSA, 1999)

- 65% of 12th graders disapprove of consuming five or more drinks once or twice each weekend. (National Center on Addiction and Substance Abuse, 1996)

- You may be alive today because the legal drinking age is 21. The National Highway Traffic Safety Administration (NHTSA) estimates these laws have saved over 18,820 lives from 1975–1999. (NHTSA, 1999)

- Females process alcohol differently than males; smaller amounts of alcohol are more intoxicating for females regardless of their size. (NHTSA, 1990)

- The same amount of alcohol is in a 12-ounce bottle of beer, a 12-ounce wine cooler, and a 5-ounce glass of wine.

- Among male high school students, 39% say it is acceptable for a boy to force sex with a girl who is drunk or high. (U.S. Dept. of HHS, 1992)

- Even though youth are less likely than adults to drive after drinking, their crash rates are substantially higher. (NIAAA, 1996)

- Alcohol in the #1 youth drug problem (CSAP, 1996); it kills 6 times more people under 21 than all other illicit drugs combined. (PIRE, Ted Miller, Ph.D.)

Pledge For Life

Join thousands of other teens heading to prom sober this year in pledging to remain alcohol free for Prom this year. You can make a T-shirt with the pledge on the back (great idea for you, your friends, the prom committee, even teachers!) to show your commitment.

Source: "Prom: PROMise to Keep it Safe," from http://www.madd.org. Used by permission. Copyright 2004 Mothers Against Drunk Driving. All rights reserved.

Themes

Mardi Gras

- Three words: beads, beads, beads! Give out beads at the door and encourage everyone to trade for the coolest ones.

- Mix up tapes or CDs of classic jazz, bayou blues, and funky zydeco.

Crush Party

- It's way cooler than your parents' Sadie Hawkins. At a crush party everyone gets to invite his or her crush anonymously to the party. Make a sign to advertise your event. Have a few volunteers staff a table during lunch hours where students can drop a slip of paper into a jar with the name of the person they want to invite.

- Once you have all the slips of paper, make a list, including all invitees' names only once. Place an ad in your school paper inviting the crushes to come to the party. They'll feel cool and you'll have fun!

> ☞ **Remember!!**
> Tap into your creative side and plan a great alcohol-free party. You'll have fun and your friends will thank you.

- Spin great dance tunes, so that even those who don't make a love connection will still have a blast and meet new people!

Scary Movie Night

- Great for smaller groups. Hit your local video store and stock up on scary movies.

- Invite everyone to wear pajamas and to lounge.

- Buy as much junk food and soda as you can possibly stuff in your face!

Western Night

- Barbecue or cook out at a local park or campground.

- Get someone who has a pickup truck to do a hay ride.

- Make a bonfire and roast marshmallows.
- Don't forget the boots and cowboy hats!

Masquerade Party

- Not just for Halloween, costume parties can be fun anytime of year. Consider twisting the theme and having a party where everyone comes as their favorite movie star or cartoon character.
- Have a few television sets playing different movies or cartoons.
- Set up different trivia stations and give prizes to those who answer correctly.

Prom Party

- You will always remember your Prom. Work with teachers and school administrators to create an unforgettable night for everyone.
- Since Prom is a big event, make sure you start planning early. Use the resources in this guide and your night will come off without a hitch.
- Encourage the play of the National Association of Broadcasters' Celebration Prom Graduation public service announcements at your local radio and television stations.

Graduation Party

- Graduation is a passage of life for everyone and should be celebrated.
- Make a "Where we will be in 10 years" board and display it at the party.
- Create a time capsule to be opened at your 25th reunion.
- Bring your yearbooks and have a signing.

Keep Your Guests Pumped Up!

While we're sure you and your friends have sparkling personalities, it's always fun to have some sort of entertainment to bring your party to life. How do you do this? It's simple—entertainment can be anything you think people will like. Your party is limited only by your imagination. Music is an obvious necessity, but you don't need to limit yourself to a boom box and a mix CD. There are a number of ways to incorporate tunes into your event. Such as:

- **Live Music**—Concerts are a lot of fun, but people often have to spend money and travel to see good live bands on stage. Why not bring the music to them? Chances are your town has a few up-and-coming bands looking for the chance to perform for an audience. Ask your friends if they know anyone with a band. Go to local music stores and look for fliers advertising local acts. Call them and see if they would be willing to donate their time to perform at your party. Hey! You get a band— they get free exposure. Everybody wins. If there are a number of bands in your area, try to organize a "Battle of the Bands," which offers your guests a whole night of live music.

- **Local DJ**—If your town has a popular music radio station, try to arrange for a DJ from the station to emcee your event. They can play music, run contests, and generally keep the crowd smiling and dancing for the entire night. Or, you might try contacting a local nightclub and see if their DJ will spin a few discs for your party. You can promote the party as if it were a major club event, which will surely get the attention of your peers. You may know of friends who want to be DJs and have their own equipment. If you do, consider having a DJ contest.

- **Theme Music Night**—If you look in your local newspaper, you'll see that most of the major clubs and hot spots sponsor theme nights (such as "80s Night" or "Disco Night") to bring people into their club. These are proven themes that always draw a big crowd and guarantee a great time. One idea would be to host a "Salsa Night," where you play Latin dance music, serve Latin American appetizers and tropical fruit juices such as guava or mango, and decorate with a Latin theme. With so many styles of music and dress, you're bound to find something great.

- **Local Celebrity**—Maybe you won't be able to land your favorite television show babe or stud on your guest list (not that you shouldn't try). But there's a good chance that people with some degree of local fame would be willing to show up to your party, sign a few autographs, and maybe hang out for a dance or two. Good sources are local sports teams or television and radio stations that have a community relations department willing to donate time to a good cause. You can also contact area theaters and even talent agencies. Maybe a Hollywood superstar grew up nearby. You'll never get them to your event if you don't ask. If there are no celebrities in sight, try a celebrity look-alike contest.

• **Karaoke Night**—Karaoke is always a party favorite. Who needs outside celebrities when your community probably has a bunch of stars just waiting to be discovered? Karaoke is always a fun time, as people young and old just relish the chance to sing a few oldies for an enthusiastic crowd. All you have to do is rent a karaoke machine from your local entertainment supply store and plug it in. This is an option that doesn't cost a lot of money and is a whole lot of fun.

• **Sports Tournament**—Get your boom box and get out to a nearby park to stage your own olympic-sized sporting events. Have everyone sign up in teams to play volleyball, basketball, tennis, or whatever you like best! Those who don't want to play can cheer on their friends and help serve food and drinks to the weary players.

Chapter 10

Religious Beliefs and Service Attendance Lower Alcohol Use

Religious Beliefs And Substance Use Among Youths

- In 2002, about 8 million youths (33 percent) aged 12 to 17 attended religious services 25 times or more in the past year.

- More than 78 percent of youths (19 million) reported that religious beliefs are a very important part of their lives, and 69 percent (17 million) reported that religious beliefs influence how they make decisions.

- Youths aged 12 to 17 with higher levels of religiosity were less likely to have used cigarettes, alcohol, or illicit drugs in the past month than youths with lower levels of religiosity.

Prior research suggests that religiosity serves as a protective factor for substance use and that higher levels of religiosity are associated with lower levels of substance use among youths.[1] The National Survey on Drug Use and Health (NSDUH), formerly the National Household Survey on Drug Abuse (NHSDA), includes questions about cigarette, alcohol, and illicit drug use during the 30 days prior to the survey interview. "Any illicit drug" refers

About This Chapter: The information in this chapter is from "Religious Beliefs and Substance Use Among Youths," *The National Survey on Drug Use and Health (NSDUH) Report*, Substance Abuse and Mental Health Services Administration (SAMHSA), January 30, 2004.

Table 12.1. Percentages Of Youths Aged 12 To 17 Reporting Religious Factors, By Gender And Race/Ethnicity: 2002

	Attended 25 Or More Religious Services In The Past Year	Religious Beliefs Are A Very Important Part of Their Lives	Religious Beliefs Influence How They Make Decisions
Total	33.0	78.2	69.0
Gender			
Male	31.3	74.4	66.3
Female	34.7	62.1	71.9
Race/Ethnicity			
White	36.9	76.4	67.1
Black	28.1	85.2	77.2
Hispanic	24.3	79.5	69.1

Source: SAMHSA 2002 NSDUH.

to marijuana or hashish, cocaine (including crack), inhalants, hallucinogens, heroin, or prescription-type drugs used nonmedically. Youths also were asked to indicate how often they attended religious services, whether their religious beliefs are a very important part of their lives, and whether their religious beliefs influence how they make decisions.[2,3] Responses were analyzed by gender and race/ethnicity.[4]

Religious Factors Among Youths

In 2002, 33 percent of youths aged 12 to 17 (about 8 million) attended religious services 25 times or more in the past year (Table 12.1). Slightly more than 78 percent, or 19 million youths, reported that religious beliefs are a very important part of their lives. In addition, 69 percent, or 17 million youths, reported that religious beliefs influence how they make decisions. Among youths, females were more likely than males to attend religious services, to report that religious beliefs are a very important part of their lives, and to indicate that religious beliefs influence how they make decisions (Table 12.1). White youths were more likely to attend religious services 25 times or more in the past year than black or Hispanic youths. However, black youths were more likely to report that religious beliefs are a very important part of their lives, and that religious beliefs influence how they make decisions compared with white and Hispanic youths.

Religious Service Attendance And Substance Use

In 2002, youths aged 12 to 17 who attended religious services 25 times or more in the past year were less likely to have used cigarettes, alcohol, or illicit drugs in the past month than youths who attended less than 25 religious services in the past year. For example, 7 percent of youths who attended religious services 25 times or more in the past year used illicit drugs in the past month compared with approximately 14 percent of youths who attended religious services less than 25 times in the past year (Table 12.2).

Importance Of Religious Beliefs In Life And Substance Use

Youths aged 12 to 17 who reported that religious beliefs are a very important part of their lives were less likely to have used cigarettes, alcohol, or illicit drugs in the past month than youths who reported that religious beliefs are not a very important part of their lives. For example, 15 percent of youths who reported that religious beliefs are a very important part of their

Table 12.2. Percentages Of Youths Aged 12–17 Reporting Past Month Substance Use, By Past Year Religious Service Attendance: 2002

Substance	Fewer Than 25 Religious Services	25 Or More Religious Services
Cigarettes	15.6	7.8
Any Alcohol	20.0	13.3
Any Illicit Drug	13.9	7.1

Source: SAMHSA 2002 NSDUH.

lives used alcohol in the past month compared with 27 percent of youths who reported that religious beliefs are not a very important part of their lives (Table 12.3).

Table 12.3. Percentages Of Youths Aged 12–17 Reporting Past Month Substance Use, By Whether Or Not Religious Beliefs Are A Very Important Part Of Their Lives: 2002

Substance	Not Very Important	Very Important
Cigarettes	22.4	10.4
Any Alcohol	26.9	15.2
Any Illicit Drug	20.5	9.2

Source: SAMHSA 2002 NSDUH.

Table 12.4. Percentages Of Youths Aged 12–17 Reporting Past Month Substance Use, By Whether Or Not Religious Beliefs Influence How They Make Decisions: 2002

Substance	Do Not Influence Decisions	Influence Decisions
Cigarettes	22.3	8.9
Any Alcohol	26.5	13.8
Any Illicit Drug	19.4	8.2

Source: SAMHSA 2002 NSDUH.

Religious Beliefs' Influence On Decisions And Substance Use

Youths aged 12 to 17 who reported that religious beliefs influence how they make decisions also were less likely to have used cigarettes, alcohol, or illicit drugs in the past month than youths who reported that religious beliefs do not influence how they make decisions. For example, 9 percent of youths who reported that religious beliefs influence how they make decisions used cigarettes in the past month compared with approximately 22 percent of youths who reported that religious beliefs do not influence how they make decisions (Table 12.4).

End Notes

1. Petraitis, J., Flay, B. R., Miller, T. Q., Torpy, E. J., & Greiner, B. (1998). Illicit substance use among adolescents: A matrix of prospective predictors. *Substance Use & Misuse*, 33, 2561–2604.

☞ Remember!!

Studies from the National Center on Addiction and Substance Abuse at Columbia University have also shown that teens who attend religious services are less likely to use alcohol.

2. Youths were asked to indicate how many times in the past 12 months they attended religious services, excluding special occasions, such as weddings or funerals. Response options were (a) 0 times, (b) 1 to 2 times, (c) 3 to 5 times, (d) 6 to 24 times, (e) 25 to 52 times, and (f) more than 52 times.

3. Youths were asked whether their religious beliefs are a very important part of their lives. They also were asked whether their religious beliefs influence how they make decisions in their lives. Response options for both questions were (1) strongly disagree, (2) disagree, (3) agree, and (4) strongly agree. For this report, responses were coded as "not very important" (responses 1 and 2) and "very important" (responses 3 and 4) and as "do not influence" (responses 1 and 2) and "influence" (responses 3 and 4).

4. Non-Hispanic Asian, American Indian or Alaska Native, and Native Hawaiian or other Pacific Islander youths were excluded from the racial/ethnic comparisons due to small sample sizes.

The National Survey On Drug Use And Health (NSDUH)

The National Survey on Drug Use and Health (NSDUH) is an annual survey sponsored by the Substance Abuse and Mental Health Services Administration (SAMHSA). Prior to 2002, this survey was called the National Household Survey on Drug Abuse (NHSDA). The 2002 data are based on information obtained from 68,126 persons aged 12 or older, including 23,645 youths aged 12 to 17. The survey collects data by administering questionnaires to a representative sample of the population through face-to-face interviews at their place of residence. The NSDUH Report prepared by the Office of Applied Studies (OAS), SAMHSA, and by RTI (Research Triangle Institute) in Research Triangle Park, North Carolina.

Information and data for this chapter are based on the following publication and statistics:

• Office of Applied Studies. (2003). Results from the 2002 National Survey on Drug Use and Health: National findings (DHHS Publication No. SMA 03–3836, NHSDA Series H–22). Rockville, MD: Substance Abuse and Mental Health Services Administration. Also available on-line: http://www.DrugAbuseStatistics.samhsa.gov.

Because of improvements and modifications to the 2002 NSDUH, 2002 estimates should not be compared with estimates from the 2001 or earlier versions of the survey to examine changes over time.

Chapter 11

When Teens Drink, Parents May Pay

In his role as director of a youth commission in suburban Boston, Jon Mattleman meets parents whose teenagers have been caught drinking. Although the parents know underage drinking is illegal, their reactions sometimes surprise him.

"They'll be defensive about it, they'll rationalize it," says Mr. Mattleman, who works in Needham, Massachusetts. "They'll say, 'I did the same thing when I was a kid.'" A few even provide the liquor themselves, reasoning that if teens drink at home, parents can supervise—and lock up their car keys.

Now tolerant parents like these are becoming the latest targets in a national battle against underage drinking. After years of focusing on bars and liquor stores that serve underage drinkers, community leaders and law-enforcement officials are broadening their approach, holding parents accountable if they allow liquor to be served to minors in their home.

"We can't blame teenagers for the problem when it's adults who are providing the alcohol to them," says Ferris Morrison, project manager for the North Carolina Initiative to Reduce Underage Drinking. "A lot of the problem is that parents just don't see alcohol as a problem."

About This Chapter: Text in this chapter is from "When teens drink, parents may pay," by Marilyn Gardner, *Christian Science Monitor*, September 6, 2000. © 2000 Christian Science Publishing Society. Republished with permission of the Christian Science Publishing Society, permission conveyed through Copyright Clearance Center, Inc.

Laws Aim At Adults' Role

Efforts to change that attitude are wide-ranging. Some states are passing tougher "social host" and "adult responsibility" laws. Others are holding community meetings to educate parents and teenagers. In addition, 10 states, the District of Columbia, and Puerto Rico have formed coalitions to reduce underage drinking, funded by the Robert Wood Johnson Foundation.

Rep. John Mica (R) of Florida and Rep. Lucille Roybal-Allard (D) of California introduced a bill in Congress to establish a national media campaign to prevent underage drinking. An existing antidrug media campaign does not warn against alcohol.

Although the use of illegal drugs is down among young people, more than 10 million teenagers drink, according to a study released by the Substance Abuse and Mental Health Services Administration. Nearly 7 million engaged in binge drinking last year. The average age for a first drink is 13, even though drinking under the age of 21 is illegal.

Many parents strongly support efforts to prevent underage drinking, of course. But others view it simply as a rite of passage.

Some parents raised in the 1960s and '70s "take a little more cavalier approach to underage drinking," says David LeVasseur, co-chairman of the Connecticut Coalition to Stop Underage Drinking. "We all know parents who say, 'Well, at least it's just alcohol and not marijuana or cocaine.'" In fact, parents who tolerate teen drinking are not necessarily devoid of moral intention. Some see teen alcohol use as almost inevitable, and argue that providing a supervised environment for the activity is the most responsible approach.

But letting youths use "just" alcohol carries its own perils. Beyond drunk driving, experts point out that youthful drinking can contribute to unwanted pregnancies, sexually transmitted diseases, vandalism, and violence. Alcohol abuse is linked to as many as two-thirds of all sexual assaults and date rapes among teenagers and college students.

Students obtain alcohol in many ways: getting older friends and siblings to buy it for them, raiding parents' liquor cabinets, and bribing customers outside package stores. Adding to the temptation are relatively low prices. A single serving of alcohol can cost less than bottled water or bottled juice.

✤ **It's A Fact!!**

Laws Hold Adults Responsible If They Provide Alcohol To Minors

Adult Responsibility Laws

Adult responsibility laws make it illegal for any person to sell, furnish, or provide any alcoholic beverages to anyone under the age of 21 years. (It may be lawful for parents to provide alcohol to their children in their home or under certain circumstances, i.e., holidays, religious celebrations).

Dram shop or social host laws make adults 21 and older liable for the actions of those under the legal drinking age, i.e., criminal or civil liability against a host who provided alcohol to a minor and that minor was involved in an incident resulting in physical or bodily harm. (Source: "Community How To Guide On Underage Drinking Prevention," National Highway Traffic and Safety Administration, March 2001.)

Keg Registration

Keg registration laws require vendors to record the keg purchaser's name, address, telephone number, and driver's license number, along with the address at which the keg is to be served. Keg identification numbers are also issued and recorded, much like license plates on cars, but nearly impossible to remove. Keg purchasers must sign a form acknowledging that they understand the penalties for serving underage drinkers. Every retailer should have visible signs informing the public that it is illegal to supply alcoholic beverages to youth. If police are called to a disturbance or party where underage youth are consuming alcohol served from a keg, the keg identification number can be used to determine who supplied the keg and appropriate sanctions can be imposed, whether the responsible party is an individual adult or a retailer. Keg registration can be effective in deterring sales to underage youth or adults who supply alcohol to underage youth. (Source: "Partners in Prevention," National Highway Traffic and Safety Administration, July 2002.)

Parents Have Key Role

But it is parental attitudes that can have the most profound effect on young people. "Many kids say, 'We drink because adults let us drink,'" explains Bonnie Holmes, executive director of the Maryland Underage Drinking Prevention Coalition. "Kids have told us over and over, 'We laugh at these parents [who allow teenagers to drink in their homes] all the way to the next party. If we can drink in your house, why can't we drink at the park or at the football game under the bleachers?'"

As a result, many states are cracking down with tougher laws:

• In Minnesota, those convicted under a recent Zero Adult Providers (ZAP) law can be jailed, fined, or sued for damages. Homeowner's insurance policies do not cover this liability, because it involves an illegal act. Those found guilty must pay out of pocket.

• In North Carolina, anyone convicted of providing alcohol to underage persons will be fined a minimum of $250 and assigned 25 hours of community service.

• In Maryland, adult providers can be charged up to $1,000 for a first offense.

The upshot: No longer can parents claim to be ignorant of what is going on in their home, saying, "Oh, I was up in the bedroom or down in the basement."

Family advocates point out the importance of changing attitudes, helping parents understand that youthful drinking is not the norm. "We need to say to adults, 'Most adults don't provide alcohol to teenagers, and most teenagers don't drink,'" Ms. Morrison says.

Community Campaigns

In Connecticut, towns are organizing public meetings to educate parents. "We're trying to increase awareness that parents take on an incredible liability potential when they condone and provide alcohol for an in-home party," says Mr. LeVasseur.

And in Needham, Massachusetts, the Needham Youth Commission has created a 12-hour program to help parents of teens. "Letting parents know that they put themselves at risk will have an impact," Mattleman says.

Teenagers, too, are playing a role. Some 435 high school students proposed solutions to Washington lawmakers at a national youth summit on preventing underage drinking, hosted by Mothers Against Drunk Driving.

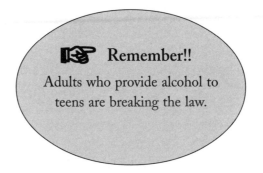

☞ Remember!!
Adults who provide alcohol to
teens are breaking the law.

Chapter 12

Reduce Youth Access To Alcohol

Why Raise Alcohol Excise Taxes To Protect Underage Youth?

In its report released on September 10, 2003, *Reducing Underage Drinking: A Collective Responsibility*, the National Academy of Sciences recommended increasing alcohol excise taxes to curb underage drinking. The report listed rationales for increasing the taxes. This chapter provides research evidence to support each reason.

"Underage drinking imposes particularly high average social costs..."

- One study estimates the total economic cost of alcohol use by underage drinkers in America amounts to nearly $53 billion a year. This includes more than $29 billion in alcohol-related violent crime costs, over $19 billion in traffic crashes, and over $1.5 billion in suicide attempts (fatal and nonfatal). If this cost were shared equally by each congressional district, the amount would total more than $120 million per district.[1]

About This Chapter: This chapter includes "Why Raise Alcohol Excise Taxes to Protect Underage Youth?" October 2003, and "Enforcing Underage Drinking Laws," April 2001; both reprinted with permission from the Center for Science in the Public Interest Alcohol Policies Project. All rights reserved. For more information please visit http://cspinet.org/booze.

- Alcohol is a factor in the four leading causes of death among persons ages 10 to 24: (1) motor-vehicle crashes, (2) unintentional injuries, (3) homicide, and (4) suicide.[2]

- Young people who begin drinking before age 15 are four times more likely to develop alcohol dependence than those who begin drinking at age 21.[3]

- For college students, lower beer prices are related to higher incidences of trouble-making with police and other authorities, property damage, getting into an argument or a fight, and taking advantage of or being taken advantage of sexually.[4]

"Raising excise tax rates, and hence prices, is a strategy that has strong and well-documented prevention effects on underage drinking."

- Young adults are more responsive to price increases than adults.[5]

- Beer prices inversely correlate with youths' decisions to drink.[6]

♣ It's A Fact!!
Teen Access To Alcohol

The National Center on Addiction and Substance Abuse at Columbia University reports that:

- Each year approximately 3.3 million students between the ages of 12 and 17 start drinking.

- One significant contributing factor to underage drinking is easy access to alcohol. In 2001, 70.6 percent of eighth graders, 87.7 percent of tenth graders, and 94.3 percent of twelfth graders said it is "fairly easy" or "very easy" to obtain alcohol.

- One study found that adults over the age of 21 were the primary source of alcohol for teens in the ninth and twelfth grades and for older teens, 18–20 year olds.

- Other studies suggest that it is fairly easy for teens to purchase alcohol from commercial establishments. One survey of teens found that approximately two-thirds of teenagers who drink report that they can buy their own alcohol.

Source: "Teen Tipplers: American's Underage Drinking Epidemic," Reprinted with permission from the National Center on Addiction and Substance Abuse (CASA) at Columbia University, http://www.casacolumbia.org. © 2002. All rights reserved.

- Frequency and quantity of underage alcohol consumption is inversely related to the price of alcohol.[7]

- In a survey of self-reported responses, high school students admit to reducing their overall alcohol use because of price increases.[8]

- Research shows that higher taxes increase the probability of attending and graduating from a four-year college or university. According to the study, raising the state beer tax from $0.10 per case to $1.00 per case would increase the probability of graduating from college by 6.3 percent.[9]

- College students are less likely to transition from abstainers to moderate drinkers or from moderate drinkers to heavy drinkers if alcohol prices are high.[10]

- The Centers for Disease Control and Prevention found that a beer-tax increase of 20 cents per six-pack would reduce gonorrhea rates by 8.9 percent and syphilis rates by 32.7 percent.[11]

- Higher beer taxes are associated with lower rates of traffic fatalities. For every one percent increase in the price of beer, the traffic fatality rate declines by 0.9 percent.[12]

"A designated portion of the funds generated by the taxes can be earmarked for preventing and reducing underage drinking."

- Nearly 82 percent of adults favor an increase of five cents per drink in the tax on beer to pay for programs to prevent minors from drinking and to increase alcohol treatment programs.[13]

- Few states are taking advantage of alcohol excise tax collections by earmarking revenues to pay for important treatment and prevention programs that, because of budget shortfalls, have been forced to make cuts.[14]

- A recent report found that 24 states earmarked the revenues from alcohol taxes and sales to various state programs in 1997. Some examples of programs to which the money went include public schools in Idaho, the school aid fund in Michigan, and health insurance programs in Oregon.[15]

References

1. Levy, D.T., Miller, T.R., Spicer, R. & Stewart, K. (1999). *Underage Drinking: Intermediate Consequences and their Costs.* Pacific Institute for Research and Evaluation working paper. June 1999.

2. Grunbaum, J., Kann, L., Kinchen, S.A., Williams, B.I., Ross, J.G., Lowry, R., & Kolbe, L.J. Youth risk behavior surveillance—United States, 2001. In: *Surveillance Summaries,* June 28, 2002. *MMWR* 2002;51(No. SS-4):1-64.

3. Grant, B.F. & Dawson, D.A. (1997). Age at Onset of Alcohol Use and its Association with DSM-IV Alcohol Abuse and Dependence: Results from the National Longitudinal Alcohol Epidemiologic Survey. *Journal of Substance Abuse.* 9:103-110.

4. Grossman, M. & Markowitz, S. (2000). *Alcohol regulation and violence on college campuses.* Research report. National Bureau of Economic Research. January 2000.

5. Chaloupka, F.J., Grossman, M. & Saffer, H. (2002). The effects of price on alcohol consumption and alcohol-related problems. *Alcohol Research & Health.* 26(1):22-34.

6. Cook, P.J. & Moore, M.J. (2002). The economics of alcohol abuse and alcohol-control policies. *Health Affairs.* 21(2):120-133.

7. Grossman, M., Chaloupka, F.J., Saffer, H. & Laixuthai, A. (1994). Effects of alcohol price policy on youth: A summary of economic research. *Journal of Research on Adolescence.* 4(2):347-364. Cook, P.J. & Moore, M.J. (1993). Drinking and schooling. *Journal of Health Economics.* 12:411-429.

8. Lockhart, S.J., Beck, K.H. & Summons, T.G. (1993). Impact of higher alcohol prices on alcohol-related attitudes and perceptions of suburban, middle class youth. *Journal of Youth and Adolescence.* 22(4):441-454.

9. Cook, P.J. & Moore, M.J. (1993). Drinking and schooling. *Journal of Health Economics.* 12:411-429.

10. Williams, J., Chaloupka, F. & Wechsler, H. (2002). *Are there differential effects of price and policy on college students' drinking intensity?* ImpacTeen. Research Paper Series, No. 16. January 2002. Online: http://impacteen.org/ab_RPNo16_2002.htm

11. Chesson, H., Harrison, P. & Kassler, W.J. (2000). Sex under the influence: The effect of alcohol policy on sexually transmitted disease rates in the United States. *Journal of Law and Economics.* XLIII:215-238.

12. Ruhm, C.J. (1996). Alcohol policies and highway vehicle fatalities. *Journal of Health Economics.* 15(4):435-454.

13. Harwood, E.M., Wagenaar, A.C. & Zander, K.M. (1998). *Youth access to alcohol survey: Summary report.* Princeton, NJ: Robert Wood Johnson Foundation. Online: http://www.rwjf.org/publications/publicationsPdfs/Youth_Access_to_Alcohol_Survey.pdf

14. Ensuring Solutions to Alcohol Problems (2003). "Few States Dedicate Alcohol Excise Tax to Fund Alcohol Treatment Programs, New Analysis Shows How Critical Programs Can Be Saved By Little-Known Revenue Source." Press Release. May 29, 2003. Online: http://www.ensuringsolutions.org/pages/052903.html

15. Fiscal Planning Services Inc. (2002). *Dedicated State Tax Revenues: A Fifty-State Report.* Bethesda, MD. Online: http://www.ncsl.org/programs/fiscal/pmtaxrev.pdf

Enforcing Underage Drinking Laws

There is no doubt that underage drinking is a major public health problem in the United States. In 1998, about 10.4 million current drinkers were between the ages of 12 and 20.[1] More than five million of these individuals were binge drinkers.[1] One study estimates the total economic cost of alcohol use by underage drinkers in America amounts to nearly $53 billion a year. This includes more than $29 billion in alcohol-related violent crime costs, over $19 billion in traffic crashes, and over $1.5 billion in suicide attempts (fatal and nonfatal).[2]

Table 12.1. Cost Of Underage Drinking (In Millions)[2]

Violent Crime	$29,368
Traffic Crashes	$19,452
Suicide Attempts	$1,512
Treatment	$1,008
Fetal Alcohol Syndrome	$493
Drowning	$426
Alcohol Poisonings	$340
Burns	$189
Total	$52,788

To address the growing cost to society associated with underage drinking, Congress appropriated $50 million, over a two-year period, to the Department of Justice's Office of Juvenile Justice and Delinquency Prevention (OJJDP) to fund the Enforcing the Underage Drinking Laws Program (formerly the Combating Underage Drinking Program). In fiscal years 1998 and 1999 the program provided block grants, discretionary funds, and training and technical assistance to state and local jurisdictions in an effort to help develop comprehensive and coordinated initiatives to enforce state laws that prohibit the sale of alcoholic beverages to minors and to prevent the purchase or consumption of alcoholic beverages by individuals under the age of 21.[3]

Enforcement of state and local laws has proven highly effective in the past. According to the National Highway Traffic Safety Administration, since 1975 over 18,000 young lives have been saved by minimum drinking-age laws.[4] Implementing zero tolerance laws, vigorous use of compliance checks, and increases in alcoholic-beverage excise taxes have also been found to be effective in curbing youth alcohol consumption.[5]

OJJDP Recommendations For Reducing Youth Access To Alcohol

In an effort to assist state and local governments to identify "gaps" in their current efforts to reduce youth access to alcohol, OJJDP offers a guide highlighting the "best practices" for regulating underage drinking. The guide contains the following recommendations:

Commercial Availability[6]

- Ban commercial sales and gifts to minors
- Restrict the location of alcohol outlets
- Restrict alcohol sales at community events
- Restrict the age of alcohol servers and sellers
- Restrict minors' access to bars and nightclubs
- Install and use driver license scanners
- Regulate home delivery and Internet/mail-order sales
- Mandate responsible beverage service programs
- Carry out compliance check programs

Social/Public Availability[6]

- Restrict noncommercial furnishing of alcohol to minors
- Implement beer keg registration
- Implement "shoulder-tap" enforcement programs (shoulder tap enforcement deters adult strangers from buying alcohol for minors)
- Implement teen party ordinances
- Restrict and monitor teen parties at motels and hotels
- Establish alcohol restrictions in public locations
- Apply appropriate penalties to illegal transactions in noncommercial settings

Minors In Possession Of Alcohol[6]

- Ban possession by minors in public and private locations
- Use "Cops in Shops" programs sparingly ("Cops in Shops" uses undercover law enforcement officers in commercial establishments)

- Implement and enforce zero-tolerance laws

- Ban false identification

- Apply appropriate penalties to minors in possession

References

> **☞ Remember!!**
> Laws and fees which make it harder for people under 21 to drink are saving lives.

1. Substance Abuse and Mental Health Services Administration. *Summary of Findings from the 1998 National Household Survey on Drug Abuse*, U.S. Department of Health and Human Services, August 1999.

2. Levy, D.T., Miller, T. R., Spicer, R., & Stewart, K. *Underage Drinking: Intermediate Consequences and their Costs*, Pacific Institute for Research and Evaluation working paper, June 1999.

3. McKinney, K. *Enforcing the Underage Drinking Laws Program*, Office of Juvenile Justice and Delinquency Prevention, May 1999.

4. National Highway Traffic Safety Administration. *Traffic Safety Facts 1998: Young Drivers*, U.S. Department of Transportation, 1999.

5. Pacific Institute for Research and Evaluation. *Strategies to Reduce Underage Alcohol Use: Typology and Brief Overview*, in support of the OJJDP Enforcing the Underage Drinking Laws Program, 1999.

6. Pacific Institute for Research and Evaluation. *Regulatory Strategies for Preventing Youth Access to Alcohol: Best Practices*, prepared for the Office of Juvenile Justice and Delinquency Prevention National Leadership Conference, July 11-14, 1999.

Chapter 13

Preventing Alcohol Abuse Through Positive Youth Development

A number of youth serving organizations are turning to positive youth development as a way to deal with problems involving alcohol use. Positive youth development differs from prevention in that it focuses on a young person's strengths and his or her ability to make healthy, responsible decisions and be a productive member of society. Prevention programs, by and large, focus on preventing specific behaviors. Rather than labeling young people at risk, positive youth development is an asset building approach.

In 2002 4-H convened "The National Conversation on Youth Development in the 21st Century" to celebrate the 4-H movement's centennial year. The vision statement for that conversation gives a good description of positive youth development.

> Youth development: the natural process of growing up and developing one's capabilities, which is too important to be left to chance. Positive youth development occurs from an intentional process that promotes

About This Chapter: Text in this chapter is excerpted from "National Youth Resource Center Ideas and Suggestions." Copyright 2003 National Commission Against Drunk Driving. Reprinted with permission. Additional text under the heading "Too Smart To Start," is from "SAMHSA Launches National Program to Keep Pre-Teens from Alcohol," Substance Abuse and Mental Health Services Administration (SAMHSA), News Release, April 20, 2004.

positive outcomes for young people by providing support, relationships, and opportunities. Youth development takes place in families, peer groups, schools, and in neighborhoods and communities, and prepares young people to meet the challenges of adolescence and adulthood through a coordinated, progressive series of research-based experiences that help them to become socially, morally, emotionally, physically, and intellectually competent.

According to the National Youth Development Information Center, youth development generally has the following elements:

- Focuses on the positive

- Urges personal responsibility for making a difference

- Is proactive

- Mobilizes the public as well as all youth-serving organizations in a community

- Views youth as resources

- Has a vision-building perspective

- Advocates cooperation within the community

- Unleashes the caring potential of all the residents and organizations so that public resources can be focused on areas of greatest need

> ✔ Quick Tip
> The positive developmental approach views young people as resources and builds on their strengths and capabilities.

Rather than seeking to stop young people from engaging in risky behaviors, like underage drinking, youth development programs address the basic needs that are critical to survival and healthy development. These include:

- Safety and structure

- Belonging and membership

- Self-worth and an ability to contribute

- Independence and control over one's life

- Closeness and several good relationships

- Competence and mastery

According to the Younger Americans Act Policy Proposal, National Collaboration for Youth, effective programs have the following characteristics:

- Youth centered

- Staff and activities engage young people's diverse talents, skills, and interest

- Build on a young person's strengths and involve them in planning and decision-making

- Knowledge centered and show youth that learning is a reason to be involved

- Provide opportunities to connect with a wide array of adult and peer mentors

The goal is to build a resilient young person. In their 1992 report, "A Matter of Time," the Carnegie Council on Adolescent Development, a resilient individual has the following attributes:

- Social competence

- Problem-solving skills

- Autonomy (sense of self-identity and an ability to act independently and to exert control over his or her environment)

- Sense of purpose and of a future

A positive youth development program works on three levels:

- Help individual youth build positive characteristics

- Ensures there is at least one caring, consistent adult in each young person's life

- Develops a sense of security in the lives of all young people

♣ **It's A Fact!!**

Tips For Youth

- It is illegal in all 50 states and the District of Columbia to drink alcohol if you are under 21.

- If you have respect for yourself, your friends will respect your right to be you. Respect yourself enough not to do something you know is not right.

- To be treated like an adult, you have to act like one. This means following the rules your parent/guardian establishes for you, obeying the law, and making responsible decisions.

- Alcohol is just a temporary solution to your problems. If you have a problem, find someone to talk to such as a friend, a sibling, or a teacher.

- Involve yourself in positive activities.

- Not everyone drinks. On college campuses, less than 40% of young people drink.

- Encourage your school/community organizations to host alcohol and drug-free activities.

- Be a leader, not a follower.

- Work with groups in your area to spread the message that it is cool to be sober.

- Choosing not to drink does not make your less cool than others. It is a sign of self-pride and maturity.

- Never ride with a drunk driver. The driver may seem okay to drive, but do not risk your life—take the person's keys if necessary.

- Remember alcohol lessens inhibitions. You could do something you do not want to do which could ruin a bright and promising future.

Tips For Communities

- Use community centers/halls to host non-alcohol parties for under-21 youth in your area. Specify all rules before you begin the party including starting and ending times. Circulate regularly during the party, checking all rooms of the center and the parking lot. Do not allow young people to leave and re-enter.

- Establish a citizen hotline to report underage drinking parties to police departments and alcohol beverage (ABC) agencies. Work with local law enforcement and ABC personnel to enforce underage drinking laws.

- Testify in public hearings on the importance of strong underage drinking laws.

- Work with parents and community groups to share information and co-ordinate activities. Publicize liquor establishments that continually sell to underage youth in a community newsletter, flyers, and the newspaper.

- Volunteer to work with youth at teen centers and after-school programs to help them develop peer leadership and peer pressure resistance skills.

- Create and sponsor mini-grants for use by student groups and schools for prevention activities. Local businesses can provide funds.

- Write letters to the editor on the need for more attention to the issue of underage drinking.

- Send letters congratulating the local police department on their underage drinking enforcement efforts.

- Sponsor "Parent Pledges" which indicate no alcohol is allowed in the home by youth under-21.

Tips For Schools

- Establish a firm "no use" policy for participation in all team activities. Enforce the policy with no exceptions.

- Use school cafeteria/gymnasium to host non-alcohol parties for high school students. Rotate these events throughout the school year and in the summer to different schools in your area.

- Circulate regularly during parties, check all halls and parking lot. Do not let any student leave and re-enter. Admit students with school identification from your area.

- Film the school's football and basketball games. Host a party following the game and show the game film. Showing the film will serve as an attraction for athletes and others.

- Host "open gym" or "lock ins" for area youth at your high school.

- Work with your local law enforcement officials to educate youth on the legal consequences of underage drinking.

- Develop media literacy training in your school to educate young people about the effects of alcohol advertising.

- Develop creative ways to convey the "no use" message, i.e., drama club, drunk driving simulator.

- Sponsor competitions among youth such as posters, songs, or videos that focus on solutions to underage drinking.

- Develop and coordinate education programs aimed at parents and/or guardians regarding underage drinking issues.

- Sponsor "Parent Pledges" which indicate no alcohol is allowed for under-21 youth. Distribute these addresses to your local PTA.

- Produce a calendar which lists positive alternatives for students.

- Recognize students who have done an outstanding job in underage drinking prevention and education.

- Develop and promote programs which increase self-esteem, leadership skills, and individual responsibility.

Too Smart To Start

April 20, 2004, Substance Abuse and Mental Health Services Administration (SAMHSA) Administrator Charles G. Curie launched a new national program to keep pre-teens, ages 9–13, from initiating alcohol consumption. The idea behind *Too Smart to Start* is to reach out to children and caregivers before children start drinking alcohol.

Too Smart to Start provides research-based strategies and materials to community groups with the objective of enhancing communication between parents and children about the harm of underage alcohol use. Materials target both the parent's views about underage drinking and those of the child, with information on alcohol use behaviors of 9–13 year-olds and strategies to deliver behavioral messages.

"SAMHSA's National Survey on Drug Use and Health shows approximately 11.6 percent of 12 year olds report using alcohol at least once in their lifetime. That percentage more than doubles by age 13 and by age 15, it is over 50 percent," SAMHSA Administrator Charles Curie pointed out. "We

---

☞ Remember!!

For Additional Information On Positive Youth Development Programs

National Youth Development Information Center
1319 F Street, N.W., Suite 601
Washington, DC 20004
Toll-Free: 877-693-4248
Fax: 202-393-4517
Website: http://www.nydic.org/nydic/

National 4-H Council
7100 Connecticut Ave.
Chevy Chase, MD 20815
Website: http://www.fourhcouncil.edu
E-mail: info@fourhcouncil.edu

Too Smart To Start
7200 Wisconsin Ave, Suite 600
Bethesda, MD 20814
Toll-Free: 800-729-6686
Website: http://www.toosmarttostart.samhsa.gov

have to reach out to 9–13 year olds now, before they drink, and provide health messages that will resonate with them, and with their parents.

SAMHSA's data show that over 2.6 million adolescents 12–17 were binging on alcohol in 2002 and 630,000 were already heavy drinkers. "Parents must understand that yes, it can be their kids," Curie said, "and that children who use alcohol early in life are at greater risk of having alcohol problems as adults."

Part Three

Underage Drinking

Chapter 14

America's Underage Drinking Epidemic

Teen Tipplers

Alcohol is far and away the top drug of abuse by America's teens. Children under the age of 21 drink 25 percent of the alcohol consumed in the U.S. More than five million high school students (31.5 percent) admit to binge drinking at least once a month. The age at which children begin drinking is dropping: since 1975, the proportion of children who begin drinking in the eighth grade or earlier has jumped by almost a third, from 27 to 36 percent. And the gender gap that for generations separated alcohol consumption by girls and boys has evaporated: male and female ninth graders are just as likely to drink (40.2 percent and 41 percent) and binge drink (21.7 percent and 20.2 percent).

By any public health standard, America has an epidemic of underage drinking that germinates in elementary and middle schools with children nine to 13-years old and erupts on college campuses where 44 percent of students binge drink and alcohol is the number one substance of abuse—

About This Chapter: Text in this chapter is excerpted from "Teen Tipplers: America's Underage Drinking Epidemic," reprinted with permission from the National Center on Addiction and Substance Abuse (CASA) at Columbia University, http:// www.casacolumbia.org. © 2002. All rights reserved. Additional text under its own heading is from "Quantity and Frequency of Alcohol Use," Substance Abuse and Mental Health Services Administration (SAMHSA), 12/12/2003.

implicated in date rape, sexual harassment, racial disturbances, drop outs, overdose deaths from alcohol poisoning, and suicides. Teenagers who drink are seven times likelier to engage in sex and twice as likely to have sex with four or more partners than those who do not. Such behavior can lead to unprotected sex with the increased risk of AIDS, other sexually transmitted diseases, and pregnancy. Preliminary studies have shown that alcohol damages young minds, limiting mental and social development.

No other substance threatens as many of the nation's children. Eighty percent of high school students have tried alcohol, while 70 percent have smoked cigarettes, and 47 percent have used marijuana. Twenty-nine percent of high school seniors have used some other illegal drug such as Ecstasy.

Drinking is teen America's fatal attraction. Beer and other alcohol are implicated in the three top causes of teen deaths: accidents (including traffic fatalities and drowning), homicide, and suicide. The financial costs of underage drinking approach $53 billion in accidents, drowning, burns, violent crime, suicide attempts, fetal alcohol syndrome, alcohol poisoning, and emergency medical care. Teens who experiment with alcohol are virtually certain to continue using it. Among high school seniors who have ever tried alcohol—even once—91.3 percent are still drinking in twelfth grade. Most troubling, of high school students who have ever been drunk, 83.3 percent—more than two million teens—are still getting drunk in twelfth grade.

> ♣ **It's A Fact!!**
> High school students who drink are five times likelier to drop out of school.

The time and place to deal with binge drinking in college is in elementary and high school.

- Teen drinking is the number one source of adult alcoholism. Children who begin drinking before age 21 are more than twice as likely to develop alcohol-related problems. Those who begin drinking before age 15 are four times likelier to become alcoholics than those who do not drink before age 21.

- Underage drinkers are at greater risk of nicotine and illegal drug addiction. Teens who are heavy drinkers (consume at least five drinks on at least five occasions over 30 days) are more than 12 times likelier to use illegal drugs than those who do not drink.

How did we get here?

- Parents tend to see drinking and occasional bingeing as a rite of passage, rather than a deadly round of Russian roulette. Home—a child's or a child's friend's—is a major source of alcohol for children, especially for younger children. A third of sixth and ninth graders obtain alcohol from their own homes. Children cite other people's houses as the most common setting for drinking.

♣ **It's A Fact!!**
Just Once Is A Problem
Trying alcohol even once is dangerous. 91.3 percent of students who ever try alcohol are still drinking in twelfth grade.

- In our schools, middle and high school teachers have been reluctant to inform parents or intervene when they suspect a child or teen of drinking. College administrators and alumni have played Pontius Pilate, washing their hands and looking away, as students made beer, alcohol, and binge drinking a central part of their college experience.

- The pervasive influence of the entertainment media has glamorized and sexualized alcohol and rarely shown the ill effects of abuse. A review of 81 G-rated animated films found that in 34 percent of them alcohol use was associated with wealth or luxury and 19 percent associated alcohol with sexual activity.

- Television runs ads glorifying beer on sports programs watched by millions of children and teens. General Electric had decided that one of "the good things it will bring to life" will be hard liquor commercials on its NBC network. In its craven collaboration with the distilled spirits industry, GE has made NBC the only network to hawk hard liquor on shows watched by millions of children and teens.

- With a big push from alcohol lobbyists, the Congress has denied the White House Office of National Drug Control Policy authority to include alcohol—the number one drug of abuse by children and teens—in its media campaign and other activities to prevent drug abuse.

• The interest of the alcohol industry—especially those who sell beer—in underage drinking is understandable, if appalling. Underage drinkers are a critical segment of the alcohol beverage market. Individuals who do not drink before age 21 are virtually certain never to do so: 82.8 percent of adults who drink had their first drink of alcohol before age 21. Underage drinkers consume 25 percent of the alcohol—most often beer—sold in this country. In 1998, they accounted for up to $27 billion of the $108 billion spent on alcohol, including as much as $15 billion on beer. Without underage

---

✤ It's A Fact!!
Adolescents' Beliefs About Alcohol

• Adolescents ages 12 to 14 believe that the positive benefits of drinking (feeling good, fitting in with peers) are more likely to occur than the negative effects of drinking (feeling sick, causing serious health problems). White non-Hispanic students tend to hold more favorable beliefs about alcohol than African American students.

• Youth ages 12 to 14 who expect to gain greater social acceptance from drinking are more likely to begin to drink as well as to consume alcohol at faster rates.

• Adolescents ages 12 and 13 see other people, including their parents, as less disapproving of their engaging in drinking than do younger children.

• Fifty-six percent of students in grades 5 through 12 say that alcohol advertising encourages them to drink.

• Seventy-five percent of 8th graders and 89 percent of 10th graders believe that alcohol is readily available to them for consumption.

• Eighty percent of 12–17 year-olds surveyed think that alcohol negatively affects scholastic performance, and 81 percent believe it increases the likelihood of getting into trouble.

Source: Excerpted from "Youth and Underage Drinking: An Overview," Substance Abuse and Mental Health Services Administration (SAMHSA), 2000.

drinkers, the alcohol industry, and the beer industry in particular, would suffer severe economic declines and dramatic loss of profits.

Quantity And Frequency Of Alcohol Use

The *National Household Survey on Drug Use and Health* (NSDUH) is an annual survey sponsored by the Substance Abuse and Mental Health Services Administration (SAMHSA). Prior to 2002, this survey was called the *National Household Survey on Drug Abuse* (NHSDA). The 2002 data are based on information obtained from 68,216 persons aged 12 or older. The survey collects data by administering questionnaires to a representative sample of the population through face-to-face interviews at their place of residence.

Because of improvements and modifications to the 2002 NSDUH, estimates from the 2002 survey should not be compared with estimates from the 2001 or earlier versions of the survey to examine changes over time.

- In 2002, 51 percent of persons aged 12 or older were current drinkers.

- Current drinkers aged 12 to 17 and young adults aged 18 to 25 drank more drinks per day on the days they drank alcohol than adults aged 26 or older.

- Current drinkers aged 18 to 25 were more likely to drive under the influence of alcohol during the past year than drinkers aged 26 or older.

The 2002 *National Survey on Drug Use and Health* (NSDUH), formerly the *National Household Survey on Drug Abuse* (NHSDA), asks respondents who drank alcohol in the past 30 days (i.e., current drinkers) to report the number of days they drank alcohol in the past month and the average number of drinks consumed per day on each of the days they drank alcohol. Respondents also were asked whether they drove under the influence of alcohol during the past year. Responses were analyzed by age, gender, and race/ethnicity for comparison purposes.[1]

Prevalence Of Past 30 Day Alcohol Use

Among persons aged 12 or older, 51 percent drank alcohol in the past 30 days. Current drinking rates were higher among young adults aged 18 to 25

Table 14.1. Alcohol Use In The Past Month And Measures Of Past Month Alcohol Consumption, By Detailed Age Categories: 2002

Age Category	Percentage Using Alcohol in Past Month	Average Number of Days Used Alcohol in the Past Month	Average Number of Drinks Consumed Per Day of Use in the Past Month[1]	Average Number of Drinks Consumed Per User in the Past Month[1,2]	Total Number (in Thousands) of Drinks Consumed in the Past Month[3]
Total	51.0	8.5	3.1	29.6	3,551,565
12	2.0	3.2	2.7	11.1	923
13	6.5	3.7	2.7	20.0	5,477
14	13.4	4.5	3.5	22.5	13,136
15	19.9	4.8	4.4	30.9	25,368
16	29.0	4.8	5.0	31.2	36,303
17	36.2	5.3	5.8	39.2	56,050
18	46.3	6.0	5.4	41.2	83,274
19	51.6	7.0	5.5	47.5	100,031
20	55.5	6.9	5.0	41.0	91,026
21	70.9	7.9	4.5	40.5	116,215
22	67.0	7.8	4.6	45.3	117,303
23	66.2	7.8	4.4	41.7	105,157
24	64.9	7.2	3.8	32.5	74,239
25	64.4	7.4	3.8	32.7	70,140

[1]Respondents with missing data were excluded.

[2]The number of drinks consumed per user in the past month is defined as the product of the number of days that a respondent used alcohol in the past month and the average number of drinks consume per day on the days that alcohol was used in the past month.

[3]The total number of drinks consumed in the past month is defined as the product of the total number of persons who used alcohol in the past month and the average number of drinks consumed per user in the past month.

Source: SAMHSA, Office of Applied Studies, National Survey on Drug Use and Health, 2003.

(61 percent) than older adults aged 26 or older (54 percent) or youths aged 12 to 17 (18 percent). A higher percentage of males used alcohol during the past month (57 percent) than females (45 percent). Past month alcohol use also was higher among whites (55 percent) than American Indians or Alaska Natives (45 percent), Hispanics (43 percent), blacks (40 percent), or Asians (37 percent).

Number Of Days Drank Alcohol In The Past 30 Days

Current drinkers aged 12 or older drank on an average of 9 of the past 30 days. Among current drinkers, adults aged 26 or older drank alcohol on more days in the past 30 days (9 days) than adults aged 18 to 25 (7 days) or youths aged 12 to 17 (5 days). Current male drinkers drank on more days in the past 30 days (10 days) than current female drinkers (7 days). Among current drinkers, whites drank alcohol on more days in the past 30 days than blacks, Hispanics, or Asians.[2]

Number Of Drinks Per Day In The Past 30 Days

Current drinkers aged 12 or older drank an average of 3 drinks per day on the days they drank alcohol. Current drinkers aged 12 to 17 and young adults aged 18 to 25 drank more drinks per day on the days they drank alcohol than adults aged 26 or older. Among current drinkers, males drank 4 drinks per day compared to females who drank an average of 2 drinks per day on the days they drank alcohol. Among current drinkers, American Indians or Alaska Natives drank more drinks per day on the days they drank alcohol (6 drinks) than Hispanics (4 drinks), as well as whites, blacks, or Asians (each at 3 drinks).

Underage Drinking

In 2002, adults aged 21 or older were more likely to drink alcohol during the past 30 days (55 percent) than persons aged 12 to 20 (29 percent). Among current drinkers, adults aged 21 or older drank more days on average in the past 30 days compared with persons aged 12 to 20. However, current drinkers aged 12 to 20 drank more drinks per day on the days they drank than adults aged 21 or older.

Table 14.2. Alcohol Use In The Past Month And Measures Of Past Month Alcohol Consumption, By Demographic Characteristics: 2002

Demographic Characteristic	Percentage Using Alcohol in Past Month	Average Number of Days Used Alcohol in the Past Month	Average Number of Drinks Consumed Per Day of Use in the Past Month	Average Number of Drinks Consumed Per User in the Past Month [1,2]	Total Number (in Thousands) of Drinks Consumed in the Past Month [3]
Total	51.0	8.5	3.1	29.6	3,551,565
Age					
12–17	17.6	4.8	4.8	31.8	138,819
18–25	60.5	7.3	4.6	40.4	757,141
26 or Older	53.9	8.9	2.7	27.5	2,657,287
Gender					
Male	57.4	9.9	3.6	39.6	2,585,284
Female	44.9	6.7	2.4	17.8	972,188

Race					
Not Hispanic					
or Latino	52.1	8.7	3.0	29.4	3,160,831
White	55.0	9.0	2.9	29.6	2,698,088
Black or African					
American	39.9	7.2	2.9	28.1	301,203
American Indian					
or Alaska Native	44.7	7.3	5.9	53.5	35,312
Asian	37.1	5.5	2.5	20.1	67,602
Two or More Races	49.9	6.9	3.3	32.9	41,234
Hispanic or Latino	42.8	6.5	4.0	31.5	391,979

[1]Respondents with missing data were excluded.

[2]The number of drinks consumed per user in the past month is defined as the product of the number of days that a respondent used alcohol in the past month and the average number of drinks consume per day on the days that alcohol was used in the past month.

[3]The total number of drinks consumed in the past month is defined as the product of the total number of persons who used alcohol in the past month and the average number of drinks consumed per user in the past month.

Source: SAMHSA, Office of Applied Studies, National Survey on Drug Use and Health, 2003.

End Notes

1. Estimates for Native Hawaiian or other Pacific Islander respondents are not shown for the racial/ethnic comparisons in this report due to low precision.

2. Because of the small sample size for American Indian or Alaska Native respondents, the estimate for this group is not statistically different from estimates for any of the other racial/ethnic groups.

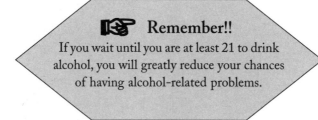

Remember!!
If you wait until you are at least 21 to drink alcohol, you will greatly reduce your chances of having alcohol-related problems.

Chapter 15

How Is Alcohol Affecting Your Life?

Drinking Can Spin Your World Around

Why should I say no to alcohol?

Alcohol is a drug and you can become addicted to it. Alcohol changes the way your mind and your body work. Even one beer can slow your reactions and confuse your thinking. This means anything that requires concentration and coordination—like driving—is dangerous when you've had a drink.

Alcohol also changes the way you act. It can make you let go of the feelings that keep you from doing things you know are risky or dangerous. This can lead you to make bad decisions—like having unsafe sex or driving when you know you shouldn't. You might think that it won't happen to you, but everyone knows someone who has said that and then ended up hurt.

What problems can alcohol cause?

Alcohol can ruin your health. The more you drink, the more damage is done. You can get alcohol poisoning if you drink too much. As the level of alcohol in your blood rises, the chemicals in your body can cause vomiting or seizures, or you may pass out.

Cirrhosis of the liver is one of the most well-known effects of alcohol abuse. Cirrhosis stops the liver from being able to clean the toxins (poisons) out of your body. Alcohol can also cause stomach ulcers that lead to internal bleeding.

Other things alcohol can do to your body:

- Make you gain weight

- Make you feel sick or dizzy

✔ Quick Tip
How Are Alcohol And Drugs Affecting Your Life?

A Self-Test For Teenagers

Purchase or public possession of alcohol is illegal for anyone under the age of 21 everywhere in the United States. Aside from the fact that you may be breaking the law by using alcohol and/or illicit drugs, if you answer yes to any three of the following questions, you may be at risk for developing alcoholism and/or dependence on another drug. If you answer yes to five of these questions, you should seek professional help immediately.

1. Do you use alcohol or other drugs to build self-confidence?

2. Do you ever drink or get high immediately after you have a problem at home or at school?

3. Have you ever missed school due to alcohol or other drugs?

4. Does it bother you if someone says that you use too much alcohol or other drugs?

5. Have you started hanging out with a heavy drinking or drug using crowd?

6. Are alcohol or other drugs affecting your reputation?

7. Do you feel guilty or bummed out after using alcohol or other drugs?

8. Do you feel more at ease on a date when drinking or using other drugs?

9. Have you gotten into trouble at home for using alcohol or other drugs?

- Give you bad breath

- Make you clumsy

- Slur your speech

- Make your skin break out

- Make you feel out of control

Would anybody care about my drinking if I were older?

Yes. Even adults are warned about the risks of alcohol.

---

10. Do you borrow money or do without other things to buy alcohol and other drugs?

11. Do you feel a sense of power when you use alcohol or other drugs?

12. Have you lost friends since you started using alcohol or other drugs?

13. Do your friends use less alcohol or other drugs than you do?

14. Do you drink or use other drugs until your supply is all gone?

15. Do you ever wake up and wonder what happened the night before?

16. Have you ever been busted or hospitalized due to alcohol or use of illicit drugs?

17. Do you turn off any studies or lectures about alcohol or illicit drug use?

18. Do you think you have a problem with alcohol or other drugs?

19. Has there ever been someone in your family with a drinking or other drug problem?

20. Could you have a problem with alcohol or other drugs?

Source: "How Are Alcohol and Drugs Affecting Your Life? A Self-Test for Teenagers," © 2003 National Council on Alcoholism and Drug Dependence, Inc. (NCADD). Reprinted with permission. For additional information, visit the NCADD website at www.ncadd.org.

Everyone I know drinks. What should I do?

Television and radio make it seem easy to avoid alcohol, but this may not be the case for you. You may be facing pressure from your friends who drink, you may be stressed out, or you may think that drinking makes people like

☞ **Remember!!**

Organizations That Can Help If Alcohol Is Affecting Your Life

Al-Anon/Alateen Family Groups
1600 Corporate Landing Parkway
Virginia Beach, VA 23454
Toll-Free: 888-425-2666
Phone: 757-563-1600
Fax: 613-723-0151
Website: http://www
.al-anon.alateen.org
E-mail: WSO@al-anon.org

Alcoholics Anonymous
General Service Office
P.O. Box 459
New York, NY 10163
Phone: 212-870-3400
Website: http://www
.alcoholics-anonymous.org

Mothers Against Drunk Driving (MADD)
National Headquarters
511 E. John Carpenter Freeway
Suite 700
Irving, TX 75062
Toll-Free: 800-438-6233
Phone: 214-744-6233
Fax: 972-869-2206
Website: http://www.madd.org

National Council on Alcoholism and Drug Dependence
20 Exchange Place, Suite 2902
New York, NY 10005
Toll-Free (24-Hour Hope Line): 800-622-2255
Phone: 212-269-7797
Fax: 212-269-7510
Website: http://www.ncadd.org
E-mail: national@ncadd.org

Students Against Destructive Decisions (SADD)
Box 800
Marlboro, MA 01752
Toll-Free: 877-723-3462
Fax: 508-481-5759
Website: http://www.saddonline.com

you. Whatever your reasons, remember that alcohol can harm your body. If you feel uncomfortable in a situation and need help saying no, get the support you need. Talk to your family doctor or another adult you trust.

How do I know I have a problem?

Drinking is a problem if it causes trouble in your relationships, school, and social activities, or how you think and feel. A drinking problem usually starts by just drinking every now and then. Eventually you may drink more and more until you have a new problem—needing a drink.

Ask yourself the following questions to find out if you have a problem with alcohol. If you answer yes to any one of them, you may have a drinking problem.

1. Do you sometimes drink more than you mean to?

2. Have you tried to cut back on your drinking and failed?

3. Do you blackout (have trouble remembering things that happened) while drinking?

4. Have your problems at school, work, or with your relationships increased since you started drinking?

5. Do you keep drinking even though you know it's causing you problems?

6. Do you drink when you feel stressed?

7. Do you drink alone?

8. Can you drink much more now than you used to be able to?

9. Do you ever feel uncomfortable when you haven't had a drink?

10. Do you drink even when it's important to stay sober?

How can I stop drinking?

The first step is to admit that you have a problem and you want to stop. Talk to your doctor, or a parent, school counselor, or spiritual leader. You can also contact Alcoholics Anonymous (AA), an organization that helps people with drinking problems get better. Visit their website at www.aa.org, or check your local phone book for an AA meeting near you.

How much alcohol is really in a drink?

Beer usually contains 3% to 5% alcohol. Wine has 9% to 16%. Hard liquor usually contains the highest levels (up to 50%). Most states consider an adult to be intoxicated, or drunk, at 0.08% blood level of alcohol. For a man who weighs 170 pounds, this might mean only 4 beers (12-ounce cans) on an empty stomach in an hour. For a woman who weighs 137 pounds, this might mean less than 3 beers in an hour. For people under 21, many states now practice zero-tolerance laws, which mean you are breaking the law if you have any alcohol in your system.

Is there anything I can do to sober up?

No. It takes time for your body to get all the alcohol out of your system. Many people think coffee can help, but it can't make you sober or speed your reaction times if you've been drinking. It can make you think you're alert when you're really not.

Chapter 16

Gender And Underage Alcohol Use

Big Differences In Why Girls And Boys Use Cigarettes, Alcohol, And Drugs

Girls and young women use cigarettes, alcohol, and other drugs for reasons different from boys, their signals and situations of higher risk differ, and they are more vulnerable to substance abuse and addiction and its consequences, according to a report released in February 2003 by The National Center on Addiction and Substance Abuse (CASA*) at Columbia University, *The Formative Years: Pathways to Substance Abuse among Girls and Young Women Ages 8-22.*

Despite promising statistics on recent declines in youth substance use, more than one quarter (27.7 percent) of high school girls currently smoke cigarettes, 45 percent drink alcohol, more than a quarter (26.4 percent) binge drink, and 20 percent use marijuana. Younger girls are smoking and drinking like boys. High school girls are almost as likely as boys to use cocaine and

About This Chapter: The text in this chapter includes an excerpt from "Big Differences in Why Girls VS Boys Use Cigarettes, Alcohol, and Drugs," reprinted with permission from the National Center on Addiction and Substance Abuse (CASA) at Columbia University, http://www.casacolumbia.org. © 2003. All rights reserved. Additional text under the heading "Alcohol Abuse In Men," is excerpted from "Alcohol and Drug Abuse in Men," National Women's Health Information Center, 11/2003. Additional text under its own heading is excerpted from "Alcohol Use Among Girls," Substance Abuse and Mental Health Services Administration (SAMHSA), 6/2000.

♣ **It's A Fact!!**

Alcohol, Women, And Men

Why the difference between women and men? Alcohol passes through the digestive tract and is dispersed in the water in the body. The more water available, the more diluted the alcohol. As a rule, men weigh more than women. In addition, pound for pound, women have less water in their bodies than men, so a woman's brain and other organs are exposed to more alcohol before it is broken down. These differences play a role in both the short- and long-term effects of alcohol on women.

Alcohol's Appeal For Teens

Among the reasons teens give most often for drinking are to have a good time, to experiment, and to relax or relieve tension. Peer pressure can encourage drinking. Teens who grow up with parents who support, watch over, and talk with them are less likely to drink than their peers.

Source: "Alcohol: A Women's Health Issue," National Institute on Alcohol Abuse and Alcoholism, (NIAAA), 2003.

inhalants. More girls are using substances at earlier ages, nearly as early as boys. Unfortunately, girls suffer consequences beyond those of boys.

"The findings from this study cry out for a fundamental overhaul of public health prevention programs," says Joseph A. Califano, Jr., CASA president and former U.S. Secretary of Health, Education and Welfare. "Unisex prevention programs—largely developed without regard to gender, often with males in mind—fail to influence millions of girls and young women. The women of America have paid a fearful price in premature death and destroyed lives for our failure to craft programs aimed at their unique needs."

Califano noted that launching prevention programs designed for girls and young women will reduce the number of women abusing and addicted to substances: "A reduction of only 25 percent would mean saving one million women from alcoholism and alcohol abuse and half a million from drug abuse and addiction."

Among risks and consequences of smoking, drinking, and drug use that the CASA report identifies as unique to girls and young women are these:

- Girls experiencing early puberty are at higher risk of using substances sooner, more often, and in greater quantities than later maturing peers; puberty is a time of higher risk for girls than boys.

- Girls are more likely than boys to be depressed, have eating disorders, or be sexually or physically abused—all of which increase the risk for substance abuse.

- Substance use can sink into abuse and addiction more quickly for girls and young women than for boys and young men, even when using the same amount or less of a particular substance.

- Girls using alcohol and drugs are likelier to attempt suicide.

- Girls and young women are likelier than boys and young men to experience more adverse health consequences. Women are more susceptible to alcohol-induced brain damage, cardiac problems, and liver disease which occur more quickly and with lower levels of alcohol consumption than with males.

- Girls are likelier than boys to abuse prescription painkillers, stimulants, and tranquilizers.

- Girls who move frequently from one home or neighborhood to another are at greater risk of using substances than boys who move frequently.

- Transitions from elementary to middle school, from middle to high school, and from high school to college are times of increasing risk for girls. Girls making the transition from high school to college show the largest increases in smoking, drinking, and marijuana use.

- Girls are more likely to be offered substances by a female acquaintance, a young female relative, or a boyfriend and to receive offers in private settings; while boys are more likely to be offered drugs by a male acquaintance, a young male relative, a parent, or a stranger and to receive these offers in public settings.

- Religion is more protective for girls than for boys.

• Parents are the first line of prevention. CASA's *Formative Years* survey
  showed that most girls (61.6 percent) who had conversations with their
  parents about substance use said that the conversation made them less
  likely to smoke, drink, or use drugs.

♣ **It's A Fact!!**

Caffeine Use Is A Risk Factor

Girls and young women who drink coffee are significantly likelier than girls and young women who do
not to be smokers (23.2 percent vs. 5.1 percent) and
drink alcohol (69.8 percent vs. 29.5 percent).
Young women who drink coffee began
smoking and drinking at earlier ages.

Alcohol Abuse In Men

Alcohol and drug abuse in men oftentimes begins early in their lives.
School years, especially high school and college years, are especially difficult
for many boys, as they are facing concerns about body image, sexuality, and
athletic performance. And at this critical time in their lives, they are more
likely than women to have more opportunities to use alcohol and drugs.

Consider how men and women react differently to drugs:

• While both men and women are equally likely to become addicted to
  cocaine, heroin, hallucinogens, tobacco, and inhalants, men are more
  likely to abuse alcohol and marijuana.

• Men become dependent on drugs more slowly than women.

• Men in drug treatment programs are more likely to have graduated
  from high school and to be employed, and have fewer other health
  problems than women.

- More men than women are alcohol dependent or have alcohol problems. And alcohol problems are highest among young adults ages 18–29 and lowest among adults ages 65 and older.

Alcoholism And Alcohol Abuse

We also know that people who start drinking at an early age—for example, at age 14 or younger—greatly increase the chance that they will develop alcohol problems at some point in their lives. Young men (and women) who abuse alcohol often take risks that endanger their health and the health of others, especially with having unsafe sex. Having unsafe sex can lead to teen pregnancy or to unwanted pregnancy, or to getting sexually transmitted diseases (STDs), such as HIV/AIDS. If you have a problem with alcohol, know that you are at risk for these diseases, which can cause serious, even life-threatening health problems.

What is alcoholism?

Alcoholism, also known as alcohol dependence, is a disease that includes the following four symptoms:

- Craving—a strong need, or urge, to drink.
- Loss of control—not being able to stop drinking once drinking has begun.
- Physical dependence—withdrawal symptoms, such as nausea, sweating, shakiness, and anxiety after stopping drinking.
- Tolerance—the need to drink greater amounts of alcohol to get high.

Research shows that the risk for developing alcoholism runs in families, but lifestyle factors, such as having friends that use or abuse alcohol, having a high amount of stress in your life, and having alcohol easily available to you also are factors. Knowing you are at risk is important, though, because then you can take steps to protect yourself from developing problems with alcohol. And with support and treatment, many people are able to stop drinking and rebuild their lives.

♣ It's A Fact!!
Women, Girls, And Alcohol

The gender gap in underage drinking has closed. Young girls are drinking more than underage boys.

- National survey data indicate that in 2002 for the first time in at least 10 years, eighth- and tenth-grade girls became more likely than their male peers to drink.

Table 16.1. Students Reporting That They Have Had A Drink In The Last 30 Days[1]

	Girls	Boys
8th-graders	20.0%	19.1%
10th-graders	35.7%	35.3%
12th-graders	45.1%	52.3%

- According to 2003 data, more ninth-grade girls consume alcohol now than do ninth-grade boys. More ninth-grade girls than ninth-grade boys also report binge drinking.

Youth Exposure To Alcohol Advertising

Girls are significantly more likely than boys to be overexposed to alcohol advertising in magazines, as seen in a study from the Center on Alcohol Marketing and Youth that analyzed alcohol advertising in magazines in 2002.

- Girls, ages 12 to 20, saw 68% more beer advertising than women of legal age on a per capita basis in magazines in 2002, while boys, ages 12 to 20, saw 29% more beer advertising than men on a per capita basis.[3]

- Girls saw 30% more distilled spirits advertising per capita than women in magazines in 2002, while boys saw almost as much as men.[4]

- Girls saw 95% more magazine advertising for low-alcohol refreshers (also called alcopops or malternatives) than women per capita in 2002, while boys saw 37% more than men. Girls' exposure to low-alcohol refresher magazine advertising increased by 216% from 2001 to 2002, while boys' exposure increased 46%.[5]

- Sixteen alcoholic beverage brands (14 distilled spirits brands, one beer, and one low-alcohol refresher brand) accounted for half of the total magazine alcohol advertising exposure of girls ages 12 to 20 in 2002. Five of these 16 brands had greater exposure in magazines to underage girls per capita than to women ages 21 to 34.[6]

Health Consequences

- Women generally drink less and less often than men. However, women drinkers are at higher risk for certain medical problems, including liver, brain, and heart damage, than are men who drink comparable amounts.[7]

- Women metabolize alcohol differently than men. When women and men of the same body weight drink the same amount of alcohol, women reach higher peak blood alcohol levels.[8]

- The USDA Dietary Guidelines reflect that women drinkers are at higher risk for alcohol-related health problems. The USDA prescribes that any alcohol use [by adults 21 and over] be done in moderation and defines moderation as no more than one drink a day for women and no more than two drinks a day for men.[9]

- Several studies have found that any consumption of alcohol increases the risk of breast cancer, and that the degree of risk rises as the level of consumption increases.[10]

Table 16.2. Ninth-Grade Students Reporting Alcohol Use[2]

	Ninth-Grade Girls	Ninth-Grade Boys
Drank alcohol in last 30 days	38.5%	33.9%
Engaged in binge drinking (5+ drinks on same occasion in last 30 days)	20.9%	18.8%

continued...

...continued from previous pages

Risky Sexual Behavior And Sexual Assault

- It is estimated that teenage girls who binge drink are up to 63% more likely to become teen mothers.[11]

- A study of students between the ages of 18 and 24 found that more than 70,000 were victims of alcohol-related sexual assault.[12]

- In a survey done of prisoners in state jails in 1997, 40% of convicted rape and sexual assault offenders said that they were drinking at the time of their crime.[13]

Domestic Violence

- Of domestic violence incidents reported by the victims, 67% involve an abusive partner who has been drinking.[14]

- A study on substance abuse and domestic violence between 1993 and 1998 found that 57% of domestic violence incidents during those six years involved only alcohol, while 10% of incidents involved both alcohol and drug use. In contrast, only 11% of domestic violence incidents during those years involved only drug use, and only 21% involved no substance abuse at all.[15]

Notes

1. L.D. Johnston, P.M. O'Malley, and J.G. Bachman, *Monitoring the Future National Survey Results on Drug Use, 1975-2002, Volume I: Secondary School Students* (Bethesda, MD: National Institute on Drug Abuse, 2003).

2. Centers for Disease Control and Prevention, "Youth 2003 Online," Available at <http://apps.nccd.cdc.gov/yrbss/ > (cited 19 July 2004).

3. David H. Jernigan, Joshua Ostroff, Craig Ross, and James A. O'Hara III, "Sex Differences in Adolescent Exposure to Alcohol Advertising in Magazines," *Arch Pediatr Adolesc Med* 158 (July 2004): 629-634.

4. "Sex Differences in Adolescent Exposure," 632.

5. "Sex Differences in Adolescent Exposure," 631-632.

6. "Sex Differences in Adolescent Exposure," 632.

7. National Institute on Alcohol Abuse and Alcoholism, "Are Women More Vulnerable to Alcohol's Effects?," *Alcohol Alert* 46 (December 1999). Available at <http://www.niaaa.nih.gov/publications /aa46.htm>.

8. U.S. Department of Health and Human Services, Public Health Service. *10th Special Report to the U.S. Congress on Alcohol and Health*, 254.

9. United States Department of Agriculture, Center for Nutrition Policy and Promotion, "Choose Sensibly," *Dietary Guidelines for Americans, 2000, 5th edition*. Available at <http://www.health.gov/dietaryguidelines/dga2000/document/choose.htm#alcohol> (cited 19 July 2004).

10. Thomas Babor et al., Alcohol: *No Ordinary Commodity* (Oxford: Oxford University Press, 2003), 69.

11. T.S. Dee, "The Effects of Minimum Legal Drinking Ages on Teen Childbearing," *The Journal of Human Resources* 36, no. 4 (2001): 824-838.

12. R. Hingson et al., "Magnitude of Alcohol-Related Mortality and Morbidity among U.S. College Students Ages 18-24," *Journal of Studies on Alcohol* 63 no. 2 (March 2002): 136-144.

13. L. Greenfield and M. Henneberg, "Alcohol, Crime, and the Criminal Justice System," *Alcohol Policy XII Conference, Alcohol & Crime: Research and Practice for Prevention* (Washington, DC: CSAP, 2000), 23-40.

14. L. Greenfield and M. Henneberg, "Alcohol, Crime, and the Criminal Justice System."

15. L. Greenfield and M. Henneberg, "Alcohol, Crime, and the Criminal Justice System."

What is alcohol abuse?

A person can abuse alcohol without actually being an alcoholic—that is, he or she may drink too much and too often, but still not be dependent on alcohol. Some of the problems linked to alcohol abuse include not being able to complete tasks for your job, school, or family; drunk-driving arrests and car crashes; and drinking-related health problems. Sometimes, even social or moderate drinking can be a problem—such as drinking and driving.

Is there a safe amount of alcohol for men?

For most adults age 21 or older, moderate alcohol use—up to two drinks per day for men seems safe. (One drink equals one 12-ounce bottle of beer or wine cooler, one 5-ounce glass of wine, or 1.5 ounces of 80-proof distilled spirits.)

You shouldn't drink at all if you:

• are younger than age 21

• plan to drive or engage in other activities that require alertness and skill (such as driving and using high-speed machinery)

• take certain over-the-counter or prescription medications (ask your health care provider or pharmacist if it is safe to drink alcohol while taking them)

• have a health problem that can be made worse by drinking

• are a recovering alcoholic

Is alcohol good for a man's heart?

Studies have shown that moderate drinkers—men who have two or less drinks per day—are less likely to die from sudden cardiac death. Sudden cardiac death usually happens when the heart begins beating too fast or chaotically to pump blood in the right way. Small amounts of alcohol might help protect the heart by cutting the risk of blood clots in the heart's arteries and by reducing problems with the heart's rhythm. Heavy drinking though, can actually increase the risk of heart failure, stroke, and high blood pressure, and cause many other health problems. If you don't drink alcohol, you should not start drinking solely to benefit your heart.

Alcohol Use Among Girls

According to the Substance Abuse and Mental Health Services Administration (SAMHSA)'s National Household Survey on Drug Abuse (NHSDA), male and female rates of alcohol use among 12- to 17-year-olds were similar in the early 1990s for the first time.[1] Girls are beginning to drink at younger ages than ever before. In the 1960s, 7 percent of new female users of alcohol were ages 10 to 14, but by the early 1990s, that figure had risen to 31 percent.[2]

Some Risk Factors For Girls Who Use Alcohol

Many of the reasons why adolescents drink are the same for boys and girls, but some factors may affect girls more than boys.

- Puberty tends to bring a higher incidence of depression among teenage girls, which can trigger alcohol use.[3] One study found symptoms of depression in one in four girls—a rate that is 50 percent higher than in boys.[4]

- Adolescent girls who are heavy drinkers (drink five or more drinks in a row on at least 5 different days in the past month) are more likely than boys to say that they drink to escape problems or because of frustration or anger.[5]

- Friends have a big influence on teenagers overall, but girls are particularly susceptible to peer pressure when it comes to drinking. Adolescent girls are more likely than boys to drink to fit in with their friends, while boys drink largely for other reasons and then join a group that also drinks.[6]

- Girls often are introduced to alcohol by their boyfriends,[7] who may be older and more likely to drink.

Why Do Males And Females Respond Differently To Alcohol?

Females process alcohol differently than males; smaller amounts of alcohol are more intoxicating for females regardless of their size. Three physiological differences may explain this:

- Females have less body water than males. When people drink, alcohol spreads into the water in their bodies. Because females have smaller amounts of body water to dilute the alcohol, they have higher concentrations of alcohol in their blood than males have after drinking identical amounts of alcohol.[8]

- An enzyme that is important in metabolizing or processing alcohol works differently in females than in males. In males, the enzyme—called alcohol dehydrogenase—breaks down much of the alcohol in the stomach so that less of it enters the circulatory system. In females, the enzyme is less active.[9]

- Changing hormone levels during the menstrual cycle may affect the rate of alcohol metabolism in females.[10]

References

1. *Substance Abuse and Mental Health Services Administration, National Household Survey on Drug Abuse, Substance Abuse Among Women in the U.S.*, Rockville, MD: U.S. Department of Health and Human Services, 1996.

2. *Ibid.*

3. The Commonwealth Fund, *The Commonwealth Fund Survey of the Health of Adolescent Girls*, New York: The Commonwealth Fund, 1997.

4. *Ibid.*

5. Donovan, J.E., "Gender differences in alcohol involvement in children and adolescents: a review of the literature," *Women and Alcohol: Issues for Prevention Research*, National Institute on Alcohol Abuse and Alcoholism, Research Monograph No. 32, Bethesda, MD, 1996.

6. *Ibid.*

☞ **Remember!!**

Alcohol is a dangerous drug for all teens; however, teen girls have a higher risk for alcohol-induced brain damage, cardiac problems, breast cancer, and liver disease which happen more quickly and at lower levels of alcohol consumption than with teen boys.

7. Jacob, T., and Leonard, K., "Family and peer influences in the development of adolescent alcohol abuse," *Development of Alcohol Problems: Exploring the Biopsychosocial Matrix of Risk*, National Institute on Alcohol Abuse and Alcoholism, Research Monograph No. 26, Bethesda, MD, 1994.

8. National Institute on Alcohol Abuse and Alcoholism, Alcohol and Women, *Alcohol Alert* No. 10, 1990.

9. *Ibid.*

10. *Ibid.*

Chapter 17

Factors That Affect Teen Drinking

National Study Links Teens' "Sense Of Self" To Alcohol, Drug Use, And Sex

How teenagers feel about themselves plays a significant role in whether they choose to drink or use other drugs, according to a report released March 2, 2004 by SADD and Liberty Mutual Group. *The Teens Today* 2003 study also reveals that a teen's "Sense of Self," can influence sexual behavior, reaction to peer pressure, and importantly, be affected by a teen's relationships with parents.

"Sense of self" is a young adults' self-evaluation on their progress in three key developmental areas: identity formation, independence, and peer relationships. The report finds that teens with a high sense of self feel more positive about their own identity, growing independence and relationships with peers than do teens with a low sense of self. Specifically, high sense of self teens reported feeling: smart, successful, responsible, and confident, and cite positive relationships with parents. Also, significantly, the study revealed that:

1. High sense of self teens are more likely to avoid alcohol and drug use;

2. Low sense of self teens are more likely to use alcohol and "harder" drugs such as ecstasy and cocaine; and,

3. Parental involvement strongly correlates with teens' sense of self and the decisions they make regarding alcohol and drug use.

"This information is critically important in helping us to better understand the role that self-definition plays in predisposing young adults to destructive decision-making, establishing a clear link between who they are and what they do," said Stephen Wallace, chairman and chief executive officer of the national SADD organization.

Among the key findings demonstrating the importance of sense of self and parental relationships:

- 62 percent of teens with a high sense of self report that their relationship with their parents helps make them feel good about themselves, while only about one-third of low sense of self teens report the same.

- Only 30 percent of high school teens whose parents provide a strong level of guidance have used drugs, compared to 48 percent of high school teens whose parents do not provide strong guidance.

- Less than half (47 percent) of high school teens whose parents provide a strong level of guidance have used alcohol, compared to 80 percent of high school teens whose parents do not provide strong guidance.

- Teens with a high sense of self report overwhelmingly that they feel respected by their parents (93 percent) and close to their parents (85 percent), while teens with a low sense of self report lower levels of respect from their parents (8 percent) and closeness to their parents (12 percent).

- Nearly two-thirds (64 percent) of teens believe it is very likely they will lose their parents' trust if caught drinking alcohol; two-thirds (67 percent) report the same with respect to drug use.

What Does This Mean For Families?

These findings are consistent with past *Teens Today* studies that have shown that teens who report regular, open communication with their parents about important issues say they are more likely to try to live up to their parents' expectations and less likely to drink, use drugs, or engage in early sexual behavior.

Paul Condrin, Liberty Mutual executive vice president, Personal Market, said, "We know that parents who cultivate a family environment that includes positive, open channels of communication with their children are much more successful at influencing their children to avoid engaging in dangerous behaviors. Now we know that helping to develop a young person's positive sense of self can go to great lengths at improving the odds that the child will avoid alcohol and drug use."

Importantly, *Teens Today* 2003 points to important steps parents can take to positively enhance their teens' sense of self.

- Support a wide sampling of interests, activities, and age-appropriate behaviors.

- Encourage separation from parents and age-appropriate independence in decision-making.

- Teach peer-to-peer social skills and facilitate (positive) peer relationships.

A teen's sense of self also relates directly to mental health and relationships with peers. For example, teens with a low sense of self are more likely than teens with a high sense of self to report regular feelings of stress and depression, weaker relationships with parents, and greater susceptibility to peer pressure.

♣ It's A Fact!!

New Survey Reveals Over One-Quarter Of Kids Ages 9 To 13 Have Been Offered Alcohol

Kids who frequently drink alcohol cite the desire "to be cool" and "boredom" as main reasons kids try alcohol.

In a new KidsHealth® KidsPoll survey of 9- to 13-year-olds, 29% of respondents reported that they had been offered alcohol at least once. Of those kids who said they had been offered alcohol, 34% said it was offered by "adults I know" and 29% said it was offered by "older kids." Three percent (3%) of respondents said they drink alcohol every week, another 3% said they drink at least every month, and 4% of kids surveyed said they drink once in a while, but not every month. Seventy-two percent (72%) of kids surveyed said they have never tried alcohol and 18% said they tried it once.

Although 86% of the total kids surveyed said teens who drink alcohol are "very un-cool," 42% of respondents who said they drink every week said teens who drink are "very cool." Only 3% of respondents who have never consumed alcohol thought teens who drink are "very cool." Further, 50% of kids who said they drink every week believe that drinking alcohol at "my age" is always OK or OK most of the time versus 2% of nondrinkers.

Approximately 700 children ages 9 to 13 participated in the KidsHealth KidsPoll on alcohol at 6 member sites of the National Association of Health Education Centers throughout the United States. The study was conducted by researchers from the Department of Health Education and Recreation, Southern Illinois University Carbondale.

The survey found interesting variations of beliefs and attitudes among kids who drink alcohol at least every week ("frequent drinkers") and those who have never tried alcohol ("non-drinkers"). These variations could provide important guidelines for programs designed to stop children who have already begun consuming alcohol from drinking.

The KidsHealth KidsPoll revealed that the main reason all respondents think kids try alcohol is "they think it will make them cool." There is, however, a major shift in beliefs between frequent drinkers and non-drinkers when it comes to the second most-popular reason kids try alcohol. Thirty-five percent (35%) of frequent drinkers say it's because "they have nothing better to do" compared to only 2% of non-drinkers. Non-drinkers' second most-popular reason, with a 17% response, was "other kids are doing it" compared to 0% of frequent drinkers.

"Giving kids fun things to do instead" was the most popular response by all kids surveyed when asked: What is the best way to keep kids from drinking alcohol? "Let them learn from their own experiences" was the second most common way cited by frequent drinkers (27%). "Have people with alcohol problems talk to them" was the second most common way cited by nondrinkers (21%).

There is also a difference between frequent and non-drinkers in their perceptions of how common drinking is among kids. Those who drink frequently perceive that "almost all the kids my age" have had more than a sip of alcohol (69%) versus non-drinkers (6%).

Source: This information was provided by KidsHealth, one of the largest resources online for medically reviewed health information written for parents, kids, and teens. For more articles like this one, visit www.KidsHealth.org, or www.TeensHealth.org. © 2004 The Nemours Center for Children's Health Media, a division of The Nemours Foundation.

Other Key Findings From The Research

Teens who regularly feel stress or depression are much less inclined than other teens to avoid high-risk behaviors such as drinking, using drugs, or engaging in early sexual activity.

- Teens who avoid drinking and drug use are more likely to have a favorable self-image.

- Regular feelings of stress and depression tend to be more common among sexually active teens than among their non-sexually active peers.

- High sense of self teens are more resistant to pressure from peers to drink, use drugs, or have sex.

- Teens' involvement with alcohol increases steadily as they mature.

- Younger teens are more likely than older teens to drink because of peer pressure.

- Older teens are more likely than younger teens to drink to escape problems.

- High sense of self teens are particularly resistant to peer pressure to drink.

- Teens who are alcohol repeaters and experimenters are much more likely than teens who are alcohol avoiders to have immediate family members who drink a lot.

High Stress Teens Twice As Likely To Smoke, Get Drunk, Use Illegal Drugs

The risk that teens will smoke, drink, get drunk and use illegal drugs increases sharply if they are highly stressed, frequently bored, or have substantial amounts of spending money, according to The National Survey of American Attitudes on Substance Abuse VIII: Teens and Parents, an annual back-to-school survey conducted by The National Center on Addiction and Substance Abuse (CASA) at Columbia University. This was the first time in its eight-year history that the survey measured the impact of these characteristics on the likelihood of teen substance abuse.

Among CASA's survey findings:

- High stress teens are twice as likely as low stress teens to smoke, drink, get drunk, and use illegal drugs.

- Often bored teens are 50 percent likelier than not often bored teens to smoke, drink, get drunk, and use illegal drugs.

- Teens with $25 or more a week in spending money are nearly twice as likely as teens with less to smoke, drink, and use illegal drugs, and more than twice as likely to get drunk.

- Teens exhibiting two or three of these characteristics are at more than three times the risk of substance abuse as those exhibiting none of these characteristics.

- More than half the nation's 12-to-17 year olds (52 percent) are at greater risk of substance abuse because of high stress, frequent boredom, too much spending money, or some combination of these characteristics.

"High stress, frequent boredom, and too much spending money are a catastrophic combination for many American teens," said CASA Chairman and President and former U.S. Secretary of Health, Education and Welfare Joseph A. Califano, Jr. "But it is a catastrophe that can be avoided through parental engagement. Parents must be sensitive to the stress in their children's lives, understand why they are bored, and limit their spending money."

Other findings of this year's survey:

- More than 5 million 12-to-17 year olds (20 percent) can buy marijuana in an hour or less; another 5 million (19 percent) can buy marijuana within a day.

- The proportion of teens that consider beer easier to buy than cigarettes or marijuana is up 80 percent from 2000 (18 percent vs. 10 percent).

- For the first time in the survey's eight-year history, teens are as concerned about social and academic pressures as they are about drugs.

- Teens at schools with more than 1,200 students are twice as likely as teens at schools with less than 800 students to be at high risk of substance abuse (25 percent vs. 12 percent).

Drug Free Schools

The proportion of students who say that drugs are used, kept, or sold at their high schools is up 18 percent over 2002 (from 44 to 52 percent). "This is a significant deterioration from last year, when most high school students attended drug free schools," Califano observed. As in previous years Catholic and other religious middle and high schools are likelier to be drug free than are public schools (78 percent vs. 58 percent). For the first time there was a large enough sample of students from secular private schools to assess their status: 76 percent of such schools are drug free.

Girls Vs. Boys

The incidence of high stress was greater among girls than boys, with nearly one in three girls saying they were highly stressed compared to fewer than one in four boys. And while girls and boys are equally likely to have

Table 17.1 Substance Abuse And Eating Disorders

Shared Risk Factors

Occur in times of transition or stress
Common brain chemistry
Common family history
Low self esteem, depression, anxiety, impulsivity
History of sexual or physical abuse
Unhealthy parental behaviors and low monitoring of children's activities
Unhealthy peer norms and social pressures
Susceptibility to messages from advertising and entertainment media

Shared Characteristics

Obsessive preoccupation, craving, compulsive behavior, secretiveness, rituals
Experience mood altering effects, social isolation
Linked to other psychiatric disorders, suicide
Difficult to treat, life threatening
Chronic diseases with high relapse rates
Require intensive therapy

more than $50 a week in spending money, girls with this much spending money are likelier than boys to smoke, drink, get drunk, and use marijuana.

Other Key Findings

- Fewer teens are associating with peers who use substances: 56 percent have no friends who regularly drink, up from 52 percent in 2002; 68 percent have no friends who use marijuana, up from 62 percent in 2002; 70 percent have no friends who smoke cigarettes, up from 56 percent in 2002.

- Teens who attend religious services at least once a week are at significantly lower risk of substance abuse.

- The average age of first use is 12 years 2 months for alcohol, 12 years 6 months for cigarettes and 13 years 11 months for marijuana.

- Between the ages of 12 and 17, the likelihood that a teen will smoke, drink, or use illegal drugs increases more than seven times and the percentage of teens with close friends who use marijuana jumps 14 times.

Link Between Alcohol And Eating Disorders

The first comprehensive examination of the link between substance abuse and eating disorders reveals that up to one-half of individuals with eating disorders abuse alcohol or illicit drugs, compared to nine percent of the general population. Conversely, up to 35 percent of alcohol or illicit drug abusers have eating disorders compared to three percent of the general population.

"For many young women, eating disorders like anorexia and bulimia are joined at the hip with smoking, binge drinking, and illicit drug use," said Califano. "This lethal link between substance abuse and eating disorders sends a signal to parents, teachers, and health professionals—where you see the smoke of eating disorders, look for the fire of substance abuse and vice versa."

The exhaustive report finds anorexia nervosa and bulimia nervosa as the eating disorders most commonly linked to substance abuse and for the first time identifies the shared risk factors and shared characteristics of both afflictions.

Stress And Substance Abuse   ♣ It's A Fact!!

Stressful events can profoundly influence drug, alcohol, and tobacco use initiation, continuation, as well as relapse. Researchers have long recognized the strong correlation between stress and drug use, particularly relapse to drug use. Our awareness of the role that stress can play in increasing ones' vulnerability to drug use is important. Exposure to stress is among the most common human experiences. It also is one of the most powerful triggers for relapse to substance abuse in addicted individuals, even after long periods of abstinence.

Stress And Drug Abuse

Stressful events may strongly influence the use of alcohol or other drugs. Stress is a major contributor to the initiation and continuation of addiction to alcohol or other drugs, as well as to relapse or a return to drug use after periods of abstinence.

Children exposed to severe stress may be more vulnerable to drug use. A number of clinical and epidemiological studies show a strong association between psychosocial stressors early in life (e.g., parental loss, child abuse) and an increased risk for depression, anxiety, impulsive behavior, and substance abuse in adulthood.

Post Traumatic Stress Disorder (PTSD) And Substance Abuse

An emerging body of research has documented a very strong association between PTSD and substance abuse. In most cases, substance use begins after the exposure to trauma and the development of PTSD, thus making PTSD a risk factor for drug abuse.

Early intervention to help children and adolescents who have suffered trauma from violence or a disaster is critical. Children who witness or are exposed to a traumatic event and are clinically diagnosed with PTSD have a greater likelihood for developing later drug and/or alcohol use disorders.

Of individuals with substance use disorders, 30 to 60 percent meet the criteria for comorbid PTSD. Patients with substance abuse disorders tend to suffer from more severe PTSD symptoms than do PTSD patients without substance use disorders.

Source: "Stress and Substance Abuse," National Institute on Drug Abuse (NIDA), NIH Pub. No. 02-5087, January 2002.

The report lists caffeine, tobacco, alcohol, diuretics, laxatives, emetics, amphetamines, cocaine, and heroin as substances used to suppress appetite, increase metabolism, purge unwanted calories, and self-medicate negative emotions.

The report found that because health professionals often overlook the link between substance abuse and eating disorders, treatment options are virtually nonexistent for these co-occurring conditions.

"Advertisers put children at greater risk of developing an eating disorder through the portrayal of unrealistic body images," noted Mr. Califano. "The average American woman is 5'4" tall and weighs approximately 140 pounds, but the average model that purportedly epitomizes our standard of beauty is 5'11" tall and weighs 117 pounds." The report found that women's magazines contain more than ten times more ads and articles related to weight loss than men's magazines, which is the same gender ratio reported for eating disorders.

The report finds that while only 15 percent of girls are overweight, 40 percent of girls in grades one through five and 62 percent of teenage girls are trying to lose weight. These girls are especially vulnerable to eating disorders and related substance abuse problems.

Other Notable Findings

- Bulimic women who are alcohol dependent report a higher rate of suicide attempts, anxiety, personality and conduct disorders, and other drug dependence than bulimic women who are not alcohol dependent.

- As many as one million men and boys suffer from an eating disorder; gay and bisexual males are at increased risk of such disorders.

Making The Link: Underage Drinking And Mental Health

Alcohol use in adolescence is associated with psychological distress and depression.

- Among 12- to 17-year-olds who were current drinkers, 31 percent exhibited extreme levels of psychological distress and 39 percent exhibited serious behavioral problems.[1]

- Twelve- to sixteen-year-old girls who were current drinkers were four times more likely than their non-drinking peers to suffer depression.[2]

The severity of behavioral problems in adolescents is significantly associated with increased likelihood of adolescent alcohol use.

- Past-month alcohol use was reported by approximately 14 percent of adolescents with low levels of behavioral problems, by 23 percent of

♣ **It's A Fact!!**
Severe Childhood Attention-Deficit/Hyperactivity Disorder (ADHD) May Predict Alcohol, Substance Use Problems In Teen Years

Scientists tracking the progress of children diagnosed with attention-deficit/hyperactivity disorder (ADHD) as they became teenagers have shed new light on the link between ADHD and the risk of developing alcohol and substance use problems. The researchers found that individuals with severe problems of inattention as children were more likely than their peers to report alcohol-related problems, a greater frequency of getting drunk, and heavier and earlier use of tobacco and other drugs. The findings indicate that childhood ADHD may be as important for the risk of later substance use problems as having a history of family members with alcoholism and other substance use disorders. The study appears in the August 2003 issue of the *Journal of Abnormal Psychology*.

ADHD is one of the most commonly diagnosed pediatric mental health disorders. It occurs in three to five percent of school-aged children. While previous research has indicated that ADHD together with a variety of other childhood behavior disorders may predispose children to drug, alcohol, and tobacco use earlier than children without ADHD, this study explores more closely specific aspects of that association.

The researchers found that significantly more of the teens diagnosed with ADHD as children reported episodes of drunkenness than their counterparts in the non-ADHD group. Nearly twice as many of the ADHD group reported having been drunk more than once in the past six months.

those with intermediate problem scores, and by 38 percent of those with significant behavioral problems.[3]

- Adolescents with serious behavioral problems were nearly three times more likely to use alcohol than those with low levels of behavioral problems.[4]

There is a link between suicide and alcohol use in adolescents.

- Twenty-eight percent of suicides by children ages 9 to 15 could be attributed to alcohol.[5]

The researchers found that the teenagers who reported more frequent episodes of drunkenness, higher alcohol problem scores, and a greater likelihood of substance abuse, were those diagnosed with more severe inattention problems in childhood. The youngsters with severe inattention were about 5 times more likely than others to use an illegal drug other than alcohol and marijuana at an early age. The researchers point out that inattention appeared to be a uniquely important variable even when the analyses considered the presence of oppositional defiant disorder (ODD) and conduct disorder (CD), factors which more typically have been considered predictive of substance use.

Although impulsivity-hyperactivity was not associated with teenage substance abuse, the authors say that better measurement of this behavior in future studies will be important. "The presence of ADHD during childhood appears to be as strong a risk factor for substance use and abuse as having a positive family history of substance use disorder. It is not specific to only one substance but cuts across alcohol, marijuana, and other drugs," says Dr. Molina. "Our findings indicate that the presence of ADHD during childhood, the severity of symptoms, and the persistence of the disorder may be risk factors for early substance use and the emergence of substance abuse disorders during the teen years."

The article "Childhood predictors of adolescent substance use in a longitudinal study of children with ADHD" appears in the *Journal of Abnormal Psychology*, August 2003, Volume 112, Number 3.

Source: News Release, August 17, 2003, National Institute on Alcohol Abuse and Alcoholism (NIAAA).

- Among eighth grade girls who drink heavily, 37 percent report attempting suicide, whereas 11 percent of girls who do not drink report attempting suicide.[6]

- Using a national school sample, a study reported that suicide attempts among heavy-drinking adolescents were three to four times greater than among abstainers.[7]

Adolescents struggling with serious emotional disturbances (SED) face even greater challenges when they use alcohol.

- Adolescents with high levels of SED were nearly twice as likely as adolescents with low levels of SED to have used alcohol in the past month.[8]

- Adolescents with high levels of SED were five times as likely as those with low levels of SED to report alcohol dependence.[9]

> ☞ **Remember!!**
> A risk factor means that something may cause you to be more inclined to drink alcohol. Drinking alcohol is still a choice. You can say no.

References

1. Substance Abuse and Mental Health Services Administration, Office of Applied Studies. *The Relationship Between Mental Health and Substance Abuse Among Adolescents.* (SMA) 99-3286. Rockville, MD: Substance Abuse and Mental Health Services Administration, 1999.

2. Hanna EZ, Hsiao-ye Y, Dufour MC, et al. *The relationship of drinking and other substance use alone and in combination to health and behavior problems among youth ages 12-16: Findings from the Third National Health and Nutrition Survey (NHANES III).* Paper presented at the 23rd Annual Scientific Meeting of the Research Society on Alcoholism, June 24-29, 2000, Denver, CO.

3. Substance Abuse and Mental Health Services Administration. *The Relationship Between Mental Health and Substance Abuse Among Adolescents.*

4. *Ibid.*

5. Unpublished data extrapolated by National Institute on Alcohol Abuse and Alcoholism from State Trends in Alcohol Mortality, 1979-1992; *US Alcohol Epidemiologic Data Reference Manual*, Volume 5. Rockville, MD: National Institute on Alcohol Abuse and Alcoholism, 1996.

6. Windle M, Miller-Tutzauer C, Domenico D. Alcohol use, suicidal behavior, and risky activities among adolescents. *J Res Adolesc* 2(4):317-330, 1992.

7. *Ibid.*

8. Substance Abuse and Mental Health Services Administration. *The Relationship Between Mental Health and Substance Abuse Among Adolescents.*

9. *Ibid.*

Chapter 18

Alcohol Advertising Target Teens

Alcohol Advertising Influences Attitudes, Beliefs, And Behaviors

- Young people view approximately 20,000 commercials each year, of which nearly 2,000 are for beer and wine.[1] For every "just say no" or "know when to say when" public service announcement, teens will view 25 to 50 beer and wine commercials.[2]

- In 2000, brewers spent more than $770 million on television ads and $15 million more on radio.[3]

- Since dropping its own TV ad ban in 1996, liquor-industry expenditures on broadcast commercials (primarily on cable TV) have skyrocketed from $3.5 million to more than $25 million in 2000.[4]

- Diageo, maker of Smirnoff Vodka, Captain Morgan's Rum, and Cuervo Tequila, has announced plans to spend as much as $1 billion on television liquor ads over the next five years.[5]

About This Chapter: The text in this chapter is from "Alcohol Advertising and Young People," July 2002. Reprinted with permission from the Center for Science in the Public Interest Alcohol Policies Project, http://cspinte.org/booze/. © 2002. All rights reserved. Additional text under the heading "The Effects Of Alcohol Advertising On Young People," is excerpted from "10th Special Report to the U.S. Congress on Alcohol and Health," National Institute on Alcohol Abuse and Alcoholism (NIAAA), June 2000.

Alcoholic-Beverage Industry "Responsibility" Guidelines Are A Sham

- Even under NBC's much-ballyhooed—and now withdrawn—proposed "responsibility" guidelines for hard liquor ads, millions of underage persons would be exposed to commercials for hard liquor, as they have been exposed for decades to appealing, funny, and seductive spots for beer. Advertising trade professionals have labeled the "85% adult audience" standard as virtually meaningless, pointing out that nearly every nighttime NBC show would qualify (72% of the U.S. population is 21 or over).[6]

  ✤ **It's A Fact!!**
  Research based on survey data indicates that children who like alcohol advertisements intend to drink more frequently as adults.

- Voluntary advertising guidelines for the beer and liquor industries allow their ads to reach audiences that are half under the minimum legal drinking age.

- Those guidelines also explicitly permit advertisements that reach and influence underage persons, so long as they are directed primarily to adults.

References

1. Strasburger, V.C. & Donnerstein, E. (1999). Children, adolescents, and the media: Issues and solutions. *Pediatrics*, 103 (1):129-139.

2. *Ibid.*

3. Adams Business Media. (2001). *Beer Handbook*. Norwalk, CT.

4. Adams Business Media. *Liquor Handbook*. Norwalk, CT.

5. Chura, H. & Friedman, W. (May 13, 2002). Diageo moves forward with network plan: Marketer to run $200 million in liquor ads on TV consortium. *Advertising Age*.

6. Friedman, W. (January 7, 2002). Nearly all NBC prime-time shows qualify for liquor ads. Observers: Network's new policies may unleash a flood of booze promos. *Advertising Age.*

The Effects Of Alcohol Advertising On Young People

Survey research on alcohol advertising and young people consistently indicates small but significant connections between exposure to and awareness of alcohol advertising and drinking beliefs and behaviors. Children and adolescents who view, or are made aware of, alcohol advertisements hold more favorable beliefs about drinking, intend to drink more frequently as adults, and are more likely to be drinkers than are other young people. They also have greater knowledge of alcohol brands and slogans.

Although these effects on young people are small, they may be important. The small effects may reflect the fact that individual differences in exposure to advertising are relatively slight given the high frequency of advertising in the environment. Because the environment is saturated with alcohol advertising, most people are exposed to many advertisements each year, with very little variation in individual exposure. In addition, as the number of exposures

---

❖ It's A Fact!!
Alcohol Counter-Advertising

Counter-advertising is used to balance the effects that alcohol advertising may have on alcohol consumption and alcohol-related problems. This type of advertising includes:

- Print or broadcast advertisements (e.g., public service announcements)

- Product warning labels

To dilute the influence of alcohol advertising, broadcast and print counter-advertising and warning labels present factual information and persuasive messages to the public.

Source: "Alcohol Counter Advertising and the Media," National Institute on Alcohol Abuse and Alcoholism, 8/2002.

increases of time, the incremental impact of each single, additional advertisement diminishes. That is the incremental effect of any single advertisement is greater if, for example, it is only the tenth advertisement to which a person has been exposed as opposed to the hundredth advertisement, which, in turn, would have a greater impact that the thousandth. These considerations suggest that research on the effects of alcohol advertising should include studies of young children who have had little exposure to it and for whom the greatest impact can be expected.

Taken as a whole, the survey studies provide some evidence that alcohol advertising may influence drinking beliefs and behaviors among children and adolescents. This evidence, however, is far from conclusive. The cross-sectional design of most of the published studies limits the ability to establish cause-and-effect relationships. Although alcohol advertising may predispose young people to drink, the reverse may be true instead. That is, young people who look favorably on drinking may seek information about alcohol and thus be more attentive to alcohol advertisements.

☞ Remember!!
Base your decision about alcohol use on facts, research, and good advice—not advertisements.

Part Four

Alcohol's Effects On The Body

Chapter 19

Long-Term Health Consequences Of Using Alcohol

Anatomy 101

Virtually every organ system is affected by alcohol. Drinking in moderation may cause problems to one's body, and drinking heavily over the years can cause irreversible damage. However, most diseases caused by excessive drinking can be prevented. Examples of alcohol's effect on organ function follow.

Liver

Even moderate social drinkers can experience liver damage. Diseases such as fatty liver, hepatitis, or cirrhosis can develop from heavy alcohol consumption.

Fatty liver is the earliest stage of alcoholic liver disease. In this condition, liver cells become swollen with fat globules and water. If drinking is stopped at this point however, the liver is capable of healing itself.

Hepatitis is an inflammation of the liver, which causes soreness and swelling. Hepatitis can be caused by many things, such as drinking too much

About This Chapter: The text in this chapter is from "Anatomy 101," National Institute on Alcohol Abuse and Alcoholism (NIAAA), 2003. Additional text under its own heading "Alcohol and Bone Health," is from National Institutes of Health Osteoporosis and Related Bone Diseases–National Resource Center, revised 8/2001.

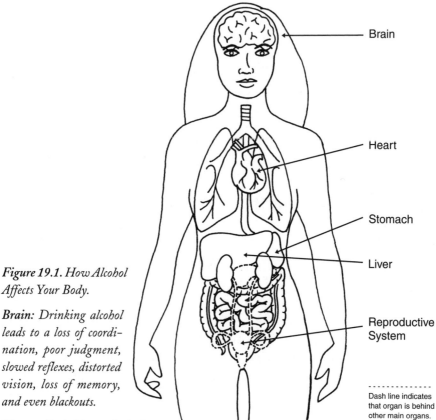

Brain

Heart

Stomach

Liver

Reproductive
System

- - - - - - - - - - - - -
Dash line indicates
that organ is behind
other main organs.

Figure 19.1. How Alcohol Affects Your Body.

Brain: *Drinking alcohol leads to a loss of coordination, poor judgment, slowed reflexes, distorted vision, loss of memory, and even blackouts.*

Heart: *Drinking alcohol could cause your blood pressure to rise, increase your heart rate, cause your heart to beat abnormally, and can increase the size of your heart.*

Stomach: *You're putting empty calories into your body, which could cause weight gain. If you drink too much, you may vomit because alcohol is toxic. Drinking alcohol can also cause stomach ulcers and cancer.*

Liver: *Drinking alcohol could cause diseases such as cirrhosis (sir-o-sis). It also can cause hepatitis (inflamed liver), or even liver cancer, which weakens the liver's ability to clot and keep your blood free from poisons and bacteria.*

Reproductive System: *Heavy drinking can cause painful periods, heavy flow, discomfort before your period (PMS), and irregular periods (not getting your period when you're supposed to). Drinking also raises the risk of getting sexually assaulted and having unsafe sex.*

Source: Excerpted from "How Alcohol Affects Your Body," National Women's Health Information Center, February 2004 (figure redrawn for Omnigraphics by Alison DeKleine).

alcohol and taking some medications. Viruses are also a cause for hepatitis. Advanced liver damage makes it difficult for your body to break down waste products (such as bilirubin) in your blood, therefore causing jaundice, a condition where your skin turns a yellow-orange color. Waste products in the bloodstream can also cause itching, nausea, fever, and body aches.

Another serious liver disease is cirrhosis that can develop by exposure to harmful chemicals. However, the most common cause of cirrhosis in this country is drinking too much alcohol. This is better known as alcoholic cirrhosis. Alcoholic cirrhosis causes the cells of the liver to be damaged beyond repair. As liver cells die, scar tissue forms. When this scar tissue builds up, blood can't flow through the liver properly. Normally, toxins and wastes in the blood get filtered (cleaned) out when blood passes through the liver. If scar tissue keeps blood from flowing normally through the liver, the blood doesn't get filtered. Toxins and wastes can build up in the body. This can lead to mental confusion, agitation, or tremors (shaking). In serious cases it can even lead to coma. Once scarring has progressed, nothing can be done to repair the liver or cure cirrhosis. Treatment is aimed at avoiding further damage to the liver and preventing and treating complications such as bleeding from broken blood vessels. Liver transplantation is the only option.

More than 25,000 Americans die each year from chronic liver disease. Experts say that about 70 percent are due, at least in part, to alcohol abuse. Transplants, an effective treatment for diseased livers, are not easy to come by, especially if you are currently drinking.

Heart

The heart has the important job of getting oxygen to every cell in the body. Accomplishing this task is not that easy for such a small organ, as it weighs between 7 and 15 ounces.

Some research has indicated that having some alcohol can provide health benefits to the heart. However, drinking alcohol, even in moderation, can create health risks such as a slight rise in blood pressure. High blood pressure associated with heavy drinking makes the heart work harder than it needs to and can be a key risk factor for coronary heart disease, leading to heart attacks and strokes. In addition, with increased intake of alcohol, levels of some fats in the blood can become elevated (high blood triglycerides), which could cause heart problems.

Excessive drinking of alcohol (binge drinking) can also lead to stroke and other serious health problems. These other problems can include cardiomyopathy (disease of the heart muscle), cardiac arrhythmia (abnormal contraction patterns of the heart), and sudden cardiac death.

Stomach

The stomach is designed to process and transport food. Ingesting healthy foods makes this organ run smoothly.

After ingestion, alcohol travels down the esophagus into the stomach, where some of it is absorbed into your bloodstream. The unabsorbed alcohol continues to move through the gastrointestinal tract. The majority of it will enter the small intestine and get absorbed into the bloodstream through the walls of the small intestine, or it can stay in the stomach and cause irritation.

While in the stomach, alcohol acts as an irritant and increases digestive juices (hydrochloric acid) that are secreted from the stomach lining. Intoxicating amounts of alcohol can halt the digestive process, robbing the body of vital vitamins and minerals. Chronic irritation may lead to damage to the lining of the stomach.

Drinking alcohol and taking medication that causes stomach irritation, such as aspirin, can cause gastritis (inflammation of the stomach lining), ulcers, and severe bleeding.

Brain

The human brain is like a command center for the body. It alerts body parts and organs when something should happen and how to react. It only takes about 30 seconds for the first amounts of alcohol to reach the brain after ingestion. Once there, alcohol acts primarily on nerve cells deep in the brain.

The most highly developed part of the brain is the cerebral cortex, which encompasses about two-thirds of the brain mass and lies over and around most of the remaining structures of the brain. It is responsible for thinking, reasoning, perceiving, and producing and understanding language. The cerebral cortex is divided into specific areas involved in vision, hearing, touch, movement, and smell. The nerves in these parts of the brain talk to each other by electrical impulses that are enabled by neurotransmitters.

Alcohol acts as a depressant to the central nervous system and causes some neurotransmitters to become inhibited. Judgment and coordination, two processes of the central nervous system, become impaired.

Heavy drinking can inhibit the firing of the nerve cells that control breathing, a condition known as respiratory depression. This condition can be fatal. Even if the inhibition of the respiratory nerve cells does not cause death, drinking excessive alcohol may cause vomiting. When drunk and unconscious, a person may inhale fluids that have been vomited, resulting in death by asphyxiation.

Research now shows that significant brain development continues through adolescence. Therefore, alcohol may have quite different toxic effects on adolescent brains than on those of adults. Heavy alcohol use can impair brain function in adolescents, and it is unclear at present whether the damage is reversible.

Alcohol And Bone Health

The negative effects of alcohol consumption on bone have long been recognized. Chronic heavy drinking has been identified as a significant risk factor for various diseases, including osteoporosis.

Alcohol And Nutrition

Calcium is important for many functions in the body, where it serves as a key nutrient in the maintenance of bone density. More than 99 percent of the body's calcium is stored in the bones and teeth. The remaining one percent is found in the blood. Blood levels of calcium depend upon how much of this nutrient is consumed in the diet, how well the nutrient is absorbed, and how much of it is excreted. Calcium balance is regulated by many factors, including parathyroid hormone (PTH) and vitamin D.

Alcohol disrupts calcium balance in many ways. To begin with, alcohol exposure increases PTH levels. In cases of chronic alcohol abuse, blood levels of parathyroid hormone can remain elevated, resulting in a strain on the body's calcium reserves. In alcoholics, continuous elevations in parathyroid hormone can precipitate the condition known as secondary hyperparathyroidism, the effects of which further deplete calcium stores.

Alcohol can inhibit the production of enzymes found in the liver and kidney that convert the inactive form of vitamin D to its active form. This interference in vitamin D metabolism results in an impairment of calcium absorption. Vitamin D deficiency can lead to osteomalacia, a bone condition associated with pain, fractures, and deformity. Alcohol also increases magnesium excretion, an effect that can further negatively impact bone health.

♣ **It's A Fact!!**

Alcohol can weaken your immune system and make you more likely to get sick or develop diseases.

Source: "Girl Power!: Alcohol Effects," U.S. Department of Health and Human Services, available at http://www.girlpower.gov/girlarea/bodyfx/alcohol.htm.

Alcohol, Hormones, And Other Metabolic Effects

Chronic heavy drinking can result in hormonal deficiencies in both men and women. Alcoholic men tend to produce less testosterone, a hormone known for its positive effect on bone density. Low testosterone levels have been linked to decreased activity of osteoblasts, the cells that stimulate bone formation.

In pre-menopausal women, chronic alcohol exposure can result in irregular menstrual cycles, an occurrence that increases osteoporosis risk. Conversely, in post-menopausal women, alcohol increases the conversion of testosterone into estradiol, a hormone commonly used to prevent bone loss after menopause. For this reason, alcohol consumption may actually have a positive effect on bone density in women after menopause.

Alcoholics have been shown to have high levels of cortisol, a corticosteroid. Excessive levels of cortisol have been linked to decreased bone formation and increased bone resorption. Corticosteroids impair calcium absorption which leads to an increase in PTH secretion, which can result in further bone loss.

Bone loss is evident in a large number of individuals that drink heavily. Alcohol appears to have a direct toxic effect on osteoblasts, suppressing bone formation. On the other hand, osteoclasts (cells responsible for the resorption or breakdown of bone) may be stimulated by alcohol exposure.

Falls And Fractures

Due to the effects of alcohol on balance and gait, alcoholics tend to fall more frequently than the general population. Heavy alcohol consumption has been associated with an increased risk of fracture, including hip fracture. An analysis of alcohol use in an arm of the Framingham study concluded that heavy alcohol consumption increased hip fracture risk in both men and women. As expected, older alcoholics are at substantially greater risk of fractures than younger alcoholics.

Vertebral fractures, which tend to be uncommon in individuals under fifty years of age, are more prevalent in those younger than fifty who abuse alcohol. Additionally, alcohol consumption is linked to other types of fracture, including those of the wrist and ribs.

The Benefits Of Abstinence

The most effective treatment for alcohol-induced bone changes is abstinence. Abstinence in alcoholics seems to result in a rapid recovery of osteoblast function. Moreover, studies demonstrate that bone loss may be partially restored when alcohol abuse is discontinued.

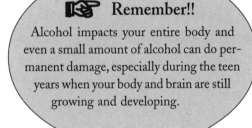

☞ **Remember!!**
Alcohol impacts your entire body and even a small amount of alcohol can do permanent damage, especially during the teen years when your body and brain are still growing and developing.

Chapter 20

Myths Versus Facts About Alcohol And The Liver

What Are The Myths Vs. Facts About Alcohol And The Liver?

Most people are confused about the relationship between alcohol and the liver. The American Liver Foundation has found that there is much misunderstanding on this subject. Because myths can be harmful, here are straight answers to some of the most common questions about alcohol and the liver.

Does alcohol cause liver disease?

Yes, but it is only one of the many causes, and the risk depends on how much you drink and over how long a period. There are more than 100 liver diseases. Known causes include viruses, hereditary defects, and reactions to drugs and chemicals. Scientists are still investigating the causes for the most serious liver diseases.

How much alcohol can I safely drink?

Because some people are much more sensitive to alcohol than others, there is no single right answer that will fit everyone. Generally, doctors recommend that if you drink, don't drink more than two drinks per day. Remember, you need to be 21 to drink legally.

Are there dangers from alcohol besides the amount that is consumed?

Yes. Even moderate amounts of alcohol can have toxic effects when taken with over-the-counter drugs containing acetaminophen. If you are taking over-the-counter drugs, be especially careful about drinking and don't use an alcoholic beverage to take your medication. Ask your doctor about precautions for prescription drugs.

> ✎ **Weird Words**
>
> <u>Cirrhosis</u>: Normal liver cells are damaged and replaced by scar tissue. This scarring keeps the liver from performing many of its vital functions.
>
> <u>Detoxification</u>: Removal or recovery of a poison in the body.
>
> <u>Hepatitis</u>: An inflammation of the liver.
>
> <u>Metabolism</u>: Chemical and physical changes that occur in body tissues and organs.

Can social drinkers get alcoholic hepatitis?

Yes. Alcoholic hepatitis is frequently discovered in alcoholics, but it also occurs in people who are not alcoholics. People vary greatly in the way their liver reacts to alcohol.

What kinds of liver diseases are caused by too much alcohol?

Alcoholic hepatitis is an inflammation of the liver that lasts one to two weeks. Symptoms include loss of appetite, nausea, vomiting, abdominal pain and tenderness, fever, jaundice, and sometimes, mental confusion. It is believed to lead to alcoholic cirrhosis over a period of years. Cirrhosis involves permanent damage to the liver cells. Fatty liver is the earliest stage of alcoholic liver disease. If the patient stops drinking at this point, the liver can heal itself.

How can alcoholic hepatitis be diagnosed?

Alcoholic hepatitis is not easy to diagnose. Sometimes symptoms are worse for a time after drinking has stopped than they were during the drinking episode. While the disease usually comes on after a period of fairly heavy drinking, it may also be seen in people who are moderate drinkers. Blood tests may help in diagnosis. Proof is established best by liver biopsy. This involves taking a tiny specimen of liver tissue with a needle and examining it under a microscope. The biopsy is usually done under local anesthesia.

Are men or women more likely to get alcoholic hepatitis?

Women appear to be more likely to suffer liver damage from alcohol. Even when a man and woman have the same weight and drink the same amount, the woman generally has a higher concentration of alcohol in the blood because she has relatively more body fat and less water than the man, and her body handles alcohol differently.

Do all alcoholics get alcoholic hepatitis and eventually cirrhosis?

No. Some alcoholics may suffer seriously from the many physical and psychological symptoms of alcoholism but escape serious liver damage. Alcoholic cirrhosis is found among alcoholics about 10–25% of the time.

♣ It's A Fact!!

True Or False?

- Many victims of liver disease are not alcoholics.
- Even moderate social drinkers may risk liver damage.
- People who never drink alcoholic beverages may still get serious liver problems.

Answer: All statements are true.

How many did you get right? If you were surprised by the answers, don't be discouraged. You are not alone.

Is alcoholic hepatitis different from fatty liver?

Yes. Anyone who drinks alcohol heavily, even for a few days, will develop a condition in which liver cells are swollen with fat globules and water. This condition is called fatty liver. It may also result from diabetes, obesity, certain drugs, or severe protein malnutrition. Fatty liver caused by alcohol is reversible when drinking of alcohol is stopped.

Does alcoholic hepatitis always lead to cirrhosis?

No. It usually takes many years for alcoholic hepatitis to produce enough liver damage to result in cirrhosis. If alcoholic hepatitis is detected and treated early, cirrhosis can be prevented.

Is alcoholic hepatitis dangerous?

Yes. It may be fatal, especially if the patient has had previous liver damage. Those who have had nutritional deficiencies because of heavy drinking may have other ailments. These medical complications may affect almost every system in the body. It is important to recognize and treat alcoholic cirrhosis early, so that these life-threatening consequences are prevented.

How can alcoholic hepatitis be prevented?

The best treatment is to stop drinking. Treatment may also include prescribed medication, good nutrition, and rest. The patient may be instructed to avoid various drugs and chemicals. Since the liver has considerable ability to heal and regenerate, the prognosis for a patient with alcoholic hepatitis is very hopeful—if he or she totally abstains from drinking alcohol.

Is cirrhosis different from alcoholic hepatitis?

Yes. Hepatitis is an inflammation of the liver. In cirrhosis, normal liver cells are damaged and replaced by scar tissue. This scarring keeps the liver from performing many of its vital functions.

What causes cirrhosis?

There are many causes for cirrhosis. Long-term alcohol abuse is one. Chronic hepatitis is another major cause. In children, the most frequent causes are biliary atresia, a disease that damages the bile ducts, and neonatal hepatitis. Children with these diseases often receive liver transplants.

Many adult patients who require liver transplants suffer from primary biliary cirrhosis. We do not yet know what causes this illness, but it is not in any way related to alcohol consumption.

Cirrhosis can also be caused by hereditary defects in iron or copper metabolism or prolonged exposure to toxins.

♣ It's A Fact!!
Basic Facts About The Liver

Your liver, the largest organ in your body, weighs about three pounds and is roughly the size of a football. It lies in the upper right side of your abdomen, situated mostly under the lower ribs. The normal liver is soft and smooth and is connected to the small intestine by the bile duct, which carries bile formed in the liver to the intestines.

Nearly all of the blood that leaves the stomach and intestines must pass through the liver. Acting as the body's largest chemical factory, it has many functions, including:

- The production of clotting factors, blood, proteins, bile, and more than a thousand different enzymes
- The metabolism of cholesterol
- The storage of energy (glycogen) to fuel muscles
- Maintenance of normal blood sugar concentration
- The regulation of several hormones
- The detoxification of drugs and poisons including alcohol

It is no wonder that liver disease can cause widespread disruption of body function. While many liver diseases can occur, one of the most important problems is cirrhosis.

Should alcoholics receive a liver transplant?

Some medical centers will not transplant alcoholics because they believe a substantial percentage will return to drinking. Other centers require abstinence from drinking at least six months before and after surgery, plus enrollment in a counseling program.

Cirrhosis: Many Causes

What is cirrhosis?

Cirrhosis is a term that refers to a consequence of chronic liver diseases in which normal liver cells are damaged and replaced by scar tissue, decreasing the amount of normal liver tissue. The distortion of the normal liver structure by the scar tissue interferes with the flow of blood through the liver. It also handicaps the function of the liver, which, with the loss of normal liver tissue, leads to failure of the liver to perform some of its critically important functions.

> ♣ **It's A Fact!!**
> Alcohol by itself, in large amounts, is a poison that can cause cirrhosis.

Can the condition responsible for cirrhosis be identified?

Causes of cirrhosis can be identified by certain factors.

In alcoholic cirrhosis:

- History of regular and excessive alcoholic intake
- Physical and behavioral changes
- Examination of liver tissue obtained by needle biopsy under local anesthesia

In active viral hepatitis infection:

- Blood tests
- Liver biopsy

Does heavy drinking always lead to cirrhosis?

While almost everyone who drinks excessive amounts of alcohol sustains some liver damage, it does not necessarily develop into cirrhosis. In those individuals who drink one-half to one pint (8 to 16 ounces) of hard liquor per day (or the equivalent in other alcoholic drinks), for 15 years or more, about one-third develop cirrhosis, another third develop fatty livers, while the remainder have only minor liver problems.

In general, the more you drink, the greater the frequency and regularity of excessive intake, the more likely that cirrhosis will result. A poor diet, long considered to be the main factor in the development of cirrhosis in the alcoholic, is probably only a contributing factor.

Can social drinkers get cirrhosis?

Some individuals who are social drinkers, not alcoholics, can develop cirrhosis. Factors affecting the development of cirrhosis include:

- The amount of alcohol consumed

- The regularity of intake

- Natural tendency

- Perhaps the state of nutrition

It is not known why some individuals are more prone to adverse reactions to alcohol than others. Women are less tolerant of alcohol than men. Researchers believe that this is because men have a greater ability than women to break down the alcohol for elimination. Studies show that a much higher percentage of women, consuming less alcohol than men, go on to cirrhosis.

Does hepatitis always result in cirrhosis?

Some patients with chronic viral hepatitis develop cirrhosis. There are five known types of viral hepatitis, each caused by a different virus.

- Acute hepatitis A and acute hepatitis E do not lead to chronic hepatitis.

- Acute hepatitis B leads to chronic hepatitis infection in approximately 5% of adult patients. In a few of these patients, the chronic hepatitis B progresses to cirrhosis.

- Acute hepatitis D infects individuals already infected by hepatitis B.

• Acute hepatitis C becomes chronic in approximately 80% of adults. A minority of these patients (20–30%) will progress to cirrhosis, typically over many years.

♣ It's A Fact!!
Signs And Symptoms Of Cirrhosis

The onset of cirrhosis is often silent with few specific symptoms to identify what is happening in the liver. As continued scarring and destruction occur, the following signs and symptoms may appear:

• Loss of appetite

• Nausea and vomiting

• Weight loss

• Enlargement of the liver

• Jaundice—yellow discoloration of the whites of the eyes and skin occurs because bile pigment can no longer be removed by the liver

• Itching—due to the retention of bile products in the skin

• Ascites—abdominal swelling due to an accumulation of fluid caused by the obstruction of blood flow through the liver

• Vomiting of blood—frequently occurs from swollen, ruptured varices (veins that burst) in the lower end of the esophagus due to the increased pressure in these vessels caused by scar tissue formation

• Increased sensitivity to drugs—due to the inability of the liver to inactivate them

• Encephalopathy (impending coma)—subtle mental changes advancing to profound confusion and coma

Many patients may have no symptoms and are found to have cirrhosis by physical examination and laboratory tests, which may have been performed in the course of treatment for unrelated illnesses.

How is cirrhosis treated?

Treatment depends on the type and stage of the cirrhosis. It aims to stop the progress of the cirrhosis, reverse (to whatever extent possible) the damage that has already occurred, and treat complications that are disabling or life-threatening.

Stopping or reversing the process requires removal of the cause: In alcoholic cirrhosis treatment includes abstention from alcohol, and an adequate, wholesome diet.

How can I avoid cirrhosis?

Do not drink to excess: Avoid the use of alcoholic beverages. Alcohol destroys liver cells. How well damaged cells regenerate varies with each individual. Prior injury to the liver by unknown and unrecognizable viruses or chemicals can also affect the regeneration process.

Take precautions when using man-made chemicals: The liver must process many chemicals that were not present in the past. More research is needed to determine the effects on the liver of many of these compounds. When using chemicals at work, in cleaning your home, or working in your garden:

- Be sure there is good ventilation

- Follow directions for use of all products

- Never mix chemical products

- Avoid getting chemicals on the skin, where they can be absorbed, and wash promptly if you do

- Avoid inhaling chemicals

- Wear protective clothing

- Seek medical advice

Remain under supervision of a physician if you develop viral hepatitis until your recovery is assured.

How might cirrhosis affect other diseases I might have or treatment of them?

The responsibility of the liver for the proper functioning of the whole body is so great that the chronic disease of the liver may modify the body's responses to a variety of illnesses. Abnormal function of the liver in cirrhosis may:

- Affect the dose of medicine required in the treatment of other conditions

- Affect the treatment of diabetes

- Alter the response of the body to infection

- Alter tolerance for surgical procedures

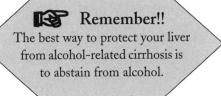

☞ Remember!!
The best way to protect your liver from alcohol-related cirrhosis is to abstain from alcohol.

Patients with cirrhosis are particularly prone to develop fatal bacterial infections, kidney malfunctions, stomach ulcers, gallstones, a type of diabetes, and cancer of the liver.

What are my prospects for reasonable health and survival with treatment?

Treatment at this stage, with proper adherence to the physician's recommendations, leads to improvement in the majority of cases and the patient is able to pursue a normal life and activities.

When cirrhosis is not discovered until extensive damage has resulted, the outlook may be less favorable for improvement, and complications such as ascites and hemorrhage are more likely to be encountered.

The liver is a large organ and is able to perform its vital functions despite some damage. It also has the ability to repair itself to a limited degree. Cells that die are replaced by new cells. If the cause of cirrhosis can be removed, these factors provide hope for both improvement and carrying on a normal life.

Chapter 21

Adolescent Drinking Impairs Brain Function

Alcohol Hits Teen Brains Hard

A report issued in 2003 by the National Academy of Sciences (NAS) contains disturbing news about the dangers of underage drinking. The national report confirms a large amount of earlier research linking alcohol use with damage to the adolescent brain.

Aaron White, Ph.D., assistant research professor in the department of psychiatry and behavioral sciences at Duke University Medical Center, says the report confirms just how hazardous alcohol is to a young person's brain.

"There's an incredible amount of development taking place in the brain during the teenage years," he says. "Because of this, it's not surprising that alcohol and perhaps other drugs affect the teenage brain differently than the adult brain."

About This Chapter: This chapter includes "Alcohol Hits Teen Brains Hard," reprinted with permission from the Duke University Medical Center News Office, September 23, 2003. © 2003 Duke University Medical Center. All rights reserved. Text under the heading "Introducing Your Brain" is from "The Brain and Addiction," National Institute on Drug Abuse (NIDA), 2003. Text under its own heading is from "Teenage Brain: A Work In Progress," National Institute of Mental Health, NIH Publication No. 01-4929, 2001. Text under "Underage Drinking And Academic Performance," is from "Making the Link: Underage Drinking and Academic Performance," Substance Abuse and Mental Health Services Administration (SAMHSA) and Leadership to Keep Children Alcohol Free, revised August, 2002.

♣ It's A Fact!!

How Alcohol Affects The Brain

- **Alcohol interferes with brain cell communication.** Intoxication and other short-term effects of alcohol are caused largely by temporary, reversible changes in specific receptors and associated molecules. With repeated (chronic) alcohol exposure, long-lasting changes occur in receptors and in the series of chemical interactions they signal. Receptor changes are only one example of many permanent changes in the brain caused by the presence of alcohol.

- **Alcohol reduces the overall level of brain activity.** This is the main reason that alcohol is thought of as a depressant.

- **Alcohol alters serotonin transmission.** Serotonin is involved in the regulation of attention, emotion, and motivation. Depression is a common disorder that occurs with alcoholism.

- **Alcohol consumption and stress are linked.** Exposure to stress may lead to the beginning and continued use of alcohol. Many researchers believe that alcohol's stress-relieving effect is what prompts most people to drink. While alcohol use may temporarily relieve the symptoms of stress, chronic drinking not only can lead to alcohol-related problems, it may increase the unwanted effects of stress, leaving the brain in a state of permanent stress. This effect may help explain why even after months or years of not drinking alcohol, alcoholics are likely to drink during stressful life events.

Source: Adapted from "Neuroscience Research and Therapeutic Targets," *Alcohol Alert*, No. 61, National Institute on Alcohol Abuse and Alcoholism (NIAAA), April 2004.

White, who is also a resident psychologist at the Durham, NC, Veterans Administration Medical Center, says alcohol affects several different parts of a young person's brain. "We're just beginning to figure this out," he says. "We've known for a long time that in adults who abuse alcohol, there is damage throughout the brain, including an area called the frontal lobes, which are critically involved in planning, decision-making, impulse control, voluntary motor behavior, and language.

"We think there is similar damage taking place in adolescents, but the extent of the damage seems to be greater than in older drinkers. In teenagers, these regions get hit very hard by alcohol."

White adds, "We also have some evidence that a structure called the hippocampus, which plays a critical role in memory formation, also suffers some damage as a result of alcohol abuse during adolescence. Unfortunately, the changes that are taking place in the hippocampus during the teenage years make it more sensitive to alcohol."

The NAS report suggests that teenagers' heavy alcohol use could possibly do long-term, or even permanent damage, says White. "If we look at the cognitive abilities of teenagers who are in drug and alcohol treatment, for at least three weeks after an adolescent's last drink, they show memory impairments and other cognitive deficits."

Introducing Your Brain

The brain is the command center of your body. It weighs about three pounds, and has different centers or systems that process different kinds of information.

The brainstem is the most primitive structure at the base of your brain. The brainstem controls your heart rate, breathing, and sleeping; it does the things you never think about.

Various parts or lobes of the brain process information from your sense organs: the occipital lobe receives information from your eyes, for example. And the cerebral cortex, on top of the whole brain, is the "thinking" part of you. That's where you store and process language, math, and strategies: It's the thinking center. Buried deep within the cerebral cortex is the limbic system, which is responsible for survival: It remembers and creates an appetite for the things that keep you alive, such as good food and the company of other human beings.[1, 2] The cerebellum is responsible for things you learn once and never have to think about, such as balance when walking or how to throw a ball.

How Does Your Brain Communicate?

The brain's job is to process information. Brain cells called neurons receive and send messages to and from other neurons. There are billions of neurons in the human brain, each with as many as a thousand threadlike branches that reach out to other neurons.

In a neuron, a message is an electrical impulse. The electrical message travels along the sending branch, or axon, of the neuron. When the message reaches the end of the axon, it causes the release of a chemical called a neurotransmitter. The chemical travels across a tiny gap, or synapse, to other neurons.

> ### ♣ It's A Fact!!
> Studies show that patients with a history of chronic alcohol consumption have smaller, lighter, more shrunken brains than nonalcoholic adults of the same age and gender.
>
> Source: "Imaging and Alcoholism: A Window on the Brain," *Alcohol Alert*, No. 47, National Institute on Alcohol Abuse and Alcoholism (NIAAA), April 2000.

Specialized molecules called receptors on the receiving neuron pick up the chemical. The branches on the receiving end of a neuron are called dendrites. Receptors there have special shapes so they can only collect one kind of neurotransmitter.

In the dendrite, the neurotransmitter starts an electrical impulse. Its work done, the chemical is released back into the synapse. The neurotransmitter then is broken down or is reabsorbed into the sending neuron.[1, 2]

Neurons in your brain release many different neurotransmitters as you go about your day thinking, feeling, reacting, breathing, and digesting. When you learn new information or a new skill, your brain builds more axons and dendrites first, as a tree grows roots and branches. With more branches, neurons can communicate and send their messages more efficiently.[1]

References

1. National Institute on Drug Abuse. *The Brain: Understanding Neurobiology Through the Study of Addiction* (http://science-education.nih.gov/Customers.nsf/highschool.htm): NIH Pub. No. 00-4871.

2. National Institute on Drug Abuse. *Brain Power! The NIDA Junior Scientists Program* (http://www.nida.nih.gov/JSP/JSP.html): NIH Pub. No. 01-4575. Bethesda, MD: NIDA, NIH, DHHS. 2000.

Teenage Brain: A Work In Progress

New imaging studies are revealing—for the first time—patterns of brain development that extend into the teenage years. Although scientists don't know yet what accounts for the observed changes, they may parallel a pruning process that occurs early in life that appears to follow the principle of use-it-or-lose-it—neural connections, or synapses, that get exercised are retained, while those that don't are lost. At least, this is what studies of animals' developing visual systems suggest. While it's known that both genes and environment play major roles in shaping early brain development, science still has much to learn about the relative influence of experience versus genes on the later maturation of the brain.

The newfound appreciation of the dynamic nature of the teen brain is emerging from MRI (magnetic resonance imaging) studies that scan a child's brain every two years, as he or she grows up. Individual brains differ enough that only broad generalizations can be made from comparisons of different individuals at different ages. But following the same brains as they mature allows scientists a much better view into developmental changes.

In the first such longitudinal study of 145 children and adolescents, reported in 1999, the National Institute on Mental Health (NIMH)'s Dr. Judith Rapoport and colleagues were surprised to discover a second wave of overproduction of gray matter, the thinking part of the brain—neurons and their branch-like extensions—just prior to puberty.[1] Possibly related to the influence of surging sex hormones, this thickening peaks at around age 11 in girls, 12 in boys, after which the gray matter actually thins some.

Prior to this study, research had shown that the brain overproduced gray matter for a brief period in early development—in the womb and for about the first 18 months of life—and then underwent just one bout of pruning.

Researchers are now confronted with structural changes that occur much later in adolescence. The teen's gray matter waxes and wanes in different functional brain areas at different times in development. For example, the gray matter growth spurt just prior to puberty predominates in the frontal lobe, the seat of executive functions—planning, impulse control, and reasoning.

Unlike gray matter, the brain's white matter—wire-like fibers that establish neurons' long-distance connections between brain

✎ Weird Words

Amygdala: A brain center that regulates fear and other reactions.

Frontal Lobe: The area of the brain that controls movement, problem solving, memory, language, judgment, emotions, impulse control, and social and sexual behavior.

Gray Matter: The thinking part of the brain.

Maturation: Completed growth and development.

Myelin: A layer of insulation that covers nerve fibers, making them more efficient, just like insulation on electric wires improves their conductivity.

Parietal Lobe: Located behind the frontal lobe in the brain and responsible for the sensations of temperature, touch, pressure, and pain from the skin. It is involved in understanding speech and in using words to express thoughts and feelings.

Puberty: A time of rapid physical growth which changes a child into an adult with sexual characteristics and the ability to reproduce.

Synapse: A membrane or receptor cell that connects nerve cells.

Temporal Lobe: The area of the brain that organizes things you hear, smell, touch, taste, and see.

White Matter: The nerve fibers in the brain and spinal cord that make the connections between regions in the brain.

regions—thickens progressively from birth in humans. A layer of insulation called myelin progressively envelops these nerve fibers, making them more efficient, just like insulation on electric wires improves their conductivity.

Advancements in MRI (magnetic resonance imaging) image analysis are providing new insights into how the brain develops. Researchers report a wave of white matter growth that begins at the front of the brain in early childhood, moves rearward, and then subsides after puberty. Striking growth spurts can be seen from ages 6 to 13 in areas connecting brain regions specialized for language and understanding spatial relations, the temporal and parietal lobes. This growth drops off sharply after age 12, coinciding with the end of a critical period for learning languages.

While this work suggests a wave of brain white matter development that flows from front to back, animal, functional brain imaging, and postmortem studies have suggested that gray matter maturation flows in the opposite direction, with the frontal lobes not fully maturing until young adulthood. To confirm this in living humans, the UCLA researchers compared MRI scans of young adults, 23–30, with those of teens, 12–16.[2] They looked for signs of myelin, which would imply more mature, efficient connections, within gray matter.

As expected, areas of the frontal lobe showed the largest differences between young adults and teens. This increased myelination in the adult frontal cortex likely relates to the maturation of cognitive processing and other executive functions. Parietal and temporal areas mediating spatial, sensory, auditory, and language functions appeared largely mature in the teen brain. The observed late maturation of the frontal lobe conspicuously coincides with the typical age-of-onset of schizophrenia—late teens, early twenties— which is characterized by impaired executive functioning.

Another series of MRI studies is shedding light on how teens may process emotions differently than adults. Using functional MRI (fMRI), a team led by Dr. Deborah Yurgelun-Todd at Harvard's McLean Hospital scanned subjects' brain activity while they identified emotions on pictures of faces displayed on a computer screen.[3] Young teens, who characteristically perform poorly on the task, activated the amygdala, a brain center that mediates fear and other gut reactions, more than the frontal lobe. As teens grow older, their brain activity during this task tends to shift to the frontal lobe, leading to more reasoned perceptions and improved performance. Similarly, the researchers saw a shift in activation from the temporal lobe to the frontal lobe during a language skills task, as teens got older. These functional changes paralleled structural changes in temporal lobe white matter.

While these studies have shown remarkable changes that occur in the brain during the teen years, they also demonstrate that the teenage brain is a very complicated and dynamic arena, one that is not easily understood.

References

1. Giedd JN, Blumenthal J, Jeffries NO, et al. Brain development during childhood and adolescence: a longitudinal MRI study. *Nature Neuroscience*, 1999; 2(10): 861-3.

♣ It's A Fact!!
Alcohol-Related Brain Damage In Young Women

A study in the February 2001 issue of *Alcoholism: Clinical & Experimental Research* used a type of magnetic resonance imaging (MRI) to closely examine brain function in young alcoholic women. The main finding was that alcohol-dependent women showed less activation in brain areas that are needed for spatial tasks like puzzles, maps, and mechanics, and for working with information that is held mentally, like doing math inside your head or making sense of a lecture or set of complex instructions. The brain parts that showed the differences are in areas that we need for finding our way around, and working with all the information we are bombarded with in everyday life. These findings suggest that even young and physically healthy individuals, particularly if they are female, risk damaging their brains through chronic, heavy use of alcohol.

Source: "Specifying Alcohol-Related Brain Damage in Young Women," Addiction Technology Transfer Center, 2001; available at http://www.nattc.org/asme/details.asp?ID=012b.

2. Sowell ER, Thompson PM, Holmes CJ, et al. In vivo evidence for post-adolescent brain maturation in frontal and striatal regions. *Nature Neuroscience*, 1999; 2(10): 859-61.

3. Baird AA, Gruber SA, Fein DA, et al. Functional magnetic resonance imaging of facial affect recognition in children and adolescents. *Journal of the American Academy of Child and Adolescent Psychiatry*, 1999; 38(2): 195-9.

Underage Drinking And Academic Performance

Research Shows That Drinking Alcohol Impairs Brain Function And Adolescent Memory

- Studies indicate that alcohol-dependent teens showed impaired memory, altered perception of spatial relationships, and verbal skill deficiencies.[1]

- It takes less alcohol to damage a young brain than to damage a fully mature one, and the young brain is damaged more quickly.[2]

Drinking Alcohol Negatively Affects Students' Academic Performance

- Students with high truancy rates were far more likely than students with low truancy rates to be drinkers or to get drunk.[3]

- Heavy drinkers and binge drinkers ages 12 to 17 were twice as likely to say their school work is poor than those who did not drink alcohol in the past month.[4]

- High school students who use alcohol or other drugs frequently are up to five times more likely than other students to drop out of school.[5]

- Among eighth graders, students with higher grade point averages reported less alcohol use in the past month.[6]

- Students drinking alcohol during adolescence have a reduced ability to learn, compared with those youth who do not drink until adulthood.[7]

- In a national survey of over 55,000 undergraduate students from 132 two and four-year colleges in the United States, 23.5 percent of students reported performing poorly on a test or assignment, and 33.1 percent said they had missed a class due to alcohol use in the previous 12 months.[8]

- College students who were frequent binge drinkers were eight times more likely than non-binge drinkers to miss a class, fall behind in schoolwork, get hurt or injured, and damage property.[9]

References

1. Brown SA, Tapert SF, Granholm E, et al. Neurocognitive functioning of adolescents: effects of protracted alcohol use. *Alcohol Clin Exp Res* 24(2):164-171, 2000.

2. Swartzwelder HS, Wilson WA, Tayyeb

✤ It's A Fact!!

Early Alcohol Use Is Linked To Academic Achievement And Future Earning Power.

- Studies indicate that alcohol-dependent teens showed impaired memory, altered perception of spatial relationships, and verbal skill deficiencies.

- Seniors' college plans and frequent alcohol use are linked: 4.8 percent of seniors planning on none or under 4 years of college reported daily drinking, versus only 3.1 percent of seniors planning to complete 4 years of college. Binge drinking was reported by 34 percent of the first group of seniors versus 27.2 percent of the second group.

- According to a study on the economic costs of alcohol and drug abuse in the United States, males with a history of alcohol dependence who began drinking before age 15 earned less than those who began drinking later.

Source: "Making the Link: Underage Drinking and the Future of Children," Substance Abuse and Mental Health Services Administration (SAMHSA) and Leadership to Keep Children Alcohol Free, revised November 2003.

MI. Age-dependent inhibition of long-term potentiation by ethanol in immature versus mature hippocampus. *Alcohol Clin Exp Res* 19(6):1480-1485, 1995.

3. O'Malley PM, Johnston LD, Bachman JG. Alcohol use among adolescents. *Alcohol Res Health* 22(2):85-93, 1998.

4. Greenblatt JC. *Patterns of alcohol use among adolescents and associations with emotional and behavioral problems.* Office of Applied Studies Working Paper. Rockville, MD: Substance Abuse and Mental Health Services Administration, 2000.

5. The National Center on Addiction and Substance Abuse at Columbia University. *Malignant Neglect: Substance Abuse and America's Schools.* New York: Columbia University, 2001.

6. O'Malley, et al. *Alcohol use among adolescents.*

7. Swartzwelder, et al. *Age-dependent inhibition.*

8. Core Institute. *2000 Statistics on Alcohol and Other Drug Use on American Campuses.* Carbondale, IL: Southern Illinois University at Carbondale, 2000.

9. Wechsler H, Dowdall G, Maenner G, et al. Changes in binge drinking and related problems among American college students between 1993 and 1997: Results of the Harvard School of Public Health College Alcohol Study. *J Am Coll Health*, 47(9):57-68, 1998.

☞ **Remember!!**

Teen brains are still growing and developing. Any use of alcohol can cause brain damage which may affect your future schooling and employment options.

Chapter 22

Alcohol Intoxication

General Effects Of Alcohol Intoxication

- **General Effect:** Alcohol is a downer that reduces activity in the central nervous system. The alcohol intoxicated person exhibits loose muscle tone, loss of fine motor coordination, and often has a staggering "drunken" gait.

- **Eyes:** The eyes may appear somewhat glossy and pupils may be slow to respond to stimulus. At high doses pupils may become constricted.

- **Vital Signs:** At intoxicating doses, alcohol can decrease heart rate, lower blood pressure and respiration rate, and result in decreased reflex responses and slower reaction times.

- **Skin:** Skin may be cool to the touch (but the user may feel warm), profuse sweating may accompany alcohol use.

- **Observation:** Loose muscle tone, loss of fine motor coordination, odor of alcohol on the breath, and a staggering "drunken" gait. See Table 22.1 for dose-specific effects.

About This Chapter: Text in this chapter is reprinted with permission from "Effects of Alcohol Intoxication" by the Indiana Prevention Resource Center at Indiana University, http://www.iprc.indiana.edu. © Copyright 2004 The Trustees of Indiana University. All rights reserved.

✎ Weird Words

Dysphoria: Feeling anxious, depressed, or uneasy.

Euphoria: Feeling extremely happy and carefree.

Inhibition: A person's control of their own behavior.

Intoxicated: The physical condition of a person who has drunk a large amount of alcohol in a short amount of time.

Table 22.1. Dose-Specific Effects Of Alcohol Intoxication Related To The Blood Alcohol Concentration (BAC)

BAC	Dose-Specific Effects*
0.02–0.03%	No loss of coordination, slight euphoria and loss of shyness. Depressant effects are not apparent.
0.04–0.06%	Feeling of well-being, relaxation, lower inhibitions, sensation of warmth. Euphoria. Some minor impairment of reasoning and memory, lowering of caution. **Driving skills may be impaired at this level of intoxication.**
0.07–0.09%	Slight impairment of balance, speech, vision, reaction time, and hearing. Euphoria. Judgment and self-control are reduced, and caution, reason, and memory are impaired. **Driving skills are always impaired at this level of intoxication.**
0.10–0.125%	Significant impairment of motor coordination and loss of good judgment. Speech may be slurred; balance, vision, reaction time, and hearing will be impaired. Euphoria. **It is illegal to operate a motor vehicle in all states at this level of intoxication.**

Dose-Specific Effects Of Alcohol Intoxication

The effects of alcohol intoxication are greatly influenced by individual variations among users. Some users may become intoxicated at a much lower blood alcohol concentration (BAC) level than is shown.

☞ Remember!!

When intoxicated, a person does not function well physically and may make disastrous decisions.

Table 22.1. Continued

BAC	Dose-Specific Effects*
0.13–0.15%	Gross motor impairment and lack of physical control. Blurred vision and major loss of balance. Euphoria is reduced and dysphoria is beginning to appear.
0.16–0.20%	Dysphoria (anxiety, restlessness) predominates, nausea may appear. The drinker has the appearance of a "sloppy drunk."
0.25%	Needs assistance in walking; total mental confusion. Dysphoria with nausea and some vomiting.
0.30%	Loss of consciousness.
0.40% and up	Onset of coma, possible death due to respiratory arrest.**

* The effects of alcohol intoxication are greatly influenced by individual variations among users. Some users will be intoxicated at a much lower BAC than is shown above.

** Death can occur at lower BAC in some individuals.

Source: Adapted from: Bailey, William J., *Drug Use in American Society*, 3rd ed., Minneapolis: Burgess, 1993.

Chapter 23

Alcohol Poisoning

Excessive drinking can be hazardous to everyone's health! It can be particularly stressful if you are the sober one taking care of your drunk roommate who is vomiting while you are trying to study for an exam.

Some people laugh at the behavior of others who are drunk. Some think it's even funnier when they pass out. But there is nothing funny about the aspiration of vomit leading to asphyxiation or the poisoning of the respiratory center in the brain, both of which can result in death.

Do you know about the dangers of alcohol poisoning? When should you seek professional help for a friend? Sadly enough, too many students say they wish they would have sought medical treatment for a friend. Many end up feeling responsible for alcohol-related tragedies that could have easily been prevented.

Common myths about sobering up include drinking black coffee, taking a cold bath or shower, sleeping it off, or walking it off. But these are just myths, and they don't work. The only thing that reverses the effects of alcohol is time—something you may not have if you are suffering from alcohol poisoning. And many different factors affect the level of intoxication of an individual, so it's difficult to gauge exactly how much is too much.

About This Chapter: The information in this chapter is from "Students and College Drinking: Alcohol Poisoning," National Institute on Alcohol Abuse and Alcoholism (NIAAA), April 3, 2002.

What Happens To Your Body When You Get Alcohol Poisoning?

Alcohol depresses nerves that control involuntary actions such as breathing and the gag reflex (which prevents choking). A fatal dose of alcohol will eventually stop these functions.

It is common for someone who drank excessive alcohol to vomit since alcohol is an irritant to the stomach. Then there is the danger of choking on vomit, which could cause death by asphyxiation in a person who is not conscious because of intoxication.

You should also know that a person's blood alcohol concentration (BAC) can continue to rise even while he or she is passed out. Even after a person stops drinking, alcohol in the stomach and intestine continues to enter the bloodstream and circulate throughout the body. It is dangerous to assume the person will be fine by sleeping it off.

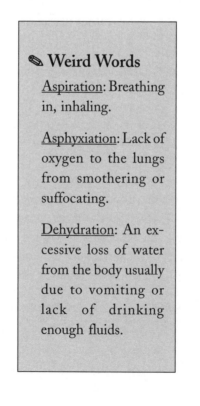

✎ **Weird Words**

Aspiration: Breathing in, inhaling.

Asphyxiation: Lack of oxygen to the lungs from smothering or suffocating.

Dehydration: An excessive loss of water from the body usually due to vomiting or lack of drinking enough fluids.

Critical Signs For Alcohol Poisoning

- Mental confusion, stupor, coma, or person cannot be roused

- Vomiting

- Seizures

- Slow breathing (fewer than eight breaths per minute)

- Irregular breathing (10 seconds or more between breaths)

- Hypothermia (low body temperature), bluish skin color, paleness

What Should I Do If I Suspect Someone Has Alcohol Poisoning?

- Know the danger signals.

- Do not wait for all symptoms to be present.

- Be aware that a person who has passed out may die.

- If there is any suspicion of an alcohol overdose, call 911 for help. Don't try to guess the level of drunkenness.

What Can Happen To Someone With Alcohol Poisoning That Goes Untreated?

- Victim chokes on his or her own vomit

- Breathing slows, becomes irregular, or stops

- Heart beats irregularly or stops

- Hypothermia (low body temperature)

- Hypoglycemia (too little blood sugar) leads to seizures

- Untreated severe dehydration from vomiting can cause seizures, permanent brain damage, or death

Even if the victim lives, an alcohol overdose can lead to irreversible brain damage. Rapid binge drinking (which often happens on a bet or a dare) is

especially dangerous because the victim can ingest a fatal dose before becoming unconscious.

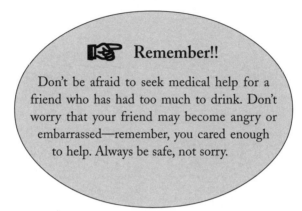

☞ Remember!!

Don't be afraid to seek medical help for a
friend who has had too much to drink. Don't
worry that your friend may become angry or
embarrassed—remember, you cared enough
to help. Always be safe, not sorry.

Chapter 24

Alcohol, Pregnancy, And Fetal Alcohol Syndrome

Alcohol Use And Pregnancy

Maternal prenatal alcohol use is one of the leading preventable causes of birth defects and developmental disabilities.

- Children exposed to alcohol during fetal development can suffer a wide array of disorders, from subtle changes in intelligence quotient (IQ) to profound mental retardation. They can also suffer growth retardation in varying degrees and be born with birth defects of major organ systems. One of the most severe effects of drinking during pregnancy is fetal alcohol syndrome (FAS).

- Approximately one in 30 pregnant women in the United States reports risk drinking (seven or more drinks per week, or five or more drinks on any one occasion). Drinking alcohol at these levels poses a

About This Chapter: This chapter includes text from "Alcohol Use and Pregnancy," National Center on Birth Defects and Developmental Disabilities (NCBDDD), 9/2002. Additional text under its own heading is from "New Study Finds Babies Born to Mothers Who Drink Alcohol Heavily May Suffer Permanent Nerve Damage," *NIH News*, National Institute of Child Health and Human Development (NICHD), 3/8/2004. Additional text under its own heading is from "Fetal Alcohol Information," National Center on Birth Defects and Developmental Disabilities (NCBDDD), updated 4/2002.

serious health threat to the unborn fetus.

- More than half of all women of childbearing age in the United States report that they drink alcohol. Also, more than half of all pregnancies are unplanned. Although early pregnancy is a particularly vulnerable time, damage to the fetus' developing organ systems can occur throughout pregnancy as a result of continued alcohol exposure.

> ✎ **Weird Words**
>
> Fetal: Relating to an unborn baby, (i.e., fetal growth, fetal distress).
>
> Prenatal: Before birth.
>
> Fetal Alcohol Syndrome: Birth defects caused by alcohol consumption by the mother during the pregnancy.

- Fortunately, FAS and other prenatal alcohol-related disorders are 100% preventable—if a woman does not drink alcohol while she is pregnant. Women should avoid drinking if they are pregnant, planning to become pregnant, or at risk of becoming pregnant (i.e., sexually active and not using an effective form of birth control).

Study Finds Babies Born To Mothers Who Drink Alcohol Heavily May Suffer Permanent Nerve Damage

Newborns whose mothers drank alcohol heavily during pregnancy had damage to the nerves in their arms and legs, according to a study by researchers at the National Institute of Child Health and Human Development (NICHD), one of the National Institutes of Health. The study was conducted in collaboration with researchers at the University of Chile. The nerve damage was still present when the children were reexamined at one year of age.

The study is the first to examine whether exposure to alcohol before birth affects the developing peripheral nervous system—the nerves in the arms and legs, rather than in the brain or spinal cord. The study appears in the March 2004 issue of the *Journal of Pediatrics*.

"Infants born to mothers who drink heavily during pregnancy are known to be at risk for mental retardation and birth defects, said Duane Alexander,

M.D., director of the NICHD. "This is the first study to show that these infants may suffer peripheral nerve damage as well."

Adults who drink excessive amounts of alcohol can experience peripheral neuropathy, a condition that occurs when nerves involved in communication between the central nervous system (the brain and spinal cord) and the rest of the body are damaged. This can lead to tingling sensations, numbness, pain, or weakness.

The NICHD–University of Chile Alcohol and Pregnancy Study compared 17 full-term, newborn infants whose mothers drank heavily during pregnancy to 13 newborns not exposed to alcohol in the womb. "Heavy drinking" is defined as having four standard drinks per day (one standard drink is equivalent to one can of beer, one glass of wine, or one mixed drink). All women identified as heavy drinkers were advised that their drinking habits were potentially dangerous to their fetus and were offered help from an alcohol counseling clinic to stop drinking alcohol or to cut down on their drinking.

All of the children underwent a complete neurological exam followed by testing of the nerves in their upper and lower limbs. The researchers stimulated the nerves using a machine that passed a very mild electric current through the skin and then recorded the electrical activity of the nerves to determine if they were normal or damaged. (The procedure uses a current mild enough not to cause pain.) The nerve studies were performed when the children were about one month old and again when they were 12 to 14 months old.

The children exposed to alcohol before they were born experienced significant problems in conducting a message through the nerves—both at one month and one year of age. The alcohol-exposed children did not experience any catch-up or improvement in nerve function by the time they reached their first birthday.

"The finding that the nerve damage persisted when the children were a year old suggests that alcohol may cause permanent damage to developing nerves," said James L. Mills, MD, MS, director of the study and chief of the Pediatric Epidemiology Section in the Division of Epidemiology, Statistics, and Prevention Research at the NICHD. "Because the children were evaluated before they could talk, they were unable to tell us if they had symptoms such as pain or numbness. We are continuing to follow these children to determine what effect this nerve damage will have on normal nerve function and whether it will lead to weakness or problems with touch sensation or fine motor skills later in life."

Fetal Alcohol Information

What is fetal alcohol syndrome (FAS)?

Prenatal exposure to alcohol can cause a spectrum of disorders. One of the most severe effects of drinking during pregnancy is fetal alcohol syndrome (FAS). FAS is one of the leading known preventable causes of mental retardation and birth defects. If a woman drinks alcohol during her pregnancy, her baby can be born with FAS, a life-long, physically and mentally disabling condition. FAS is characterized by:

1. Abnormal facial features

2. Growth deficiencies

3. Central nervous system (CNS) problems

♣ **It's A Fact!!**

Birth defects associated with prenatal exposure to alcohol can occur in the first 3 to 8 weeks of pregnancy, before a woman even knows that she is pregnant.

People with FAS may have problems with learning, memory, attention span, communication, vision, and/or hearing. These problems often lead to difficulties in school and problems getting along with others. FAS is a permanent condition. It affects every aspect of an individual's life and the lives of his or her family. However, FAS is 100% preventable—if a woman does not drink alcohol while she is pregnant.

Many terms have been used to describe children who have some, but not all, of the clinical signs of FAS. Three terms are fetal alcohol effects (FAE), alcohol-related neurodevelopmental disorder (ARND), and alcohol-related birth defects (ARBD). FAE has been used to describe children who have all of the diagnostic features of FAS, but at mild or less severe levels. In 1996, the Institute of Medicine (IOM) replaced FAE with the terms ARND and

ARBD. Those with ARND may have functional or mental problems linked to prenatal alcohol exposure. These include behavioral and/or cognitive abnormalities. Examples are learning difficulties, poor school performance, and poor impulse control. They may have difficulties with mathematical skills, memory, attention, and/or judgment. Those with ARBD may have problems with the heart, kidneys, bones, and/or hearing.

How common is FAS?

The reported rates of FAS vary widely. These different rates depend on the population studied and the surveillance methods used. CDC studies show FAS rates ranging from 0.2 to 1.5 per 1,000 live births in different areas of the United States. Other prenatal alcohol-related conditions, such as alcohol-related neurodevelopmental disorder (ARND) and alcohol-related birth defects (ARBD) are believed to occur approximately three times as often as FAS.

What are the characteristics of children with FAS?

FAS is the severe end of a spectrum of effects that can occur when a woman drinks during pregnancy. Fetal death is the most extreme outcome. FAS is a disorder characterized by abnormal facial features and growth, and central nervous system (CNS) problems. If a pregnant woman drinks alcohol but her child does not have all of the symptoms of FAS, it is possible that her child has an alcohol-related neurodevelopmental disorder (ARND). Children with ARND do not have full FAS, but may demonstrate learning and behavioral problems caused by prenatal exposure to alcohol. If you think a child may have FAS or other alcohol-related effects, contact a doctor. Children with FAS or ARND may have the following characteristics or exhibit the following behaviors:

- small for gestational age or small in stature in relation to peers
- facial abnormalities such as small eye openings
- poor coordination
- hyperactive behavior
- learning disabilities

- developmental disabilities (e.g., speech and language delays)

- mental retardation or low IQ

- problems with daily living

- poor reasoning and judgment skills

- sleep and sucking disturbances in infancy

Children with FAS are at risk for psychiatric problems, criminal behavior, unemployment, and incomplete education. These secondary conditions are problems that an individual is not born with, but might acquire as a result of FAS. These conditions can be very serious, yet there are protective

---

❖ It's A Fact!!

Fetal Alcohol Syndrome

Fetal alcohol syndrome (FAS) is one of the leading known causes of mental retardation and birth defects. If a woman drinks alcohol regularly during her pregnancy, her baby can be born with FAS, a physically and mentally disabling condition.

- FAS is characterized by abnormal facial features, growth retardation, and central nervous system problems. Children with FAS have problems with learning, memory, attention span, problem solving, speech, and hearing. These deficits often lead to problems in school and problems getting along with others.

- FAS is an irreversible, lifelong condition that affects every aspect of a child's life and the lives of the child's family. However, FAS is 100% preventable—if a woman does not drink alcohol while she is pregnant.

- If a child was exposed to alcohol during pregnancy but does not have all of the symptoms of FAS, it is possible that he or she may have alcohol-related neurodevelopmental disabilities (ARND). Children with ARND may demonstrate learning and behavioral problems similar to those experienced by children with FAS.

There is no safe amount of alcohol, nor a safe time, that a woman can drink while pregnant. When a pregnant woman drinks alcohol, so does her unborn

factors that have been found to help individuals with these problems. For example, a child who is diagnosed early in life can be placed in appropriate educational classes and given access to social services that can help the child and his or her family. Children with FAS who receive special education are more likely to achieve their developmental and educational potential. In addition, children with FAS need a loving, nurturing, and stable home life in order to avoid disruptions, transient lifestyles, or harmful relationships. Children with FAS who live in abusive or unstable households or become involved in youth violence are much more likely to develop secondary conditions than children with FAS who have not had such negative experiences.

---

baby. There is no safe dose of alcohol in pregnancy, and there does not appear to be a safe time during pregnancy for drinking. Therefore, it is recommended that women abstain from drinking at any time during pregnancy or if they are planning a pregnancy, since many women do not know they are pregnant for the first several weeks. Even if a woman is not planning a pregnancy, she should limit alcohol consumption if she is sexually active and not using effective contraception because she may be pregnant and not know it.

- All drinks containing alcohol can hurt an unborn baby. A standard 12-ounce can of beer has the same amount of alcohol as a 4-ounce glass of wine or a 1-ounce shot of straight liquor. In addition, some alcoholic drinks, such as malt beverages, wine coolers, and mixed drinks, often contain more alcohol than a 12-ounce can of beer.

- If a pregnant woman does drink, it is never too late for her to stop. The sooner a pregnant woman stops drinking, the better it will be for both her baby and herself.

- There is no cure for FAS. However, with early identification and diagnosis, children with FAS can receive services that can help increase their well-being.

Source: National Center on Birth Defects and Developmental Disabilities (NCBDDD), 2002.

How can we prevent FAS?

FAS and other prenatal alcohol-related conditions are completely preventable—if a woman does not drink alcohol while she is pregnant or could become pregnant. If a woman is drinking during pregnancy, it is never too late for her to stop. The sooner a woman stops drinking, the better it will be for both her baby and herself. If a woman is not able to stop drinking, she should contact her physician, local Alcoholics Anonymous, or local alcohol treatment center. The Substance Abuse and Mental Health Services Administration (SAMHSA) has a Substance Abuse Treatment Facility locator. This locator helps people find drug and alcohol treatment programs in their area. If a woman is sexually active and not using an effective form of birth control, she should not drink alcohol. She could be pregnant and not know it for several weeks or more.

Mothers are not the only ones who can prevent FAS. The father's role is also important in helping the woman abstain from drinking alcohol during pregnancy. He can encourage her abstinence from alcohol by avoiding social situations that involve drinking and by abstaining from alcohol himself. Significant others, family members, schools, health and social service organizations, and communities alike can help prevent FAS through education and intervention.

To reduce prenatal alcohol exposure, prevention efforts should target not only pregnant women who are currently drinking, but also women who could become pregnant, are drinking at high-risk levels, and are engaging in unprotected sex.

☞ Remember!!

There is no safe amount of alcohol, nor a safe time, that a woman can drink while pregnant. When a pregnant woman drinks alcohol, so does her unborn baby.

For Additional Information On Alcohol-Related Birth Defects

The Arc of the United States
1010 Wayne Ave., Suite 650
Silver Spring, MD 20910
Phone: 301-565-3842
Fax: 301-565-5342
Website: http://www.thearc.org
E-mail: Info@TheArc

National Organization on Fetal Alcohol Syndrome (NOFAS)
900 17th Street, NW, Suite 910
Washington, DC 20006
Toll-Free: 800-666-6327
Phone: 202-785-4585
Fax: 202-466-6456
Website: http://www.nofas.org
E-mail: information@nofas.org

National Center on Birth Defects and Developmental Disabilities (NCBDDD)
Fetal Alcohol Syndrome Prevention Section
Centers for Disease Control and Prevention
4770 Buford Highway N.E., MSF-49
Atlanta, GA 30341-3724
Phone: 770-488-7370
Fax: 770-488-7361
Website: http://www.cdc.gov/ncbddd

Part Five

Alcohol's Influence On Behavior And Mental Health

Chapter 25

DUI: Driving Under The Influence Of Alcohol

Teenagers, Drinking And Driving: A Quick Trip To The Grave

- Motor vehicle crashes are the leading cause of death for 15- to 20-year-old youth in the U.S.

- More than one-quarter of the drivers killed in crashes had been drinking.

"A law setting a minimum drinking age of 21 years exists in all the states," explained Jean T. Shope, senior research scientist with the Transportation Research Institute at the University of Michigan and lead author of the study. "Although it has reduced underage drinking and driving fatalities, we still have a problem."

In 1999, according to the National Highway Traffic Safety Administration, 3,561 drivers 15 to 20 years old were killed—and an additional 362,000

About This Chapter: Text in this chapter begins with an excerpt from "Teenagers, Drinking and Driving: A Quick Trip to the Grave," Addiction Technology Transfer Center National Office, 2001. Text under the heading "Information From the Insurance Institute For Highway Safety/Highway Loss Data Institute," is from "Q&A: Alcohol: General," copyright © 2004 Insurance Institute for Highway Safety, Highway Loss Data Institute. Reprinted with permission. For additional information, visit http://www.iihs.org. Additional text under its own heading is from "Determine Why There Are Fewer Young Alcohol-Impaired Drivers," Department of Transportation, National Highway Traffic Safety Administration, September 2001.

injured—in traffic crashes. Of those young drivers fatally injured, 29 percent had been drinking. Although driving after drinking is potentially deadly under any circumstances, it is particularly dangerous when teenagers do it.

"It's important to look at the context of this behavior," said James Hedlund, a consultant in traffic safety for Highway Safety North. "Not only is their drinking illegal, because the minimum drinking age in the United States is 21 years of age, but so too is their driving after drinking. Every state has a

---

♣ **It's A Fact!!**

A High Price To Pay

In addition to the legal consequences of a DUI/DWI arrest, it will cost you personally, professionally, and economically.

- If you are arrested for drinking and driving, it will cost you approximately $5,600 (Virginia Alcohol Safety Action Program, 1999).

- This is equivalent to:

  - One used car or a down payment for a new car

  - 375 compact discs

  - 800 movie tickets

  - 100 pairs of shoes

  - 185 haircuts

- When filling out a job application, you must say "yes" you have been convicted of a crime.

- Nine out of 10 insurance companies will cancel your policy forcing you to find a high-risk insurance company, which increases your premiums by $1,000–$1,500 a year.

- While a DUI/DWI can be removed from your driving record, it stays on your criminal record for life.

Source: Excerpted from "2004 Corporate Guide to Safe Celebrating and Safe Driving." Reprinted with permission from the Washington Regional Alcohol Program, http://www.wrap.org. © 2004. All rights reserved.

zero-tolerance law." Under these laws, teenage drivers detected with a blood alcohol concentration of 0.02 grams per deciliter or above will lose their driver's licenses. "So drinking after driving is doubly illegal," he said.

Information From The Insurance Institute For Highway Safety/Highway Loss Data Institute

What is "drunk driving?"

The term "drunk driving" is an inaccurate characterization of the problems caused by motorists who are impaired by alcohol. The first criminal laws targeting this problem prohibited "drunk driving," encouraging the notion that the problem involved drivers who were visibly drunk. In fact, many alcohol-impaired drivers do not appear drunk in the traditional way. Research has shown that even small amounts of alcohol can impair the skills involved in driving, but the persistent notion that the problem is predominantly one of drunk drivers has allowed many drinking drivers to decide they are not part of the problem. For these reasons, the term "alcohol-impaired driving" is a more accurate and precise description of what is commonly referred to as "drunk driving."

What does blood alcohol concentration (BAC) measure?

Blood alcohol concentration (BAC) describes the amount of alcohol in a person's blood expressed as weight of alcohol per unit of volume of blood. For example, at 0.10 percent BAC, there is 100 mg of alcohol per 100 ml of blood. For most legal purposes, however, a blood sample is not necessary to determine a person's BAC. It can be measured much more simply by analyzing exhaled breath.

What is the effect of alcohol on driving skills and crash risk?

At BACs as low as 0.02 percent, alcohol affects driving ability and crash likelihood. The probability of a crash begins to increase significantly at 0.05 percent BAC and climbs rapidly after about 0.08 percent. For drivers age 35 and older with BACs at or above 0.15 percent on weekend nights, the likelihood of being killed in a single-vehicle crash is more than 380 times higher than it is for non-drinking drivers.[1]

How many drinks does it take to reach significantly impairing BACs?

The effects of alcoholic drinks vary greatly because the rate of absorption and BACs attained varies from person to person due to such factors as weight, amount of fat tissue, and stomach contents. Nevertheless, various organizations have developed charts intended to help people estimate their BACs based on the number of drinks consumed. These tables can be used to estimate BACs, but they are subject to error.

Are beer and wine less impairing than hard liquor?

Impairment is not determined by type of drink, but rather by the amount of alcohol ingested over a specific period of time. There is a similar amount of alcohol in such standard drinks as a 12-ounce glass of beer, a 4-ounce glass of wine, and 1.25 ounces of 80-proof liquor. Beer is the most common drink consumed by people stopped for alcohol-impaired driving or involved in alcohol-related crashes.

What proportion of motor vehicle crashes involves alcohol?

The most reliable information about alcohol involvement comes from fatal crashes. In 2002, 32 percent of fatally injured drivers had BACs of at least 0.08 percent. Although alcohol may not have been a causal factor in all of the crashes, this statistic is frequently used to measure the change over time in alcohol involvement in fatal crashes.

In 2002, the National Highway Traffic Safety Administration (NHTSA) estimated that 35 percent of all traffic deaths occurred in crashes in which at least one driver or non-occupant had a BAC of 0.08 percent or more and that any alcohol was present in 41 percent of all fatal crashes in 2002.[2] Such statistics are sometimes cited as proof that a third to half of all fatal crashes are caused by "drunk driving" and that none of the crashes that involve alcohol would occur if the alcohol were not present. But this is incorrect and misleading because alcohol is only one of several factors that contribute to crashes involving drinking drivers. Furthermore, some fatally injured people in alcohol-related crashes are pedestrians with positive BACs, and these fatalities still would occur even if every driver were sober.

Alcohol involvement is much lower in crashes involving nonfatal injuries, and it is lower still in crashes that do not involve injuries at all. A study conducted during the 1960s estimated that 9 percent of drivers in injury crashes in Grand Rapids, Michigan[3]—12 percent in Huntsville, Alabama and in San Diego, according to a study from the 1970s—had BACs at or above 0.10 percent. Only 5 percent of drivers had BACs that high in non-injury crashes in the Grand Rapids study. During the same time, studies of fatally injured drivers found 40–55 percent had BACs of 0.10 percent or more.

Table 25.1. Drove Under The Influence Of Alcohol In the Past Year Among Persons Aged 12 Or Older, By Demographic Characteristics: Percentages, 2002

Demographic Characteristic	Alcohol
Total	14.2
Age	
12–17	4.0
18–25	26.6
26 or Older	13.5
Gender	
Male	18.8
Female	9.9
Hispanic Origin and Race	
Not Hispanic or Latino	14.8
White	16.2
Black or African American	9.6
American Indiana or Alaska Native	15.3
Native Hawaiian or Other Pacific Islander	11.1
Asian	5.7
Two or More Races	10.2
Hispanic or Latino	10.5

Source: SAMHSA, Office of Applied Studies, National Survey on Drug Use and Health, 2003, Table 7.75B.

Table 25.2. Drove Under The Influence Of Alcohol In The Past Year, by Detailed Age Categories: Percentages, 2002.

Age Category	Alcohol
12	0.1
13	0.4
14	0.8
15	2.1
16	7.8
17	13.8
18	18.5
19	22.7
20	24.3
21	32.4
22	30.9
23	29.9
24	29.7
25	25.9

Source: SAMHSA, Office of Applied Studies, National Survey on Drug Use and Health, 2003, Table 7.74B.

How has the problem of alcohol-impaired driving changed over time?

The incidence of alcohol-impaired driving has been reduced in recent years but remains a major problem. The NHTSA and the Institute undertook a national roadside breath survey in 1996—it was patterned after 1986 and 1973 surveys—and found that 83 percent of drivers had no measurable alcohol, a significant increase above the 74 percent rate of sober drivers in 1986 and the 64 percent rate in 1973.[4] Impairment begins even at low BACs, but increases rapidly after 0.05 percent. The proportion of drivers with high BACs has fallen, but less so in recent years. Overall, 7.7 percent of 1996 drivers had 0.05 percent BACs or higher, compared with 8.4 percent in 1986 and 13.7 percent in 1973.

Do alcohol-related crashes differ by gender?

Crashes involving men are much more likely than those involving women to be alcohol-related. Among fatally injured male drivers of passenger vehicles in 2002, 39 percent had BACs of 0.08 percent or more.[2] The corresponding proportion among women was 18 percent. Alcohol involvement in fatal crashes is highest for men ages 21–40. There have been some reports that women are becoming an increasing part of the alcohol-impaired crash problem. According to national roadside breath surveys, more women now are driving at night. The percentage of women in a weekend nighttime sample of drivers increased from 16 percent in 1973 to 26 percent in 1986 to 31 percent in 1996.[4] The increase from 1973 to 1986 was accompanied by a reduction in the percentage of women with high BACs. However, in the period between 1986 and 1996, the percentage of women drivers with high BACs has increased slightly, from 1.3 to 1.5 percent. During this period, the percentage of males with high BACs dropped from 3.9 to 3.5 percent.

When do alcohol-related crashes occur?

They happen at all hours, but alcohol involvement in crashes peaks at night and is higher on weekends than on weekdays. Among passenger vehicle drivers who were fatally injured between 9 p.m. and 6 a.m. in 2002, 59 percent had BACs at or above 0.08 percent compared with 18 percent during other hours. Forty-five percent of all fatally injured drivers on weekends (6 p.m. Friday to 6 a.m. Monday) in 2002 had BACs of 0.08 percent or more. During the rest of the week, the proportion was 25 percent.

Are most alcohol-related crashes caused by repeat offenders?

No. It is true that drivers with prior convictions for driving while impaired by alcohol are over-represented among drivers in fatal crashes. According to a federal study, drivers convicted of alcohol-impaired driving in the past three years are at least 1.8 times as likely to be in fatal crashes as drivers with no prior convictions during the same time period, and are at least four times as likely to be in fatal crashes in which drivers have high BACs (0.10 percent or more).[5] However, it is important to note that 87 percent of drivers with high BACs in fatal crashes have no alcohol convictions during the previous three years.

References

1. Zador, P.L.; Krawchuk, S.A.; and Voas, R.B. 2000. Alcohol-related relative risk of driver fatalities and driver involvement in fatal crashes in relation to driver age and gender: an update using 1996 data. *Journal of Studies on Alcohol* 61(3): 387-395.

2. Insurance Institute for Highway Safety. 2002. *Fatality facts: alcohol*. Arlington, VA. Available: http://www.highwaysafety.com/safety_facts/fatality_facts/alcohol.htm. Accessed: February 3, 2004.

3. Borkenstein, R.F.; Crowther, R.F.; Shumate, R.P.; Ziel, W.B.; and Zylman, R. 1964. *The role of the drinking driver in traffic accidents*. Bloomington, Indiana: Department of Police Administration, Indiana University.

4. Voas, R.B.; Wells, J.K.; Lestina, D.; Williams, A.F.; and Greene, M. 1998. Drinking and driving in the United States: the 1996 national roadside survey. *Accident Analysis and Prevention* 30(2): 267-275.

♣ **It's A Fact!!**
Drinking And Motor Vehicles In The U.S.

- General blood alcohol concentration (BAC) limits for drivers of non-commercial vehicles gradually declined over the past three decades, meaning that a driver can consume less alcohol now than in the 1960s before being considered legally impaired. (Editor's note: As of July 2004 all states mandated BAC limits at 0.08 g/dL.)

- Every state in the U.S. now has zero or very low BAC limits (less than 0.02 g/dL) for drivers under the legal drinking age.

- Every state in the U.S. now has BAC laws for individuals who operate motorboats for recreational purposes.

- By 2000, only a few states had mandated BAC limits for snowmobile drivers.

- As of January 1, 2000, less than half the states had mandatory minimum fines or jail time for the first offense violation of general BAC limits.

Source: Excerpted from Alcohol Epidemiology Program. *Alcohol Policies in the United States: Highlights from the 50 states*. University of Minnesota, 2000. Reprinted with permission

5. Fell, J.C. 1991. *Repeat DWI offenders: their involvement in fatal crashes.* Washington, DC: National Highway Traffic Safety Administration.

Determine Why There Are Fewer Young Alcohol-Impaired Drivers

Youth Drinking And Driving Dropped Substantially

- Youth drinking and driving has dropped substantially, as measured by drinking drivers in fatal crashes and by self-reported drinking and driving behavior. At the same time, young sober driver fatal crash involvement increased.

- Most of the decrease took place between 1982 and 1992.

- The decrease was nationwide: most states had very substantial decreases. However, states with the largest declines tended to lie on the East and West coasts. This outcome generally parallels the pattern for overall reductions in alcohol-related fatalities.

- Young drivers of all ages up to 21 reduced their drinking and driving by similar amounts. Drinking and driving decreases by high school and college age youth were similar.

- Drinking and driving decreased substantially more among youth than among older drivers.

Youth Drinking Also Dropped, But Not As Much

- Youth drinking also decreased during this period, but by less than half as much as youth drinking and driving. Youth drinking has increased gradually since about 1993, while drinking and driving has remained approximately constant.

- The decrease in youth drinking also occurred fairly uniformly across the country. By 1998, youth drinking habits were similar in all regions.

- Most youth still drink; a majority drink at least monthly; a substantial minority binge drink regularly.

Youth Have Separated Drinking And Driving More Than Older Drivers

- Youth have separated their drinking and their driving more than have drivers over 21.

- Drinking and driving has become less socially acceptable among youth than it was in 1982. Youth have accepted the designated driver concept and often use designated drivers.

Laws And Enforcement—MLDA 21 And Zero Tolerance

☞ **Remember!!**
Driving after drinking is not smart. Not only is it illegal with license suspension and fines likely, it could kill you.

- Minimum Legal Drinking Age increases caused some of the decrease. All states were required to raise their Minimum Legal Drinking Age to 21 since 1984. This reduced both youth drinking and youth drinking and driving.

- Zero tolerance laws caused a portion of the decrease. All states enacted zero tolerance laws since 1990.

Programs In States And Communities

- States and communities have conducted many, many activities directed at youth drinking and driving not involving laws and enforcement. But there is almost no direct evidence that these activities have affected youth drinking and driving.

Drinking And Driving Measures Directed At All Drivers

- In general, states that reduced overall drinking and driving the most (as measured by the reduction in alcohol-related traffic fatalities) also reduced youth drinking driver involvements in fatal crashes the most.

Other Factors

- Economic and social changes may well have influenced youth drinking and driving substantially, but no direct evidence was found.

Chapter 26

Alcohol Use Increases Risky Sexual Behavior And Assault

Alcohol And Sexual Assault

The Prevalence Of Sexual Assault And Alcohol-Involved Sexual Assault

At least one-half of all violent crimes involve alcohol consumption by the perpetrator, the victim, or both. Sexual assault fits this pattern. Researchers consistently have found that approximately one-half of all sexual assaults are committed by men who have been drinking alcohol.

Common Characteristics Of Non-Alcohol-Involved And Alcohol-Involved Sexual Assaults

Sexual assault occurs most commonly among women in late adolescence and early adulthood, although infants, as well as women in their 80s, have

About This Chapter: The text in this chapter is excerpted from "Alcohol and Sexual Assault," National Institute on Alcohol Abuse and Alcoholism (NIAAA), 2001. Additional text under its own heading is from "Substance Use and Sexual Health Among Teens and Young Adults in the U.S.," (#3213), The Henry J. Kaiser Family Foundation, February 2002. This information was reprinted with permission from the Henry J. Kaiser Family Foundation. The Kaiser Family Foundation, based in Menlo Park, California, is a nonprofit, independent national health care philanthropy and is not associated with Kaiser Permanente or Kaiser Industries.

been raped. Most sexual assaults that are reported to the police occur between strangers. These assaults, however, represent only a small proportion of all sexual assaults. At least 80 percent of sexual assaults occur among persons who know each other.

Several studies in various populations have attempted to identify typical characteristics of sexual assault. Among college students, a typical sexual assault occurs on a date, at either the man's or the woman's home, and is preceded by consensual kissing. In addition, the assault involves a single assailant who uses no weapon, but twists the woman's arm or holds her down. The woman, who believes that she has clearly emphasized her nonconsent, tries to resist through reasoning and by physically struggling.

✔ Quick Tip

If You Are Sexually Assaulted

- Get away from the attacker to a safe place as fast as you can.

- Do not wash, comb, or clean any part of your body, or change clothes if possible. Do not touch or change anything at the scene of the assault; it is a crime scene.

- Call a friend or family member you trust. You also can call a crisis center or a hotline to talk with a counselor. Do not feel ashamed or guilty. These feelings, as well as being afraid and shocked, are normal. It is important to get counseling from a trusted professional.

- Go to your nearest hospital emergency room as soon as possible. You need to be examined, treated for any injuries, and screened for possible sexually transmitted diseases or pregnancy. The doctor will collect evidence that the attacker may have left behind, like clothing fibers, hairs, saliva, or semen. A standard rape kit is usually used to help collect these things.

- You, or the hospital staff can call the police from the emergency room to file a report.

Source: "Sexual Assault," The National Women's Health Information Center, April 2001.

In a representative community sample, the typical sexual assault scenario involved a woman who was assaulted by a single assailant who was either an acquaintance or a friend and who used both verbal and physical pressure, which the woman tried to resist.

Although alcohol-involved and non-alcohol-involved sexual assaults share many characteristics, some differences exist. For example, sexual assaults involving alcohol consumption are more likely than other sexual assaults to occur between men and women who do not know each other well (e.g., strangers, acquaintances, or casual dates as opposed to steady dates or spouses). Furthermore, alcohol-involved sexual assaults tend to occur at parties or in bars, rather than in either person's home.

The Relationship Between Alcohol Consumption And Sexual Assault

Although alcohol consumption and sexual assault frequently co-occur, this does not prove that alcohol use causes sexual assault. Thus, in some cases, the desire to commit a sexual assault may actually cause alcohol consumption (e.g., when a man drinks alcohol before committing a sexual assault in order to justify his behavior). Moreover, certain factors may lead to both alcohol consumption and sexual assault. For example, some fraternities encourage both heavy drinking and sexual exploitation of women. In fact, many pathways can prompt a man to commit sexual assault, and not all perpetrators are motivated by the same factors.

Heavy alcohol consumption also has been linked to sexual assault perpetration. In studies involving two different subject groups (i.e., incarcerated rapists and college students), men who reported that they drank heavily were more likely than other men to report having committed sexual assault. General alcohol consumption could be related to sexual assault through multiple pathways.

- First, men who often drink heavily also likely do so in social situations that frequently lead to sexual assault (e.g., on a casual or spontaneous date at a party or bar).

- Second, heavy drinkers may routinely use intoxication as an excuse for engaging in socially unacceptable behavior, including sexual assault.

✎ Weird Words

Acquaintance Rape: Rape committed by someone that the victim knows, such as an acquaintance, friend, co-worker, date, or spouse. Most rapes are acquaintance rapes.

Alcohol Expectancies: A person's beliefs about the effects that alcohol consumption will have on himself or herself as well as on other people.

Alcohol Expectancy Set: The practice in laboratory research of telling participants that they have consumed alcohol, regardless of what the participants actually are given to drink.

Alcohol-Involved Rape: Rape in which the perpetrator, the victim, or both are under the influence of alcohol at the time of the incident.

Attempted Rape: An act that fits the definition of rape, in terms of the strategies used, but does not result in penetration.

Childhood Sexual Abuse: Sexual abuse that occurs to a child (the term child is generally defined as age 13 or younger).

Consensual Sex: Both the man and woman agree to sexual acts.

Date Rape: Rape committed by someone that the victim is dating. Among college students, approximately one-half of all rapes are committed by a date.

Rape: A sexual assault involving some type of penetration (i.e., vaginal, oral, or anal) due to force or threat of force; lack of consent; or inability of the victim to provide consent due to age, intoxication, or mental status. Rape laws vary by State; however, the aforementioned description conforms to the definition used at the Federal level and by most States.

Sexual Assault: The full range of forced sexual acts, including forced touching or kissing; verbally coerced intercourse; and vaginal, oral, and anal penetration. Researchers typically include in this category only acts of this nature that occur during adolescence or adulthood; in other words, childhood sexual abuse is defined separately. Both men and women can be sexually assaulted and can commit sexual assault. The vast majority of sexual assaults, however, involve male perpetrators and female victims.

Stranger Rape: Rape committed by someone that the victim does not know. Less than 20 percent of rapes are committed by strangers, although most people believe that stranger rape is the typical rape.

- Third, certain personality characteristics (e.g., impulsivity and anti-social behavior) may increase men's propensity both to drink heavily and to commit sexual assault.

Situational Factors

Some men may purposely get drunk when they want to act sexually aggressive, thinking that intoxication will provide them with an excuse for their socially inappropriate behavior.

At least 80 percent of all sexual assaults occur during social interaction, typically on a date. The fact that sexual assault often happens in situations in which consensual sex is a possible outcome means that a man's interpretation of the situation can influence his responses. Consequently, additional factors are relevant to these types of sexual assaults. For example, American men are socialized to be the initiators of sexual interactions. Consequently, if a man is interested in having sex with a woman, he is likely to feel that he should make the first move. Initial sexual moves are usually subtle in order to reduce the embarrassment associated with potential rejection. Both men and women use this indirect form of establishing sexual interest and usually manage to make their intentions clear and save face if the other person is not interested. However, because the cues are subtle and sometimes vague, miscommunication can occur, particularly if communication skills are impaired by alcohol use.

As male-female interaction progresses, a woman who has been misperceived as being interested in sex may realize that her companion is reading more into her friendliness than she intended. However, she may not feel comfortable giving a direct message of sexual disinterest, because traditional female gender roles emphasize the importance of being nice and "letting men down easy." The man, in turn, may not take an indirect approach to expressing sexual disinterest seriously.

Research on the power of stereotypes, expectancies, and self-fulfilling prophecies demonstrate that when people have an expectation about a situation or another person, they tend to observe and recall primarily the cues that fit their hypothesis and to minimize or ignore the cues that contradict their hypothesis. Consequently, when a man hopes that a woman is interested in having sex with him, he will pay most attention to the cues that fit his expectation and disregard cues that do not support his expectation. Studies with both perpetrators and victims have confirmed that the man's misperception of the woman's degree of sexual interest is a significant predictor of sexual assault.

The process just described can occur even in the absence of alcohol use. However, alcohol consumption can increase the likelihood of misperception, thereby increasing the chances of sexual assault.

Substance Use And Sexual Health Among Teens And Young Adults In The U.S.

Sexual activity and substance use are not uncommon among youth today. According to the Centers for Disease Control and Prevention, 79 percent of high-school students report having experimented with alcohol at least once, and a quarter report frequent drug use.[1, 2] Half of all 9th–11th graders have had sexual intercourse, and 65 percent will by the time they graduate.[3] While it has been difficult to show a direct causal relationship, there is some evidence that alcohol and drug use by young people is associated with risky sexual activity.

Risky Sexual Behaviors And Substance Use Sexual Initiation

Current data suggest that those who engage in any "risk behaviors" tend to take part in more than one, and that many health risk behaviors occur in combination with other risky activities.[4]

- Prior substance use increases the probability that an adolescent will initiate sexual activity, and sexually experienced adolescents are more likely to initiate substance use—including alcohol and cigarettes.[5]

- Teens who use alcohol or drugs are more likely to have sex than those who do not: Adolescents who drink are seven times more likely, while those who use illicit substances are five times more likely—even after adjusting for age, race, gender, and parental educational level.[6]

- Up to 18 percent of young people aged 13 to 19 report that they were drinking at the time of first intercourse.[7]

- Among teens aged 14 to 18 who reported having used alcohol before age fourteen, 20 percent said they had sex at age fourteen or earlier, compared with seven percent of other teens.[8]

- One-quarter of sexually active 9th–12th grade students report using alcohol or drugs during their last sexual encounter, with males more likely than females to have done so (31% vs. 19%).[3]

- For a significant proportion of adults aged 18 to 30, having sex and heavy drinking occur together in a single episode. Among men, 35 percent said they had sex when consuming five to eight drinks, compared with 17 percent of those who had one or two drinks. Among women aged 18 to 30, 39 percent had sex while consuming five to eight drinks, compared with 14 percent of women who had one or two drinks.[9]

Unprotected Sex

Thirty-eight percent (38%) of sexually active teenage women and 26 percent of women aged 20 to 24 rely on the condom as their contraceptive method, making it second only to the pill (used by 44% of teens and 52% of young adults).[10]

- Research on the association between condom use and substance use is mixed. According to one analysis of a large national sample of high school students, sexually active adolescents who use alcohol and/or drugs are somewhat less likely than other students to have used a condom the last time they had sex. However, the differences were not statistically significant after controlling for other factors.[1]

- The more substances that sexually active teens and young adults have ever tried, the less likely they are to have used a condom the last time they had sex: Among those aged 14 to 22, 78 percent of boys and 67 percent of girls who reported never using a substance said that they used a condom, compared with only 35 percent of boys and 23 percent of girls who reported ever having used five substances.[11]

- Teen girls and young women aged 14 to 22 who have recently used multiple substances are less likely to have used a condom the last time they had sex: 26 percent of young women with four recent alcohol or drug use behaviors reported using a condom at last intercourse, compared with 44 percent of those who reported no recent alcohol or drug use.[11]

Multiple Partners

- For teenagers as well as adults aged 18 to 30, having multiple sexual partners has been associated with both ever used and current use of alcohol or other substances.[11]

- Thirty-nine percent (39%) of sexually active students in 9th–12th grades who report ever using alcohol have had sex with four or more partners, compared with 29 percent of students who never drink.[6]

- Forty-four percent (44%) of sexually active students in 9th–12th grades who report ever using drugs have had sex with four or more partners, compared with 24 percent of students who use drugs.[6]

- Among sexually active young people aged 14 to 22 who used a substance the last time they had intercourse, 61 percent of men and 44 percent of women had had multiple partners

---

♣ It's A Fact!!

Is Alcohol A Date Rape Drug?

While GHB, rohypnol, and ketamine are considered date rape drugs, there are other drugs that affect judgment and behavior, and can put a person at risk for unwanted or risky sexual activity. Alcohol is one of those drugs. When a person is drinking alcohol:

- It's harder to think clearly and evaluate a potentially dangerous situation.

- It's harder to resist sexual or physical assault.

- Blackouts and memory loss may occur as a result of drinking too much alcohol.

But remember: Even if a victim of sexual assault drank alcohol, she is not at fault for being assaulted.

Source: Excerpted from "Date Rape Drugs," The National Women's Health Information Center, March 2004.

during the three months prior to being surveyed, compared with 32 percent of men and 14 percent of women who did not use drugs or alcohol the last time they had sex.[11]

- Sexually active women aged 14 to 22 who recently used alcohol or drugs four times are more likely than those who do not drink or take drugs to have had more than one sex partner in the last three months (48% compared with 8%).[11] The number of different substances women aged 14 to 22 use in their lifetimes significantly increases their likelihood of having multiple sex partners.[4] Among 18 to 22-year-old men and women, an earlier age at initiation of alcohol use is associated with the later likelihood of having multiple sex partners. For example, among those who reported having initiated alcohol use at age 10 or younger, 44 percent of men and 31 percent of women said they had had more than one sex partner in the three months prior to the survey, compared with 37 percent of men and 12 percent of women who said that they first drank alcohol at age 17 or older.[11]

Unintended Consequences

Sexually Transmitted Diseases (STDs)

- There are approximately fifteen million new cases of sexually transmitted diseases (STDs) annually in the United States. About two-thirds of new cases occur among adolescents and young adults under 25,[12, 13] a group that is also more likely to engage in both risky sexual activity and alcohol and drug use. Young women may be biologically more susceptible to chlamydia, gonorrhea, and HIV than older women.[13]

- In a single act of unprotected sex with an infected partner, a teenage woman has a one percent risk of acquiring HIV, a 30 percent risk of getting genital herpes, and a 50 percent chance of contracting gonorrhea.[14]

Unintended Pregnancy

- Substance use and unintended pregnancies often occur among the same populations.[1]

- Fifty-five percent of teenagers say that having sex while drinking or on drugs is often a reason for unplanned teen pregnancies.[1, 15]

- Almost one million adolescents—or 19 percent of those who have had sexual intercourse—become pregnant each year.[16] Among women aged 15 to 19, 78 percent of pregnancies are believed to be unintended, accounting for about one-quarter of all accidental pregnancies each year.[17]

- The pregnancy rate among women aged 20 to 24 is 183.3 per 1,000 women; it is thought that 59 percent of pregnancies in this age group are unintended.[17]

Sexual Assault And Violence

- Estimates of substance use during instances of sexual violence and rape in the general population range from 30 to 90 percent for alcohol use, and from 13 to 42 percent for the use of illicit substances.[1]

- Alcohol use by the victim, perpetrator, or both, has been implicated in 46 to 75 percent of date rapes among college students.[1] One survey of college students found that 78 percent of women had experienced sexual aggression (any type of sexual activity, including kissing, unwanted by the woman). Dates on which sexual aggression occurred were more likely to include heavy drinking or drug use than those dates that were not marked by sexually aggressive activity.[1]

- While 93% of teenage women report that their first intercourse was voluntary, one-quarter of these young women report that it was unwanted.[18]

- Seven out of ten women who first had intercourse before age 13 say it was unwanted or nonvoluntary [18]

- Compared with women in other age groups, women aged 19 to 29 report more violent incidents with intimate partners, for a rate of 21.3 violent victimizations per 1,000 women.[19]

References

1. The National Center of Addiction and Substance Abuse (CASA) at Columbia University. (1999). *Dangerous liaisons: Substance abuse and sex.*

New York, The National Center on Addiction and Substance Abuse (CASA) at Columbia University.

2. "Frequent drug use" was defined as occurring when a substance was used more than 20 times in one's lifetime.

3. The Centers for Disease Control and Prevention, Youth Risk Behavior Surveillance - United States, 1999, *Morbidity and Mortality Weekly Report*, June 2000, vol. 49.

4. Eisen M et al., *Teen Risk-Taking: Promising Prevention Programs and Approaches*, Washington DC: Urban Institute, September 2000. (YRBS data)

5. Mott FL and Haurin RJ, Linkages between sexual activity and alcohol and drug use among American adolescents, *Family Planning Perspectives*, 1988, vol. 20.

6. Analysis of 1997 YRBS data, reported in CASA, *Dangerous Liaisons: Substance Abuse and Sex*.

7. Analysis of a random telephone survey in Buffalo NY, reported in CASA, *Dangerous Liaisons: Substance Abuse and Sex*.

8. Analysis of National Longitudinal Survey of Youth Labor Market Experience, reported in CASA, *Dangerous Liaisons: Substance Abuse and Sex*.

9. Graves KL, Risky sexual behavior and alcohol use among young adults: Results from a national survey, *American Journal of Health Promotion*, 1995, vol. 10.

10. The Alan Guttmacher Institute, *Fact Sheet on Teens, Sex and Pregnancy*, Special tabulations by AGI of data from the 1995 National Survey of Family Growth, New York: AGI, 2000.

11. Santelli JS et al., Timing of alcohol and other drug use and sexual risk behaviors among unmarried adolescents and young adults, *Family Planning Perspectives*, 2001, vol. 33.

12. American Social Health Association/Kaiser Family Foundation, *Sexually Transmitted Diseases in America: How Many Cases and At What Cost?* Menlo Park, CA: The Henry J. Kaiser Family Foundation, 1998.

13 . The Centers for Disease Control and Prevention (CDC), *Tracking the Hidden Epidemics: Trends In STDs in the United States 2000*, Atlanta, GA: CDC, 2001.

14. The Alan Guttmacher Institute, *Sex and America's Teenagers*, New York: AGI, 1994.

15. Kaiser Family Foundation, *1996 KFF Survey on Teens and Sex: What they say teens today need to know and who they listen to: Chart Pack*, Menlo Park, CA: The Henry J. Kaiser Family Foundation, 1996.

16. The Alan Guttmacher Institute, *Teenage pregnancy: overall trends and state-by-state information, New York: AGI, 1999, Table 1*; Henshaw SK, U.S. Teenage pregnancy statistics with comparative statistics for women aged 20-24, New York: AGI, 1999.

17. Henshaw SK, Unintended pregnancy in the United States, *Family Planning Perspectives*, 1998, vol. 30.

18. Moore KA et al., *A Statistical Portrait of Adolescent Sex, Contraception, and Childbearing*, Washington, DC: National Campaign to Prevent Teen Pregnancy, 1998.

19. Bachman R and Saltzman LE, *Special Report from National Crime Victimization Survey: Violence Against Women Estimates from the Redesigned Survey*, Washington DC: Bureau of Justice Statistics, August 1995.

☞ **Remember!!**

Alcohol use greatly increases your chances of being involved in risky sexual encounters or sexual assault.

Chapter 27

Suicide, Depression, And Youth Drinking

Alcohol used in adolescence is associated with psychological distress and depression.

- Among 12- to 17-year-olds who were current drinkers, 31 percent exhibited extreme levels of psychological distress and 39 percent exhibited serious behavioral problems.[1]

- Twelve- to sixteen-year-old girls who were current drinkers were four times more likely than their nondrinking peers to suffer depression.[2]

- In a recent Center for Substance Abuse Treatment (CSAT) study, 48 percent of women in treatment for substance abuse had been sexually abused.[3]

The severity of behavioral problems in adolescents is significantly associated with increased likelihood of adolescent alcohol use.

- Past-month alcohol use was reported by approximately 14 percent of adolescents with low levels of behavioral problems, by 23 percent of those with intermediate problem scores, and by 38 percent of those with significant behavioral problems.[4]

About This Chapter: This information is from "Suicide, Depression, and Youth Drinking," *Prevention Alert*, Volume 5, Number 17, National Clearinghouse for Alcohol and Drug Information (NCADI), December 13, 2002.

- Adolescents with serious behavioral problems were nearly three times more likely to use alcohol than those with low levels of behavioral problems.[5]

There is a link between suicide and alcohol use in adolescents.

- Twenty-eight percent of suicides by children ages 9 to 15 could be attributed to alcohol.[6]

- Using a national school sample, a study reported that suicide attempts among heavy-drinking adolescents were three to four times greater than among abstainers.[7]

Adolescents struggling with serious emotional disturbances (SED) face even greater challenges when they use alcohol.

- Adolescents with high levels of SED were nearly twice as likely as adolescents with low levels of SED to have used alcohol in the past month.[8]

- Adolescents with high levels of SED were five times as likely as those with low levels of SED to report alcohol dependence.[9]

♣ It's A Fact!!
Teen Binge Drinking May Predict Suicide Attempt

The May 2004 journal *Alcoholism: Clinical and Experimental Research* reported a study of high school sophomores and juniors in Buffalo, New York which found that binge drinking by teens may predict suicide attempts. Michael Windle, Ph.D., lead author of the study, found that binge drinking episodes frequently precede serious suicide attempts, especially if the teen is depressed or experiencing a stressful event.

—JBS

Co-occurring disorders prompt new federal action.

- Seven to ten million Americans have at least one mental disorder in addition to an alcohol or drug disorder.

- A 5-year blueprint for action to improve recovery chances by increasing quality prevention, diagnosis, and treatment for people with co-occurring disorders was just sent to Congress by Department of Health and Human Services Secretary Tommy Thompson.[10]

References

1. Substance Abuse and Mental Health Services Administration (SAMHSA), Office of Applied Studies. *The Relationship Between Mental Health and Substance Abuse Among Adolescents.* (SMA) 99-3286. Rockville, MD: SAMHSA, 1999.

2. Hanna EZ, Hsiao-ye Y, Dufour MC, et al. The relationship of drinking and other substance use alone and in combination to health and behavior problems among youth ages 12-16: *Findings from the Third National Health and Nutrition Survey (NHANES III).* Paper presented at the 23rd Annual Scientific Meeting of the Research Society on Alcoholism, June 24-29, 2000, Denver, CO.

3. Burgdorf K, Chen X, Herrell J. *The prevalence and prognostic significance of sexual abuse in substance abuse treatment of women.* Center for Substance Abuse Treatment (CSAT), 2001.

4. SAMHSA. *The Relationship Between Mental Health and Substance Abuse Among Adolescents.*

5. *Ibid.*

6. Unpublished data extrapolated by National Institute on Alcohol Abuse and Alcoholism from *State Trends in Alcohol Mortality, 1979-1992; US Alcohol Epidemiologic Data Reference Manual, Volume 5.* Rockville, MD: National Institute on Alcohol Abuse and Alcoholism, 1996.

7. Windle M, Miller-Tutzauer C, Domenico D. Alcohol use, suicidal behavior, and risky activities among adolescents. *J Res Adolesc* 2(4):317-330, 1992.

8. SAMHSA. *The Relationship Between Mental Health and Substance Abuse Among Adolescents.*

9. *Ibid.*

10. *Report to Congress on the Prevention and Treatment of Co-Occurring Substance Abuse Disorders and Mental Disorders*, SAMHSA, 2002.

🖐 Remember!!

Alcohol does not help to solve problems and may make things worse when you are under stress or depressed. Tell someone you trust how you feel.

Chapter 28

Violence Linked To Underage Drinking

Alcohol, Violence, And Aggression

Scientists and nonscientists alike have long recognized a two-way association between alcohol consumption and violent or aggressive behavior.[1] Not only may alcohol consumption promote aggressiveness, but being a victim of aggression may lead to excessive alcohol consumption.

Extent Of The Alcohol-Violence Association

Based on published studies, Roizen[2] summarized the percentages of violent offenders who were drinking at the time of the offense as follows:

- up to 86 percent of homicide offenders

- 37 percent of assault offenders

- 60 percent of sexual offenders

- up to 57 percent of men and 27 percent of women involved in marital violence

- 13 percent of child abusers

These figures are the upper limits of a wide range of estimates.

About This Chapter: Text in this chapter is excerpted from "Alcohol, Violence, and Aggression," *Alcohol Alert*, No. 38-1997, National Institute on Alcohol Abuse and Alcoholism (NIAAA), updated October 2000.

♣ It's A Fact!!
Underage Drinking And Violence

Underage drinking is linked to violent and aggressive behavior.

- According to a national survey, youths ages 12 to 17 who reported violent behaviors in the past year reported higher rates of past year illicit drug or alcohol use compared with youths who did not report violent behaviors.[1]

- Almost 12 percent of adolescent drinkers (about 1.2 million 7th–12th graders) engage in alcohol-related physical fighting.[2]

- A national study indicates that those who began drinking before age 14 were 11 times more likely to have ever been in a fight while drinking or after drinking than adults who began drinking after the age of 21.[3]

- Youths ages 12 to 17 who had engaged in past month binge alcohol use were almost four times as likely to have carried a handgun in the past year compared with youths who had not engaged in binge drinking.[4]

Studies suggest that boys who drink are prone to fighting and sexual aggression.

- In one study, males were almost twice as likely as females to engage in alcohol-related physical fighting (15.6 percent of males and 8.0 percent of females).[5]

- Among male high school students, 39 percent say it is acceptable for a boy to force sex with a girl who is drunk or high.[6]

Studies suggest that girls who drink are more likely to be victims of self-inflicted violence.

- Among eighth grade girls who drink heavily, 37 percent report attempting suicide, whereas 11 percent of girls who do not drink report attempting suicide.[7]

- Researchers estimate that alcohol use is implicated in one- to two-thirds of sexual assault and date rape cases among teens and college students.[8]

References

1. Office of Applied Studies. Substance Abuse and Mental Health Services Administration. *NHSDA Report. Youth Violence and Substance Use, 2001 Update*. Rockville, MD: Substance Abuse and Mental Health Services Administration, 2002.

2. Swahn MH. *Epidemiology of alcohol-related fighting among adolescents*. Paper presented at the 129th Annual Meeting of the American Public Health Association, October 23, 2001, Atlanta, GA.

3. Hingson R, Heeren T, Zakocs R. Age of drinking onset and involvement in physical fights after drinking. *Pediatrics* 108(4):872-877, 2001.

4. Office of Applied Studies. Substance Abuse and Mental Health Services Administration. *NHSDA Report: Youths Who Carry Handguns*. Rockville, MD: Substance Abuse and Mental Health Services Administration, 2001.

5. Swahn. *Epidemiology of alcohol-related fighting among adolescents*.

6. Office of the Inspector General, U.S. Department of Health and Human Services. *Youth and Alcohol: Dangerous and Deadly Consequences*. Washington, DC: Health and Human Services, 1992.

7. Windle MA, Miller-Tutzauer C, Domenico D. Alcohol use, suicidal behavior, and risky activities among adolescents. *J Res Adolesc* 2(4):317-330, 1992.

8. Office of the Inspector General. Youth and Alcohol.

Source: "Making the Link: Underage Drinking and Violence," Substance Abuse and Mental Health Services Administration (SAMHSA) and Leadership to Keep Children Alcohol Free, revised March 2003.

Alcohol-Violence Relationships

Alcohol Misuse Preceding Violence

Direct Effects of Alcohol. Alcohol may encourage aggression or violence by disrupting normal brain function. One explanation is that alcohol weakens brain mechanisms that normally restrain impulsive behaviors, including inappropriate aggression.[4] By impairing information processing, alcohol can also lead a person to misjudge social cues, thereby overreacting to a perceived threat.[5] At the same time, by focusing on the sudden wish or urge (e.g. wanting to hit someone), a person may not think clearly about the future risks or consequences of acting on that impulsive idea.[6]

These results are consistent with the real-world observation that intoxication alone does not cause violence.[3]

Table 28.1. Percentage Of Youths Aged 12–17 Reporting Past Month Alcohol Use, By Whether Or Not They Participated In Violent Behaviors During The Past Year: 1999*

	No Alcohol Use	Used Alcohol One or More Times
Serious fighting at school or work	13.0	26.0
Group against group fighting	13.7	30.0
Attacking others with the intent to seriously hurt them	14.9	34.1

*Data presented differ from previously published data from the 1999 NHSDA because of corrections made to imputation procedures.

Source: National Household Survey on Drug Abuse (NHSDA) Report. Youth Violence Linked to Substance Use. 2001.

Social and Cultural Expectancies. Alcohol consumption may promote aggression because people expect it to.[4] For example, research using real and fake alcoholic beverages shows that people who believe they have consumed alcohol begin to act more aggressively, regardless of which beverage they actually consumed.[7] Alcohol-related expectancies that promote male aggressiveness, combined with the widespread perception of intoxicated women as sexually receptive and less able to defend themselves, could account for the association between drinking and date rape.[8]

In addition, a person who intends to engage in a violent act may drink to bolster his or her courage or in hopes of avoiding punishment.[9, 10]

Violence Preceding Alcohol Misuse

Childhood Victimization. Children who witness family violence may learn to imitate the roles of aggressors or victims, setting the stage for alcohol abuse and violence to persist over generations.[11]

Violent Lifestyles. Violence may happen before alcohol misuse in offenders as well as victims. For example, violent people may be more likely than nonviolent people to go to parties or be in situations that encourage heavy drinking.[12] In summary, violence may contribute to alcohol consumption, which in turn may continue violence.

Common Causes For Alcohol Misuse And Violence

In many cases, abuse of alcohol and a tendency to violence may stem from a common cause.[13] This cause may be a temperamental trait, such as a risk-seeking personality, or a social environment (e.g., delinquent peers or lack of parental supervision) that encourages or contributes to unacceptable behavior.[12]

Another example of a common cause relates to the frequent co-occurrence of antisocial personality disorder (ASPD) and early-onset (type II) alcoholism.[14] ASPD is a psychiatric disorder characterized by a disregard for the rights of others, often displayed as a violent or criminal lifestyle. Type II alcoholism is characterized by high heritability from father to son; early onset of alcoholism (often during adolescence); and antisocial, sometimes violent, behavioral traits.[15] Type II alcoholics and persons with ASPD overlap in their tendency to violence and excessive alcohol consumption and may share a genetic basis.[14]

Biological Study Of Violence

Although individual behavior is shaped in part by the environment, it is also influenced by biological factors (e.g., hormones) and ultimately planned and directed by the brain. Individual differences in brain chemistry may explain the observation that excessive alcohol consumption consistently promotes aggression in some persons, but not in others.[16]

Serotonin

Serotonin, a chemical messenger in the brain, is thought to function as a behavioral inhibitor. Thus, decreased serotonin activity is associated with increased impulsivity and aggressiveness[17] as well as with early-onset alcoholism among men.[18]

There is considerable overlap among nerve cell pathways in the brain that regulate aspects of aggression,[19] sexual behavior, and alcohol consumption.[20] This suggests a biological basis for the frequent co-occurrence of alcohol intoxication and sexual violence.

Testosterone

The steroid hormone testosterone is responsible for the development of male

✎ **Weird Words**

Aggression: Behavior that is threatening, hostile, or damaging in a physical or nonphysical way.

Antisocial Personality Disorder (ASPD): A psychiatric disorder characterized by a disregard for the rights of others, often manifested as a violent or criminal lifestyle.

Assault: A violent verbal or physical attack.

Heritability: Inherited, a physical trait passed genetically from parent to child.

Homicide: Murder.

Offender: A person who has broken a law.

Violence: Behavior that intentionally inflicts, or attempts to inflict, physical harm.

primary and secondary sexual characteristics. High testosterone concentrations in criminals have been associated with violence, suspiciousness, and hostility.[21, 22]

In humans, violence occurs largely among adolescent and young adult males, who tend to have high levels of testosterone compared with the general population. Young men who exhibit antisocial behaviors often "burn out" with age, becoming less aggressive when they reach their forties.[23] By that age, testosterone concentrations are decreasing, while serotonin concentrations are increasing, both are factors that tend to restrain violent behavior.[24]

References

1. Reiss, A.J., Jr., & Roth, J.A., eds. *Understanding and Preventing Violence*. Vol. 3. Washington, DC: National Academy Press, 1994.

2. Roizen, J. Epidemiological issues in alcohol-related violence. In: Galanter, M., ed. *Recent Developments in Alcoholism*. Vol. 13. New York: Plenum Press, 1997. pp. 7-40.

3. Pernanen, K. *Alcohol in Human Violence*. New York: Guilford Press, 1991.

4. Gustafson, R. Alcohol and aggression. *J Offender Rehabil* 21(3/4):41-80, 1994.

5. Miczek, K.A., et al. Alcohol, GABAA-benzodiazepine receptor complex, and aggression. In: Galanter, M., ed. *Recent Developments in Alcoholism*. Vol. 13. New York: Plenum Press, 1997. pp. 139-171.

6. Cook, P.J., & Moore, M.J. Economic perspectives on reducing alcohol-related violence. In: Martin, S.E., ed. *Alcohol and Interpersonal Violence*. NIAAA Research Monograph No. 24. NIH Pub. No. 93-3496. Rockville, MD: NIAAA, 1993. pp. 193-212.

7. Bushman, B.J. Effects of alcohol on human aggression: Validity of proposed explanations. In: Galanter, M., ed. *Recent Developments in Alcoholism*. Vol. 13. New York: Plenum Press, 1997. pp. 227-243.

8. Lang, A.R. Alcohol-related violence: Psychological perspectives. In: Martin, S.E., ed. *Alcohol and Interpersonal Violence.* NIAAA Research Monograph No. 24. NIH Pub. No. 93-3496. Rockville, MD: NIAAA, 1993. pp. 121-148.

9. Collins, J.J. Alcohol and interpersonal violence: Less than meets the eye. In: Wolfgang, M.E., eds. *Pathways to Criminal Violence.* Newbury Park, CA: Sage Publications, 1989. pp. 49 67.

10. Fagan, J. Intoxication and aggression. In: Tonry, M., & Wilson, J.Q., eds. *Crime and Justice.* Vol. 13. Chicago: Univ. of Chicago Press, 1990. pp. 241-320.

11. Brookoff, D., et al. Characteristics of participants in domestic violence: Assessment at the scene of domestic assault. *JAMA* 277(17):1369-1373, 1997.

12. White, H.R. Longitudinal perspective on alcohol use and aggression during adolescence. In: Galanter, M., ed. *Recent Developments in Alcoholism.* Vol. 13. New York: Plenum Press, 1997. pp. 81-103.

13. Jessor, R., & Jessor, S.L. *Problem Behavior and Psychosocial Development.* New York: Academic Press, 1977.

14. Virkkunen, M., et al. *Serotonin in alcoholic violent offenders.* Ciba Foundation Symposium 194:168-182, 1995.

15. Cloninger, C.R., et al. Inheritance of alcohol abuse: Cross-fostering analysis of adopted men. *Arch Gen Psychiatry* 38:861-868, 1981.

16. Higley, J.D., et al. A nonhuman primate model of type II excessive alcohol consumption? Part 1. Low cerebrospinal fluid 5-hydroxyindoleacetic acid concentrations and diminished social competence correlate with excessive alcohol consumption. *Alcohol Clin Exp Res* 20(4):629-642, 1996.

17. Virkkunen, M., & Linnoila, M. Serotonin and glucose metabolism in impulsively violent alcoholic offenders. In: Stoff, D.M., & Cairns, R.B., eds. *Aggression and Violence.* Mahwah, NJ: Lawrence Erlbaum, 1996. pp. 87-100.

18. Higley, J.D., & Linnoila, M. A nonhuman primate model of excessive alcohol intake: Personality and neurobiological parallels of type I- and type II-like alcoholism. In: Galanter, M., ed. *Recent Developments in Alcoholism.* Vol. 13. New York: Plenum Press, 1997. pp. 192-219.

19. Alexander, G., et al. Parallel organization of functionally segregated circuits linking basal ganglia and cortex. *Annu Rev Neurosci* 9:357-381, 1986.

20. Modell, J.G., et al. Basal ganglia/limbic striatal and thalamocortical involvement in craving and loss of control in alcoholism. *J Neuropsychiatry Clin Neurosci* 2(2):123-144, 1990.

21. Dabbs, J.M., Jr., et al. Salivary testosterone and cortisol among late adolescent male offenders. *J Abnorm Child Psychol* 19(4):469-478, 1991.

22. Virkkunen, M., et al. CSF biochemistries, glucose metabolism, and diurnal activity rhythms in alcoholic, violent offenders, fire setters, and healthy volunteers. *Arch Gen Psychiatry* 51:20-27, 1994.

23. Robins, L.N. *Deviant Children Grown Up.* Baltimore: Williams & Wilkins, 1996.

24. Brown, G.L., & Linnoila, M.I. CSF serotonin metabolite (5-HIAA) studies in depression, impulsivity, and violence. *J Clin Psychiatry* 51(4)(suppl):31-43, 1990.

☞ **Remember!!**
Drinking alcohol can increase feelings of anger and decrease the ability to make good choices. Alcohol adds fuel to the fire of violence.

Chapter 29

Heavy And Binge Drinking Among Under-age Persons

The Brain Risks Of Binge Drinking

Nervous system degeneration has been commonly thought to occur during alcohol withdrawal. A new study has confirmed that nervous system damage can occur during a binge pattern of drinking. Damage to the olfactory bulb, responsible for smell, occurred after just two days of binge drinking. Damage to other regions of the brain occurred after just four days of binge drinking.

Scientists agree that alcohol is toxic and that chronic alcohol abuse can damage all organs—including the brain—to various degrees. There is less agreement, however, on whether or how much nervous system degeneration is triggered by alcohol's toxicity during alcohol consumption or by the hyperexcitability caused by withdrawal from alcohol. A study in the April 2002 issue of *Alcoholism: Clinical & Experimental Research* uses rodents to examine

About This Chapter: Text in this chapter is from "The Brain Risks of Binge Drinking," Addiction Technology Transfer Center, 2002. Text under its own heading is from "Binge Drinking Among Underage Persons," Substance Abuse and Mental Health Services Administration (SAMHSA) Office of Applied Studies, April 11, 2002. Additional text under the heading "The Binge Drinking Epidemic At College Campuses," is excerpted from "The Binge Drinking Epidemic," *Prevention Alert*, Vol. 5, No. 6, May 10, 2002, SAMHSA's National Clearinghouse for Alcohol and Drug Information.

what effects just a few days of the equivalent of binge drinking can have on neuronal function.

"Most studies of alcohol-induced brain damage have looked at humans who have been alcoholic for decades or rats treated with alcohol for six to 18 months," said Fulton T. Crews, Director of the Center for Alcohol Studies at the University of North Carolina and corresponding author for the study. "Our study shows significant damage in several regions of the brain after only four days, that it occurs during intoxication, and that the process is similar to a dark-cell degeneration that is primarily necrotic." Necrosis refers to the pathologic death of cells or a portion of tissue or organ due to irreversible damage.

"This study shows significant damage in the olfactory bulb after just 2 days of heavy drinking," said Crews, "which is a short period of time relative to the decades of drinking that alcoholics do, and may be an important early process in the progression from experimentation with alcohol to addiction. In addition, the major current hypothesis regarding alcohol-induced brain damage suggests that damage occurs during withdrawal. Our findings indicate that alcohol-induced brain damage occurs during intoxication."

Michael A. Collins, professor of biochemistry at Loyola University Chicago, added that even though chronic alcohol abuse damages all organs to greater or lesser degrees, most attention has been paid to liver damage, largely because it is easier for doctors to

♣ It's A Fact!!

- In 2000, almost one in five underage persons aged 12 to 20 was a binge drinker, drinking five or more drinks on the same occasion on at least one day in the past 30 days.

- The rate of binge drinking among underage persons was almost as high as among adults aged 21 or older.

- Underage persons who reported binge drinking were 7 times more likely to report using illicit drugs during the past month than underage persons who did not binge drink.

detect and measure, and can eventually lead to liver failure death. However, he added, "a study of relatively young alcoholics published some time ago in the British journal *Lancet* showed that indicators of relatively permanent cognitive damage, measured by neuropsychological tests, actually showed up earlier than clinical signs of liver damage. Sadly, when the brain loses its excitable cells, for all practical purposes they are gone for good. In the day-to-day life of an alcoholic, this means a decreased ability to learn, to recall, to make decisions, and perhaps to sense and appreciate life in its fullest."

According to some estimates, said Collins, alcohol abuse in the United States is perhaps the third or fourth most common cause of brain damage, and may be even higher in other countries. "Given this," he said, "it is surprising that the mechanisms of brain neuronal degeneration due to a widely abused neuro-toxicant are so understudied and therefore still somewhat obscure. Certainly this has implications for a college student contemplating a weekend of binge drinking. Seriously, though, it is possible that neuronal degeneration after a couple of days of heavy intoxication in the rat might translate to the human drinker who is not even a chronic alcohol abuser. There is no firm proof of this at present, and we would need brain imaging to determine whether acute short-term binge drinking in people could be permanently deleterious to olfactory or other neurons."

Reference

Obernier, J.A., Bouldin, T.W., & Crews, F.T. (2002, April). Binge ethanol exposure in adult rats causes necrotic cell death. *Alcoholism: Clinical & Experimental Research*, 26(4).

Binge Drinking Among Underage Persons

The 2000 National Household Survey on Drug Abuse (NHSDA) questioned more than 70,000 persons aged 12 or older nationwide, including almost 35,000 persons aged 12 to 20, regarding their frequency and quantity of drinking or use of any illicit drug during the month before the survey. Respondents aged 18 to 22 were also asked about their college enrollment status.

✎ Weird Words

Binge Drinking: Drinking five or more drinks on the same occasion on at least 1 day in the past 30 days. Occasion is meant at the same time or within a couple of hours of each other.

Cognitive: Learning functions of the brain.

Heavy Alcohol Use: Drinking five or more drinks on the same occasion on each of 5 or more days in the past 30 days; all heavy alcohol users are also binge alcohol users.

Illicit Drug: Any use of illegal drugs, such as marijuana/hashish, cocaine (including crack), inhalants, hallucinogens (including PCP and LSD), or heroin, or any prescription-type drug not prescribed by a doctor.

Non-Medical Drug Use: Using a drug that was not prescribed by a doctor or taking a drug only for the experience or feeling it causes.

Binge Drinking Among Underage Persons Compared With Those Aged 21 Or Older

According to the 2000 NHSDA, an estimated 46 million persons aged 12 or older were binge drinkers. Of these, almost 7 million were younger than 21, the legal drinking age. The proportion of underage persons aged 12 to 20 who were binge drinkers (19 percent) was similar to that among adults aged 21 or older (21 percent) for whom alcohol use is legal. The percentage of underage persons who binged on alcohol increased with age, from 1 percent of 12 year olds to 39 percent of 20 year olds (Table 29.1). Youths aged 12 to 16 had lower rates of binge drinking than the total population aged 12 or older, but persons aged 17 to 20 were more likely to report binge drinking during the past 30 days than the total population aged 12 or older.

Table 29.1. Percentages Of Persons Aged 12–20 Reporting Past Month Binge Alcohol Use,* By Age: 2000

Age	Percent Reporting Past Month Binge Alcohol Use
12	1.0
13	3.0
14	6.0
15	12.6
16	17.9
17	22.9
18	30.9
19	34.8
20	38.6

*Binge alcohol use is defined as drinking five or more drinks on the same occasion on at least 1 day in the past 30 days. By "occasion" is meant at the same time or within a couple of hours of each other.

Source: SAMHSA 2000 NHSDA.

Table 29.2. Percentages Reporting Past Month Binge Alcohol Use,* By Age Group And Gender: 2000

Age Group And Gender	Percentage Reporting Past Month Binge Alcohol Use
Male 12–20	21.3
Female 12–20	15.9
Male 21 or Older	29.8
Female 21 or Older	13.0

*Binge alcohol use is defined as drinking five or more drinks on the same occasion on at least 1 day in the past 30 days. By "occasion" is meant at the same time or within a couple of hours of each other.

Source: SAMHSA 2000 NHSDA.

Table 29.3. Alcohol Use, Binge Alcohol Use, And Heavy Alcohol Use In The Past Month Among Persons Aged 12 Or Older, By Demographic Characteristics: Percentages, 2002.

Demographic Characteristic	Any Alcohol Use	Binge Alcohol Use	Heavy Alcohol Use
Total	51.0	22.9	6.7
Age			
12–17	17.6	10.7	2.5
18–25	60.5	40.9	14.9
26 or Older	53.9	21.4	5.9
Gender			
Male	57.4	31.2	10.8
Female	44.9	15.1	3.0
Hispanic Origin and Race			
Not Hispanic or Latino	52.1	22.6	6.9
White	55.0	23.4	7.5
Black or African American	39.9	21.0	4.4
American Indiana or Alaska Native	44.7	27.9	8.7
Native Hawaiian or Other Pacific Islander	*	25.2	8.3
Asian	37.1	12.4	2.6
Two or More Races	49.9	19.8	7.5
Hispanic or Latino	42.8	24.8	5.9

*Low precision; no estimate reported.

Note: *Binge alcohol use* is defined as drinking five or more drinks on the same occasion (i.e., at the same time or within a couple of hours of each other) on at least 1 day in the past 30 days. *Heavy alcohol use* is defined as drinking five or more drinks on the same occasion on each of 5 or more days in the past 30 days; all heavy alcohol users are also binge alcohol users.

Source: SAMHSA, Office of Applied Studies, National Survey on Drug Use and Health, 2003.

The difference between males and females was less among those aged 20 or younger (21 percent males vs. 16 percent females) than among those aged 21 or older (30 percent males vs. 13 percent females) (Table 29.2). Underage females were more likely to report binge drinking (16 percent) than were females aged 21 or older (13 percent). Among underage persons, fewer Asians and blacks reported binge drinking than Hispanics, American Indians/Alaska Natives, or whites.

♣ It's A Fact!!
Teen Binge Drinking May Predict Suicide Attempt

A study of high school sophomores and juniors in Buffalo, New York found that binge drinking may predict suicide attempts especially if the teen also experiences depression or a stressful event. Michael Windle, Ph.D., indicated that binge drinking episodes frequently precede serious suicide attempts making binge drinking a good predictor of suicide. The study findings were reported in the May 2004 journal *Alcoholism: Clinical and Experimental Research.*

—JBS

Binge Drinking And Illicit Drug Use Among Minors

In 2000, underage persons who reported binge drinking (43 percent) were more likely to report past month use of any illicit drug than were their peers who did not binge drink (6 percent). Underage persons who reported binge drinking were almost 9 times more likely to have used marijuana/hashish during the past month and were more than 6 times more likely to have used any illicit drug other than marijuana during the past month compared with underage persons who did not binge drink. Underage binge drinkers were 11 times more likely to have used hallucinogens during the past month and 6 times more likely to have used psychotherapeutic drugs non-medically during the past month than underage persons who did not binge drink.

Teens Who Work Are More Likely To Drink Heavily

♣ **It's A Fact!!**

Teens who work more than ten hours per week are more likely to engage in heavy or binge drinking, according to a recent study by the Prevention Research Center of the Pacific Institute for Research and Evaluation (PIRE). The study results, published in the January 2004 issue of the *Journal of Adolescent Health*, are particularly troubling in light of the recent report to Congress made by the Institute of Medicine and the National Research Council which indicated that underage drinking costs the U.S. more than $53 billion per year in addition to thousands of personal tragedies and destructive behavior such as violence, suicide, unwanted pregnancies, sexual assault, and academic failure. Underage drinking also increases the likelihood of alcohol abuse and dependency, and other negative consequences.

"One of the most consistent and troubling discoveries is that the more adolescents work, the more they drink," says M.J. Paschall, Ph.D., the author of the study and a research scientist at the Prevention Research Center of PIRE. He goes on to explain that while the study indicates that working more than 10 hours per week significantly increases the risk of heavy drinking (defined as five or more drinks on one occasion), working fewer than ten hours per week does not appear to lead to more drinking.

Dr. Paschall explained that employment increases teens' access to alcohol through greater personal income, which allows them to purchase alcohol directly or obtain it indirectly through others. "Working also means that the teens spend more time with older peers and adults who drink. This increases their belief that alcohol use and heavy drinking are common and socially acceptable," says Dr. Paschall. In 2002 almost 80% of high school seniors had consumed alcohol at least once in their lifetime, 50% had consumed alcohol within the past 30 days, and 30% had consumed enough within the past 30 days to be intoxicated.

The study, which was funded by the National Institute on Drug Abuse, also found that teens who work more than ten hours per week have a lower level of school commitment, a lower grade point average, and are less motivated to attend college than those who work fewer hours per week. There is evidence that low school commitment and poor academic performance are at least partly the result of heavy alcohol use.

Source: Reprinted with permission from the Prevention Research Center of the Pacific Institute for Research and Evaluation (PIRE). January 2004. For additional information, visit http://www.pire.org.

The Binge Drinking Epidemic At College Campuses

A recent study of the Harvard School of Public Health of 119 college campuses shows that two out of five college students drink five drinks in a row at least once every two weeks—specifically, 44 percent of collegians binge drink. This figure did not change from 1993 to 1999. However, frequent bingers (bingeing three or more times in the past two weeks) are on the rise. They comprised 20 percent of college students in 1993 and by 1999, the figure was 23 percent. More troubling, drinking at women's colleges grew substantially, from 24 percent in 1993 to 32 percent in 1999 (frequent drinking doubled—from 5 percent to 12 percent).

More For Alcohol Than Books

College is clearly a catalyst for alcohol use. In fact, young adults ages 18 to 22 who don't go to college drink less than those who do. Age 21—the age most collegians graduate from college—is the peak age for binge drinking across the typical American life span. Past month drinking actually increases into the middle years, but is more moderate in intake.

To give some sense of the magnitude of college drinking, 12 million undergraduates drink 4 billion cans of beer or 55 six packs each a year. About 25 percent of college students find drinking hurts their grades and school work. Drinking is twice as heavy at frat houses than outside them. Fraternity members average 14 drinks a week versus 6 drinks by non-fraternity members.

What Happens To The Brain And Body?

Studies show that more than 35 percent of adults with an alcohol problem developed symptoms—such as binge drinking—by age 19. Long-term use risks liver damage, pancreatitis, certain cancers, and literal shrinkage of the brain. Alcohol use is the second-leading cause of dementia; one simply ages quicker on alcohol. In 1998, there were 15,935 alcohol-related deaths in vehicular crashes. Though most college drinkers would deny it, young people do die solely from drinking. In 1995, 318 people ages 15 to 24 died from alcohol poisoning alone, many of them after a night binge at college. At the University of Virginia, a tradition that has seniors drinking a fifth of hard liquor at the final game of the football season (the so-called Fourth-year Fifth) has killed 18 students since 1990.

Alcohol Affects Women More

Many women appear to have reduced levels of the gastric enzyme that metabolizes alcohol—in short, it leaves their system more slowly. At the same time, less alcohol does more short-term, as well as long-term, damage to women's health than men's. Annually more than 70,000 college students are victims of alcohol-related sexual assault or date rape. Two-thirds of binge drinkers report reckless behavior such as unprotected sex, unplanned sex, or driving while drunk.

Selling Alcohol To Youth

Alcohol is a $115 billion industry in the United States; bingers account for 76 percent of beer sales nationwide. Studies show that underage—that is, illegal—drinkers account for 10 percent of the alcohol market, or $10 billion annually. Among recent ploys to lure youth into drinking are so-called alcopops beverages—sweet, fruity lemonades and other drinks laced with liquor—and zippers, fruity gelatin shots containing 12 percent alcohol.

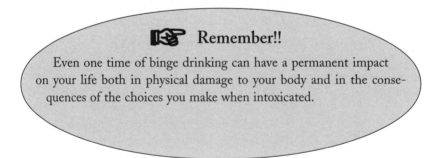

☞ Remember!!

Even one time of binge drinking can have a permanent impact on your life both in physical damage to your body and in the consequences of the choices you make when intoxicated.

Chapter 30

Drugs And Alcohol: A Dangerous Combination

The Simple Facts

There are hundreds of studies, crammed with millions of words, examining the subject of alcohol-drug interactions from every conceivable angle. Still, if you had to summarize them all, you could do it with a single word: Don't. Because the simple fact is that alcohol is a drug, and like every other drug, has potential for risks both large and small. And when it's used with other drugs, the risk index for booze jumps right off the chart. Just consider:

- Government reports rank alcohol-drug combinations as the leading cause of drug-related deaths in the United States, and have for decades.

- Complications caused by combination-drug interactions send another 160,000 Americans to emergency rooms every year for poisoning or overdose treatment.

Those are pretty simple facts. Want another? Then try this one: A majority of all the poisonings and overdoses that take place every year are accidents, plain and simple. They involve normal, everyday people using normal, everyday medicines—folks who just didn't realize that Drink A (a Tequila Mockingbird, say, from the local Mai Tai Hut) interacts with Drug B (Flagyl®, for example) to produce Effect C (cramps, vomiting) until after it did.

That's why we've put together this chapter. Because the hardest fact to swallow is this: Most drug-and-alcohol mishaps could be avoided if the people involved only knew what might happen before it did happen. The fact that they often don't only makes the rest of what we'll be talking about in this chapter that much more critical.

Sound simple enough? Good. Stick around. It keeps getting simpler.

Simple Fact #1: Drinking And Downers Don't Mix

> ✎ **Weird Word**
>
> Synergism: The effects of two drugs taken together which are different from the effects of each drug used individually.

Simple Fact #1 flows from Funny Fact #1 (as funny as these facts ever get, anyway) of this chapter, which is that one and one doesn't always equal two. Oh, it does on a calculator, but that's because calculators can't calculate all the possible outcomes of all the dumb things that people do. And one of the dumbest things that people ever do centers around one of the most critical times that one and one doesn't equal two: When somebody adds the effects of booze to other depressant drugs.

That's because alcohol is a depressant, just like tranquilizers and sleeping pills. And like other downers, it slows bodily functions, including breathing and heart rate. And when people drink enough (or combine too much alcohol with too many downers), things slow down so much that they stop altogether.

Why? Because alcohol and downers compete for the same system of liver enzymes that break down drugs and flush them from the body. That means when two or more downers are in play at the same time, the liver can't handle the load. Result: Drug molecules are reabsorbed and recirculate throughout the body. That's when problems really kick in.

♣ **It's A Fact!!**
Rumors And Reality

Rumor: Beer and wine cause fewer "serious" problems than hard liquor.

Reality: All alcoholic beverages contain about the same amount of alcohol. Beer and wine contain more water, but have the same potential for problems.

Rumor: Cocaine and alcohol cancel each other out, enabling party people to stay straight longer.

Reality: They might think they're straight, but they're not. In fact, the body converts the breakdown products of cocaine and alcohol into a different chemical, cocaethylene, which is twice as deadly as cocaine is all by itself.

Rumor: If you take aspirin before drinking, you can avoid a hangover.

Reality: Aspirin increases the stomach's absorption of alcohol, particularly when taken an hour or so before drinking. If anything, it increases the odds of a hangover.

The scientific name for this process is synergism. It means that the effects of drugs taken together can be very different than the effects they produce solo. The difference can be like night and day. In fact, it can even determine whether a person makes it through the night to ever see another day.

Simple Fact #2: Smoking Doesn't Mix With Anything

Sniff the air inside almost any bar and you'll immediately bump into one of the most common alcohol-drug combinations: booze and cigarettes. And according to recent studies, it may also be one of our most dangerous. Because researchers now believe that drinking increases absorption of cancer-causing tobacco by-products in the body. Recent studies have shown a greater risk of cancers of the mouth, neck, and throat among drinkers who also smoke. And alcoholics who smoke heavily suffer higher levels of these cancers than heavy smokers who don't drink.

Risks linked to smoking and drinking don't stop with cigarettes, either. Today, scientists warn that an increased risk of cancer may also be linked to marijuana and alcohol, since pot contains many of the same cancer-causing chemicals as tobacco.

Table 30.1. Bomb Squad: Use With Booze And Lose

Drug Class	Trade Name(s)	Effects with Alcohol
Anti-Alcohol	Antabuse®	Severe reactions to even small amounts: headache, nausea, convulsions, coma, death.
Antibiotics	Penicillin Cyantin®	Reduces the drugs' therapeutic effectiveness.
Antidepressants	Elavil® Prozac® Tofranil® Nardil®	Increased central nervous system (CNS) depression and blood pressure changes. Combination use of alcohol with MAO inhibitors can trigger massive increase in blood pressure, resulting in brain hemorrhage and death.
Antihistamines	Allerest® Dristan®	Drowsiness and CNS depression. Impairs driving ability.
Aspirin	Anacin® Excedrin®	Can intensify alcohol's effects. Irritates stomach lining. May cause gastrointestinal pain, bleeding.
Depressants	Valium® Ativan® Halcion®	Dangerous CNS depression, loss of coordination, coma. High risk of overdose and death.
Narcotics	heroin codeine Darvon®	Serious CNS depression. Possible respiratory arrest and death.
Stimulants	amphetamine cocaine	Masks the depressant action of alcohol. May increase both blood pressure and physiological tension. Increases risk of overdose.

Long-term risks aside, though, alcohol and pot pose a multitude of immediate problems, with effects that can turn a night out on the town into a night of just being plain out of it. For one thing, each can reduce coordination and concentration and slow reaction time, all critical skills if you're performing complex tasks—driving, for example. In addition, both booze and pot can impair visual tracking ability, making it harder for a smoker or drinker to follow a moving object or perceive changes and movement in peripheral vision.

Those are just some of the factors that make piling a pot high on top of a booze buzz potentially risky. And the risk is needlessly compounded when a stoned drinker does something really dumb—like sliding behind the wheel of a car.

Simple Fact #3: Medicine Doesn't Make It As A Mixer

A hundred years ago, alcohol was the number one all-purpose cure-all in the country, the "secret" ingredient in any number of patent medicines and prescription potions. Today, alcohol isn't considered a cure or treatment for anything, or used at all medicinally, except as an ingredient in some cough and flu preparations. Because the fact is that alcohol can alter the way medicines work and often blocks or decreases their therapeutic action.

Antibiotics (a group that includes such common drugs as penicillin and tetracycline) tend to lose their effectiveness when mixed with alcohol. Other medications (including such drugs as metronidazole, or Flagyl®) can interact violently with alcohol, producing a set of unexpected (and unwelcome) side effects, such as cramps, vomiting, and headaches. And those kinds of effects can be (or fast become) a bigger problem than the original. Want to avoid problems altogether? Just do the math—and remember to subtract, rather than add.

Simple Fact #4: Up Isn't Always The Opposite Of Down

The best recipe for sobering up is hot coffee and a cold shower, right? In a word, no. In fact, dosing a drunk with caffeine, the main stimulant in coffee, is little more than a time-honored waste of time. After throwing down a few cups of Brazil's Best, a drinker may be wide awake—but every bit as drunk as before. One study even suggests that following up a liquor-ish late night with an early morning cup of joe may slow response time even more than booze alone.

Stronger stimulants, such as cocaine or amphetamines, don't straighten out a drinker, either. (They can even make things worse: Check out the "Rumors And Reality" list in the box for more.) Even worse, they can trick users into believing that they're speeding toward sobriety. Why? Because stimulants temporarily mask the depressant effects of liquor, giving drinkers a false sense of security without improving coordination or concentration, or driving skills, for that matter.

Alcohol/stimulant combinations cause other problems, too, including increased blood pressure, tension, and jitters. These effects may not always be serious in themselves, but they can contribute to a number of potential problems that nobody wants or needs.

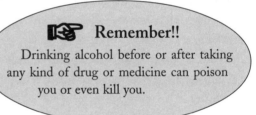

Remember!!
Drinking alcohol before or after taking any kind of drug or medicine can poison you or even kill you.

Simple Fact #5: It's Easier To Prevent Problems Than Fix Them

The truth is that there's no real trick to avoiding problems with drugs and alcohol. In fact, staying out of trouble is basically a simple matter of applying common sense about what you put in your body and when. It's an old adage, but it's as true now as ever: An ounce of prevention can prevent a ton of pain.

To reduce your risk of problems with the drugs that you take (or may be taking in the future), always remember:

• Tell your doctor about any drugs you're taking.

• Follow instructions carefully. Be sure you understand how and when to take any drug and that you're aware of potential side effects.

If you drink, find out if it's safe to drink while taking a prescription drug. If you're not sure, assume that it's not okay—and don't do it. Because the final simple fact about alcohol/drug combinations is that staying alive and staying healthy starts with staying smart.

Accidents can happen. But they don't happen as often to people who are smart enough to avoid them. And that's the simplest fact of all.

Part Six

Overcoming Alcohol Dependency

Chapter 31

Leaving Alcohol Behind

Real People, Real Struggles

John never missed a day of work, always took his kids to their sports practices, and made sure the lawn looked nice, but on weekends he spent a lot of his time drinking. He never felt quite up to par. Getting to work Monday mornings was becoming difficult. John knew he had a drinking problem, but he had a hard time asking for help.

Jessica was very shy and awkward and felt uncomfortable at parties unless she smoked some marijuana or sniffed some glue ahead of time. She knew taking drugs was becoming a pattern, but it was better than feeling her sense of loneliness. On the other hand, she thought the time was getting near when all the drugs would cause her worse pain than the loneliness.

Terry always tried to keep up with his buddies, but lately they seemed to be drinking and using other drugs all the time. Terry's father was an alcoholic and Terry had vowed he would never drink "that much." He was confused. He kept up with his buddies to prove himself a man, but if his father did the same thing to be a man, he wasn't sure it was a good idea.

About This Chapter: Text in this chapter is from "Moving Forward With Your Life!" Substance Abuse and Mental Health Service Administration–National Clearinghouse for Alcohol and Drug Information (SAMHSA–NCADI), revised 1998. Reviewed in September 2004 by Dr. David A. Cooke, MD, Diplomate, American Board of Internal Medicine.

Maria tried everything she could think of to stop drinking. She switched from beer to wine, decided not to drink until after the sun went down, took long walks whenever she felt the need to drink. But while she was pregnant, her emotions ran very high. She hated the ups and downs and longed more and more for a drink. "A little drink now and then won't hurt," she rationalized. She felt ashamed and had trouble asking for help for fear of humiliation.

Michael's mother and father told him a million times he was no good. Getting drunk proved them right. "Why bother staying sober?" he'd ask himself. He knew the answer was he didn't like himself drunk. So, he'd lay off for a month or so, but then something would get him mad and he'd start again and stay drunk for 5 or 6 days. He wanted some help. But how was he going to get it?

Susan was obsessed with drinking. She really enjoyed it and rarely associated with anyone who couldn't keep up with her drinking. She spent most of her free time in bars and restaurants known for generous drinks and became more interested in the wine list than the menu. She entertained a lot too, with plenty of people and cases of alcohol. What her guests didn't drink, she finished off. Every once in a while the thought occurred that she might be developing a problem, but she'd put it out of her mind. She didn't have to ask for help. No one would ever think she needed assistance, would they?

Recognizing The Problem

There's a good reason others may have seen your problem with alcohol or other drugs and recognized your need for help sooner than you did yourself. In a society where such problems are so stigmatized, and the person with the problem made to feel ashamed, it is easy to understand why you would want to deny that you have such a problem. In fact, this kind of denial has become so familiar that many experts associated it with alcohol and other drug dependence.

Everyone described in this chapter—including you, perhaps—is beginning to understand the seriousness of their problem and is wondering how to get help. Some will act more quickly than others to get this help. Some will actually stop drinking or taking other drugs on their own. Some will get into trouble with the law, at work, or with families or friends before they get help. But all of them need that help. They do not want to depend on alcohol or other drugs to cope with life and its problems any more than you do. Like you, they want to take charge of their lives as have millions of others who have left alcohol and other drugs behind.

If you drink to change the way you feel; to relieve boredom, anxiety, depression, anger, or low self-esteem; to gain acceptance from others; to escape life's problems; or to feel part of the good life you see in alcohol advertising, or in drinking scenes in the movies and on television, then you are not alone. These are the reasons many people give for drinking. And if you are one of the 76 million Americans who grew up in a family where there was a drinking problem, you may not have known that you had a greater chance than others of developing a problem yourself.

But figuring out why you began drinking or using other drugs is not important right now. What is important is to recognize that alcohol and/or other drugs are taking you away from the life you want, understanding how serious the problem is, and then getting help.

The Facts

There is no typical alcoholic or drug dependent person. You may be old or young; male or female; single, married, divorced, or living with someone; practice any religious observance or none; live in the country, city, or suburb; earn a lot or a little; come from any ethnic or racial background; and live any type of lifestyle.

1. If you drink heavily after a confrontation or argument, or because of emotional pain, you may feel that you need alcohol or other drugs to reduce the unpleasant feelings. But there are other ways to cope without using alcohol or other drugs—you can talk with others about your feelings, find comfort around people who want to deal with life's problems too, even yell in the shower. If these options seem difficult, you may need the help and resources provided in this chapter.

2. If it takes more and more alcohol or more and more drugs to get the same effect, you know you have a problem. You're saying the reason for drinking or drugging is to relieve painful feelings or to get high. You're trying to get away from something negative and looking for something you think is more positive. After a while, the high won't get higher and you won't be able to get rid of whatever is bothering you. In the meantime, you will have become addicted and have that added problem to

---

✔ Quick Tip

For Additional Information About Recovery From Alcohol Dependence

Alcoholics Anonymous
P.O. Box 459
New York, NY 10163
Phone: 212-870-3400
Website: http://
www.alcoholics-anonymous.org

The original 12-step self-help program with free meetings in nearly every community and more than 100 countries.

Al-Anon/Alateen Family Groups
1600 Corporate Landing Parkway
Virginia Beach, VA 23454
Toll-Free: 888-425-2666
Phone: 757-563-1600
Fax: 613-723-0151
Website: http://
www.al-anon.alateen.org
E-mail: WSO@al-anon.org

For those who have been affected by someone else's alcohol or other drug problem; also based on the AA model.

Adult Children of Alcoholics
P.O. Box 3216
Torrance, CA 90510
Phone: 310-534-1815
Website: http://
www.adultchildren.org
E-mail: info@adultchildren.org

Self-help groups for those who grew up in families with alcoholism. Send a self-addressed stamped envelope (SASE) for a list of meetings in your area.

National Institute on Alcohol Abuse and Alcoholism (NIAAA)
5635 Fishers Lane, MSC 9304
Bethesda, MD 20892
Phone: 301-435-0714
Websites: http://
www.niaaa.nih.gov;
and, http://
www.collegedrinkingprevention.gov

deal with before finding better and more positive ways of coping with your problems.

3. If you remember last night—starting out, beginning to drink, maybe having a few extra drinks before your friends arrived "just to get in the mood," feeling pretty good, having a good time, having a few more drinks—but then, that's all you remember—you've had a blackout. Blackouts are a major problem. They are linked to all those extra drinks or to the large quantity you've started to consume. Now that you know this unpleasantness clearly, you start to worry about senility, your capabilities, and the blackouts. It leads you right back to a bottle to stop the worrying and the memory of worrying. It's an addictive cycle. Worry can be useful, but you don't have to do it alone. There is help. More than 15 million Americans—1 out of every 11—suffer from a drinking problem. There also are many who use other drugs the same way. You are not alone.

4. The blackouts alarm you to the point of switching drinks, switching jobs, and switching promises to yourself. Nothing works. You're now suffering some work-related problems and beginning to have money problems. You don't tell anyone. You drink some more or use other drugs, but they don't seem to help anymore. You feel out of control. You are. Alcohol and/or other drugs have taken over your life. You know it. You also know that a little of this or a lot of that no longer takes away the worry; it is the worry. Alcohol and/or other drugs have you in serious trouble and you need immediate help. There is no turning around. Go directly for help.

5. You've begun to realize that others are talking about your drinking or drugging. Vague questions really irritate you because, although they're about what you're doing tonight, who you're going to see, or whether you got paid today, you know those questions were really to find out if you were going out to get drunk or stoned. At first you thought they were selfish and nagging, but deep down it bothers you more and more that others may care about you more than you care about yourself. Why don't they just leave you alone? Maybe they don't know how to care for you. Maybe you'll have to help them know how. It may

not be easy. It may require a great deal of honesty from yourself and others, but this is what turns the lock and lets you take control of your life again.

6. Your hands shake in the morning. You're frightened, scared, and many times terrified. You feel like a little child, alone, unhappy, miserable, and depressed. You don't care much anymore about anything. Life has passed you by and it wasn't fair. You may begin to contemplate suicide. Everyone is extremely irritated with you or has left you and it seems they didn't care. You don't eat much. Instead you drink, sometimes for several days at a time. Nothing relieves the pain, and after a while, you can't even drink very much anymore. At this point, you are in the late stages of alcoholism. While many of the physical problems may be somewhat reversed, others will not. But that doesn't mean getting help should be postponed. Thousands of men and women are recovering from the advanced stages of alcohol dependence and other drug addictions and have completely turned their lives around. They are willing to help you take charge of your life. Gather all the courage you have to ask for help. Pick up the phone and make the call.

Getting Help

Deep down in your heart you know if you have a problem. But you don't want others to think of you as bad or weak-willed or even sick, if you admit to having a problem. The fact is that if you are dependent on alcohol, you do have a progressive disease that only gets worse with time and if you do not get help you could die from it.

This is not meant to scare you. You are probably already frightened, worried about your drinking or other drug-taking, and afraid to ask for help. But it's one of the most courageous things you can do for yourself. It is difficult, but the sooner you do it, the easier it will be. It means that you have to start to value and care for yourself. It's the step to take so that all the other pieces can fall into place.

More than a million Americans like you—women and men of every possible description, who have found themselves struggling with a drinking or other drug problem—have taken charge of their lives and are free of these destructive dependencies today. As you begin investigating the kinds of help available to you, you will discover that some use one kind of help and others use a combination. Some rely more on internal strengths and seek limited guidance from others, while many find the combined wisdom and experience of others with similar problems to be of priceless value. Still others benefit from the services of professional counselors and therapists; ministers, rabbis, and priests; community agencies. You might even want to take someone with you when seeking assistance.

You can find out what kind of help is available from a health care provider, clergy, or employee assistance program (EAP). Therapists, community health and social agencies, and alcohol/other drug treatment programs also can make useful suggestions. Begin by looking under "alcohol" or "drug abuse" in your telephone directory white pages.

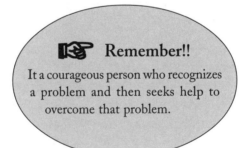

☞ Remember!!

It a courageous person who recognizes a problem and then seeks help to overcome that problem.

Chapter 32

Finding The Right Treatment Program

New Advances In Alcoholism Treatment

More than 700,000 Americans receive alcoholism treatment on any given day.[1] Over the past 20 years, modern methods of evaluating medical therapies have been increasingly applied to alcoholism treatment. This chapter focuses on the effectiveness of self-help groups, psychosocial approaches, and medications in achieving and maintaining abstinence.

Twelve-Step Self-Help Programs

Self-help groups are the most commonly sought source of help for alcohol-related problems.[2] Alcoholics Anonymous (AA), one of the most commonly known self-help groups, outlines 12 consecutive activities, or steps, that alcoholics should achieve during the recovery process. Alcoholics can become involved with AA before entering professional treatment, as a part of it, or as aftercare following professional treatment.

After one year, participants in the 12-step programs achieved more sustained abstinence and higher rates of employment compared with participants in predominantly cognitive-behavioral programs or those with courses

About This Chapter: Text in this chapter is excerpted from "New Advances in Alcoholism Treatment," *Alcohol Alert*, No. 49, National Institute on Alcohol Abuse and Alcoholism (NIAAA), updated 2/2001.

of therapy that combined both approaches.[3] The beneficial effects of AA may be attributable in part to the replacement of the participant's social network of drinking friends with a fellowship of AA members who can provide motivation and support for maintaining abstinence.[2, 4] In addition, AA's approach often results in the development of coping skills, many of which are similar to those taught in more structured psychosocial treatment settings, thereby leading to reductions in alcohol consumption .[2, 5]

Motivational Enhancement Therapy

Developed specifically for Project MATCH,* motivational enhancement therapy (MET) begins with the assumption that the responsibility and capacity for change lie within the client.[6, 7] The therapist begins by providing

✔ **Quick Tip**

A Quick Guide To Finding Effective Alcohol And Drug Addiction Treatment

If you or someone you care for is dependent on alcohol or drugs and needs treatment, it is important to know that no single treatment approach is appropriate for all individuals. Finding the right treatment program involves careful consideration of such things as the setting, length of care, philosophical approach, and your or your loved one's needs.

Twelve Questions To Consider When Selecting A Treatment Program

1. Does the program accept your insurance? If not, will they work with you on a payment plan or find other means of support for you?

2. Is the program run by state-accredited, licensed, and/or trained professionals?

3. Is the facility clean, organized, and well run?

4. Does the program encompass the full range of needs of the individual (medical: including infectious diseases; psychological: including co-occurring mental illness; social; vocational; legal; etc.)?

5. Does the treatment program also address sexual orientation and physical disabilities as well as provide age, gender, and culturally appropriate treatment services?

individualized feedback about the effects of the patient's drinking. Working closely together, therapist and patient explore the benefits of abstinence, review treatment options, and design a plan to implement treatment goals. (*Project MATCH is a national, multisite, randomized clinical trial that produced data on the outcomes of specific alcoholism treatment approaches.)

Brief Interventions

Many persons with alcohol-related problems receive counseling from primary care physicians or nursing staff in the context of five or fewer standard office visits.[8] Such treatment, known as brief intervention, generally consists of straightforward information on the negative consequences of alcohol consumption along with practical advice on strategies and community resources

6. Is long-term aftercare support and/or guidance encouraged, provided, and maintained?

7. Is there ongoing assessment of an individual's treatment plan to ensure it meets changing needs?

8. Does the program employ strategies to engage and keep individuals in longer-term treatment, increasing the likelihood of success?

9. Does the program offer counseling (individual or group) and other behavioral therapies to enhance the individual's ability to function in the family/community?

10. Does the program offer medication as part of the treatment regimen, if appropriate?

11. Is there ongoing monitoring of possible relapse to help guide patients back to abstinence?

12. Are services or referrals offered to family members to ensure they understand addiction and the recovery process to help them support the recovering individual?

Source: Substance Abuse and Mental Health Services Administration–Center for Substance Abuse Treatment (SAMHSA–CSAT), DHHS Publication No. (SMA) 02-3616, NCADI Publication No. PHD877, 2001.

to achieve moderation or abstinence.[9, 10] Most brief interventions
are designed to help those at risk for
developing alcohol-related problems
to reduce their alcohol consumption.
Alcohol-dependent patients are
encouraged to enter specialized treatment with the goal of complete abstinence.[9]

The brief intervention approach
has also been successfully applied
outside the primary care setting. Evidence suggests that 25 to 40 percent
of trauma patients may be alcohol
dependent.[11] Gentilello and col-

> ✎ **Weird Words**
>
> Abstinence: Not using something
> such as alcohol or drugs.
>
> Cognitive-Behavioral Programs:
> Therapy based on reasoning and
> talking, and identifying and
> changing behavior.
>
> Psychosocial Therapy: Therapy
> that deals with mental processes
> and social behaviors.

leagues[12] conducted a randomized controlled study among patients in a trauma
center who had detectable blood alcohol levels at the time of admission. The
researchers found that a single motivational interview at or near the time of
discharge reduced drinking levels and re-admission for trauma during 6
months of followup.[12] Monti and colleagues[13] conducted a similar randomized controlled study among youth ages 18 to 19 admitted to an emergency
room with alcohol-related injuries. After 6 months, although all participants
had decreased their alcohol consumption, the group receiving brief intervention had a significantly lower incidence of drinking and driving, traffic
violations, alcohol-related injuries, and alcohol-related problems.[13]

Brief intervention among freshman college students previously identified as being at high risk for harmful consequences of heavy drinking has
been shown to result in a significant decline in alcohol-related problems.[14, 15]

Treating Alcohol And Nicotine Addiction Together

Nicotine and alcohol interact in the brain, each drug possibly affecting
vulnerability to dependence on the other.[16] Consequently, some researchers
postulate that treating both addictions simultaneously might be an effective,
even essential, way to help reduce dependence on both.

Pharmacotherapy

More recently, research has focused on the development of medications for blocking alcohol-brain interactions that might promote alcoholism. Studies have found that some medications may be more effective for certain types of alcoholics. In conclusion, research supports the concept of using medications along with the psychosocial therapy of alcohol abuse and alcoholism.

New Advances In Alcoholism Treatment

The key change that has occurred is the advent of alcoholism clinical research, which over the past 15 years or so has made significant progress toward rigorous evaluation of both existing therapies and newly developed therapies for use in treating alcohol-related problems. Continued research on alcohol's effects in the brain and on the links between brain and behavior, which has already led to the development of medications to reduce craving, is likely to provide clinicians with a range of highly specific medications that will, when used in conjunction with behavioral therapies, improve the chance for recovery and the lives of those who suffer from alcohol abuse and dependence.

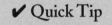

✔ Quick Tip

The U.S. Department of Health and Human Services, Substance Abuse and Mental Health Services Administration's Center for Substance Abuse Treatment (CSAT) provides a toll-free, 24-hour treatment referral service to help you locate treatment options near you. For a referral to a treatment center or support group in your area:

Center for Substance Abuse Treatment
Toll-Free: 800-662-HELP (4357)
Toll-Free TDD: 800-228-0427
Toll-Free Spanish: 800-662-9832
Website: http://findtreatment.samhsa.gov

References

1. NIAAA. *10th Special Report to the U.S. Congress on Alcohol and Health*. NIH Pub No. 00-1583. Bethesda, MD: the Institute, 2000.

2. Humphreys, K.; Mankowski, E.S.; Moos, R.H.; and Finney, J.W. Do enhanced friendship networks and active coping mediate the effect of self-help groups on substance abuse? *Ann Behav Med* 21(1):54-60, 1999.

3. Ouimette, P.C.; Finney, J.W.; and Moos, R.H. Twelve-step and cognitive-behavioral treatment for substance abuse: A comparison of treatment effectiveness. *J Consult Clin Psychol* 65(2):230-240, 1997.

4. Longabaugh, R.; Wirtz, P.W.; Zweben, A.; and Stout, R.L. Network support for drinking, Alcoholics Anonymous and long-term matching effects. *Addict* 93(9):1313-1333, 1998.

5. Morgenstern, J.; Labouvie, E.; McCrady, B.S.; Kahler, C.W.; and Frey, R.M. Affiliation with Alcoholics Anonymous after treatment: A study of its therapeutic effects and mechanisms of action. *J Consult Clin Psychol* 65(5):768-777, 1997.

6. Project MATCH Research Group. Matching alcoholism treatments to client heterogeneity: Project MATCH posttreatment drinking outcomes. *J Stud Alcohol* 58(1):7-29, 1997.

7. Miller, W.R.; Zweben, A.; DiClemente, C.C.; and Rychatrik, R.G. *Motivational Enhancement Therapy Manual*. Project MATCH Monograph Series Vol. 2. NIH Pub. No. 94-3723. Rockville, MD: NIAAA, 1995.

8. Fleming, M., and Manwell, L.B. Brief intervention in primary care settings: A primary treatment method for at-risk, problem, and dependent drinkers. *Alcohol Res & Health* 23(2):128-137, 1999.

9. NIAAA. *Alcohol Alert* No. 43: "Brief Intervention for Alcohol Problems." Bethesda, MD: the Institute, 1999.

10. DiClemente, C.C.; Bellino, L.E.; and Neavins, T.M. Motivation for change and alcoholism treatment. *Alcohol Res Health* 23(2):86-92, 1999.

11. Gentilello, L.M.; Donovan, D.M.; Dunn, C.W.; and Rivara, F.P. Alcohol interventions in trauma centers: Current practice and future directions. *JAMA* 274(13):1043-1048, 1995.

12. Gentilello, L.M.; Rivara, F.P.; Donovan, D.M.; et al. Alcohol interventions in a trauma center as a means of reducing the risk of injury recurrence. *Ann Surg* 230(4):473-483, 1999.

13. Monti, P.M.; Colby, S.M.; Barnett, N.P.; et al. Brief intervention for harm reduction with alcohol-positive older adolescents in a hospital emergency department. *J Consult Clin Psychol* 67(6):989-994, 1999.

14. Marlatt, G.A.; Baer, J.S.; Kivlahan, D.R.; et al. Screening and brief intervention for high-risk college student drinkers: Results from a 2-year follow-up assessment. *J Consult Clin Psychol* 66(4):604-615, 1998.

15. Roberts, L.J.; Neal, D.J.; Kivlahan, D.R.; Baer, J.S.; and Marlatt, G.A. Individual drinking changes following a brief intervention among college students: Clinical significance in an indicated preventive context. *J Consult Clin Psychol* 68(3):500-505, 2000.

16. Schiffman, S., and Balabanis, M. Associations between alcohol and tobacco. In: Fertig, J.B., and Allen, J.P., eds. *Alcohol and Tobacco: From Basic Science to Clinical Practice*. NIAAA Research Monograph No. 30. NIH Pub. No. 95-3531. Bethesda, MD: the Institute, 1995. pp. 17-36.

☞ Remember!!

There are many types of treatment for alcohol abuse. Ask questions and find the one that will help you. It is possible to recover from alcohol use and abuse.

Chapter 33

Everyday Detox: Taking Care Of Mind And Body

Everyday Detox: Picking Up The Pieces

Multiple Choice

You've woken up feeling

    a. the way you're feeling now,

    b. the way you felt this morning,

    c. the way you felt some other morning, or even

    d. all of the above

for the last time.

And while you might not think you're chemically dependent, you are prone to overdoing it. In fact, you've spent a big part of your life already overdoing whatever has been available to be overdone.

About This Chapter: Text in this chapter is reprinted with permission from *Everyday Detox: Picking Up the Pieces* by Jim Parker. © 2000 Do It Now Foundation. All rights reserved. Additional text under its own heading is reprinted with permission from *Cleaning Yourself Up: A Guide to Getting Your Head* by Jim Parker. © 2000 Do It Now Foundation. All rights reserved.

And though the substance you overuse is

a.   alcohol,

b.   marijuana,

c.   pills, or

d.   caffeine, sugar, and other dietary cheap thrills,

you've thought a lot lately about changing—scrapping the junk-food, junk-feeling lifestyle you've gotten strung out on, in favor of something simpler—and more real.

Congratulations! You're exactly where you need to be to create some value out of this chapter. It's about detoxifying from everyday chemicals—hard drugs and soft, controlled substances, and the ones that plop out of machines in cans. Even the one(s) you've been using for a while now.

In the sections that follow, we'll talk about ways to get off what you've been on, and how to keep your spirits up and your defense mechanisms down for as long as it takes for you to become yourself again. What you do from there is up to you—the real you. You remember him/her, don't you? Sure you do.

Facing Facts

The first step in overcoming dependency is recognizing it for what it is. That's as true for a six-cup-a-day coffee habit as it is for a 12-pack-a-day continual beer buzz or a 60 mg a day Valium addiction.

Your habit isn't any different. If it creates problems in your life—in your relationships, or your job, or your feelings about yourself—the substance you've been doing is really doing you. The point we're making has nothing to do with the pharmacological properties of specific substances. And it's not meant to imply that dropping Drug A (say, crystal meth) is no different than stopping Drug B (Jolt® Cola) in terms of risk, nor is it intended to minimize the hazards linked to detox from long-term addictions. [In fact, we strongly urge people with serious dependency issues—particularly long-term use of alcohol, cocaine, depressants, or narcotics—to consult a physician or treatment program before starting any detox regimen.]

Still, we think that there's a lot that's potentially useful in looking at substance abuse as a generic problem: generic solutions, for one thing. Stick around. And see if any of the solutions we uncover are generic enough to cover you.

Getting Off

Even though recognition is a first step in getting your life back on track, it's worth noting that simply noticing a problem doesn't make it go away. The next step in resolving chemical dependency is to bring your use under control—if you still can—or to quit using altogether. And while there are ways to contain a dependence on a psychoactive drug, there's only one way that's guaranteed to erase it, and that's to quit.

The specific forms that quitting can take can vary, depending on a user's biological and psychological make-up, the substance(s) involved, and the duration and extent of use. Example? A high-octane coffee drinker might actually increase his or her prospects for recovery by withdrawing gradually, while a cigarette smoker or crystal freak might find it impossible to quit a little at a time. An easy way to discover which way works best for you is to just quit.

Whether you're interested in cutting your use down or cutting it out altogether, it helps to discover the full extent of your involvement. And the only real way to do that is to stop doing what you've been doing and see what happens. Still, whether you go cold turkey or slip into abstinence a little at a time, the ultimate outcome of detox is usually to stay off a substance for good. And doing that takes a lot more than willpower. It takes a revolution—a real revolution of the body, mind, heart, and soul. And it's aimed at a single goal: transforming the behaviors and beliefs that became a habit which eventually turned against you.

Deconditioning The Mind

The main battlefield the revolution plays out on is in the hills and valleys and jungles of the mind. Your goal here is simple: To become aware of the terrain and begin to reverse the processes that contributed to your dependency.

Emotional traits linked to serious drug and alcohol abuse aren't that different from those underlying ordinary dependencies, especially the tendency toward compulsiveness and a low tolerance to frustration. But listing character traits doesn't explain addiction or help much to stop dependency once it's started. That takes commitment and patience—and intentional change.

Here are some issues you'll probably want to focus your intentional changes on:

- Avoid situations that trigger automatic responses, like hitting the bars during happy hour if you're a problem drinker; or making detours past candy stores if you're a chocoholic. Don't think of it as a life sentence. Think of it as the period on a life sentence.

- Learn new ways to deal with stress. Almost everything from biofeedback to meditation and visualization techniques have been tried as anti-stressors and just about everything works, if you do. Don't know how? Check the public library for books or video or audio tapes on stress management, then get busy at getting un-busy.

- Develop a social support network. Get tight with new people who can reinforce and support the changes you intend to make. Rethink the role of drug or drinking buddies, and decide whether they're going to help or hinder your commitment to change. If not, you'll need to make changes there, too.

The technical name for all this is deconditioning— breaking the stranglehold of conditioned responses learned in the past, in favor of self-generated choices more in line with the person you intend to be. Revolutionary? Yes. Easy? No.

✔ **Quick Tip**
Books To Check-Out

If you heed our earlier advice and head to the library for resources on stress management, check out the nutrition section, too. Two great overviews are Sugar Blues, by William Dufty, and The Hidden Addiction (& How to Get Free), by Janice Phelps, M.D. and Alan Nourse.

Because the simple truth is that deconditioning involves a conscious shifting of focus from past to future, from what we were to what we will be, from automaticity to awareness, from habit to choice.

It's not always easy—or comfortable. In fact, it could be the hardest thing you ever do. But people who've succeeded—and created major changes in their lives—swear that it's worth the effort. Especially when you consider the alternative.

Reconditioning The Body

Important as it is, deconditioning the mind is only half the story. Just as important are the changes you may need to make to recover your physical health. That's because substances can wreak havoc on the body, and total recovery almost always requires havoc de-wreaking. Here are some places to start.

Nutrition. Vitamin supplements can play a huge role in the early stages of detox to counteract nutritional deficiencies or metabolic problems linked to an addiction. Also important, are dietary changes aimed at correcting long-term nutritional problems. Regardless of what you may think (especially if your thinking on the subject is defined by junk and convenience food TV ads), what you put into your body has a real impact on how you feel and relate to others.

Programmers coined a word to describe the process in computers: G.I.G.O.—garbage in, garbage out. It's the same with any machine—and your body is a machine. Stop the flow of junk that you load up with and you'll see a similar halt in the flow of junk out of your life—in the form of scattered thinking and the roller-coaster emotions that come with the typical high-sugar, high-fat American diet.

A diet better suited to recovery from almost anything is one that's low in fat, low in sugar, and high in complex carbohydrates. Other recommendations:

- Drink lots of water and avoid coffee and soda.
- Lighten up on processed foods and red meats.
- Eat natural foods, especially fresh vegetables and whole grains.

Still not convinced? Get convinced.

Exercise. Physical activity is another key element in detox, since exercise conditions the body at the same time it reduces stress and enhances mood. Any type or combination of activities will do the trick, but jogging, especially, works wonders at dispelling detox-related anxiety.

In beginning your exercise program, start slowly and build up to a daily schedule that you can live with—and stay with. Start each session by stretching

---

✔ **Quick Tip**

Wake-Up Calls

Want to get out of the rut you've been stuck in? Then get into a new rut—one that you consciously choose, one that will even make the world a better place. It may still be a rut, but you'll like it better than your old one. Just don't forget to ask the desk clerk in your head for an occasional wake-up call, at least until you get over this darned amnesia.

Stuck for ideas? Try some of these:

- **Do what needs doing.** Remember that candy wrapper you kicked on the street the other day? Pick it up next time, and throw it in the trash. When you do, you will have made the world a better place by exactly one iota. It sounds small, but it adds up. (Score 10 iotas for a broken beer bottle.)

- **Smile.** You've got bills to pay, bumper-to-bumper traffic to contend with at rush hour, and a cold sore, but that's no reason to scare people with your face. If you really want to change, start by smiling at how ridiculous and wonderful and precious life is. It's another small thing, but if you take care of the small things, the big things—you know.

- **Volunteer.** Feel strongly about the spotted-owl? Legal access to medical marijuana for AIDS patients? Saving the rain forest? Connect with a local group that's trying to do something about it. If your interests are more general, call a local nursing home or shelter care facility to see who needs you. Somebody does, and helping them will help get your attention off yourself and onto something—or someone—who needs it more.

And it's nice to remember, at least once in a while, that life pays us back for the good that we do with interest.

and end with a warm-down walk or more stretching. If you've never been particularly body-conscious, you may be surprised at how much fun getting physical can be after a period of inactivity. And if you've been laying off jogging or working out for a time (while wreaking all the aforementioned havoc on yourself), you may be surprised at how far (and how fast) physical exercise goes toward getting you back in the pink—and back in charge of your life.

Staying Straight

Once you've beaten your addiction for a while, you may be tempted to prove how far you've come by handling what you couldn't handle before. Don't bother. This is the last obstacle in the path of recovery and the place where thousands of cool, smart, no-longer-recovering people went down before you.

Why stay straight? To develop your commitment to mastery in your life. Chemicals—coffee or cocaine, ephedrine or ecstasy—are a mirror-image of that mastery. Because they work fast, they make us think they're the magic in our lives, and the problem is that just isn't true.

What is true is that the last stage of detox and recovery involves making the changes we've discussed part of who you are—not just some of the time or whenever you feel the bottom's about to drop out of your life, but as a normal part of everyday life. It doesn't have to be a burden. In fact, it won't be as big a burden as some of the problems you've been through already. And it can give the rest of your life the meaning you sensed was missing all along.

Why not give it a try? After all, you really don't have that much to lose— only a few

    a. problems

    b. dependencies

    c. insecurities, or (more likely)

    d. all of the above

How many reasons do you need?

Cleaning Yourself Up

Chemical Consciousness And The Upside's Downside

What goes up must come down. It's a basic law of physics. We call it gravity, but the principle extends further than simply explaining why apples fall down. It also describes what happens to people when they pump themselves up with chemicals: Eventually, they come down, too.

It's the First Law of Chemical Consciousness—the old rebound principle. And it holds true no matter what your favorite psychoactive substance is—or used to be. Coffee or cocaine, alcohol or LSD, sooner or later you come down. And when you do, you'll notice that the First Law has a corollary: The higher you go, the further you fall. That means that once you do come down, you usually end up lower than when you started.

What do you do about it after the fact? Well, a first impulse may be to use more of the chemical you started with (or even a different one) to get back up (or down) to where you started from. That's one option. Of course, that ultimately leaves you even further down—or further up (or off) the wall, if you've been climbing one lately.

The other option is to stop the cycle completely. It's trickier, since it involves effort and patience on your part and requires putting up with feeling down long enough to let your body re-center itself. But it can be done.

That's where we come in. In this section, we'll talk about ways of breaking out of the chemical-dependency trap and discuss techniques that can make the withdrawal process easier on your body and mind. Because even though time is a factor in freeing yourself from chemicals, a lot can be done to cut that time to a minimum, and get you back on your feet again—one day and one step at a time.

Body/Mind 101

Mind and body are inseparable parts of the same basic unit; what happens to one automatically affects the other. That means that getting back to where you want to be will require paying attention to the needs of both.

✔ Quick Tip

✔ Quick Tip

Running From Problems

Along with proper nutrition, exercise does a lot to tone the body and tune the spirit. Because not only does sustained activity improve physical fitness, it also triggers a surge in the body's production of endorphins, the chemical messengers that act in the brain to increase positive feelings and reduce stress.

You might have heard about endorphins as the basis for the so-called "runner's high." It's not hype. Runners do report an expanded sense of well-being after a run. But increased endorphin levels have been linked to activities other than running.

In fact, recent research shows that any intense physical exercise can trigger the same response. That means that swimming, walking, or almost anything else that gets the heart thumping and the muscles pumping can inspire a major uplift in mood and outlook. Try it—even if you don't really feel like it. After all, you've been doing what you feel like all along. And look where it's got you.

Once you've gotten over your immediate reliance on drugs and/or alcohol (and you really do have to begin there), start with a general cleaning-up program, like the one outlined below. It's designed to give your body what it really needs—exercise, nutrition, and rest—rather than the chemical substitutes you've been using as your personal gun, whip, and chair.

Nutrition

Poor nutrition doesn't just cause poor physical health. Moodiness, irritability, restlessness, fatigue, and many other "emotional" problems are often directly linked to poor nutrition. So if you're not eating well, all you're eating is calories—and potential problems. But what does "eating well" mean? It means eating the same stuff that your mom probably tried to get you to eat a long time ago—veggies and fresh fruits and grains.

While you're at it, you might want to avoid heavily-processed foods and anything that contains ingredients you can't pronounce or spell, like polysorbate-60 or calcium disodium EDTA (whatever that is). Also, cut back on caffeine and sugar, since they're both almost guaranteed to kick in cravings for whatever you're trying to clear out of your system.

✔ Quick Tip

The 15-Minute Meditator

One of the most up-to-the-minute methods for beating stress happens to be one of the oldest. It's meditation, and in recent years, it's been dusted off and demystified and studied in depth by researchers, who consider it one of the best tools for managing everyday tension and anxiety.

Learning to meditate has never been easier, either. One researcher, Herbert W. Benson of the Harvard Medical School, offers an introduction to the basic elements of meditation in his book, *The Relaxation Response*. According to Dr. Benson, all you need to do is follow these main points:

1. Find a quiet place where you won't be disturbed for 15 minutes or so.

2. Close your eyes and relax all the muscles in your body.

3. Focus your attention on your breathing, and silently repeat the word "one" (or another single-syllable word, such as "calm") each time you exhale.

4. When thoughts intrude, simply return your focus to the word "one" as you exhale.

5. Don't push. The goal is to temporarily turn off the flood of thoughts, judgments, and interpretations that flow through our minds. And while that's the goal, don't realistically expect to do it for more than a few seconds at a time any time soon.

Still, if you try it, stick with it. Benson recommends a twice-a-day schedule (mornings and early evenings work best for most people) if you want to get good at it—and get the full range of physical and psychological benefits linked to it.

Since chemical use tends to deplete vitamins and minerals in the body (especially the B vitamins), supplements are also a great idea. It's a tricky subject, though, since all vitamins aren't the same. Some—like vitamin C and the B-complex vitamins—are water-soluble, so your body only uses what it needs and excretes the rest. Other vitamins, though, are fat-soluble (such as A, D and E), and can build up to harmful levels in the body. If you want to know more, contact a nutritionist or ask someone knowledgeable at a local health-food store.

Remember, though: Everyone has an opinion about nutrition, and what works for someone else (alfalfa sprouts on carob-chip Tofuti) may not work for you. So listen to your body. And if you don't feel your absolute best (both physically and mentally), listen some more. There's still room for improvement.

Sleep

Good-old, made-in-the-shade sleep is another key element in any body-cleansing program. There's just no substitute for the rest and revitalization that sleep can provide. It'll help you adjust psychologically to the changes you're going through and reduce feelings of burnout in the bargain. So if you really want to be responsible for yourself—and you're serious about staying off whatever you've been on—start giving your body the natural sleep it needs.

If insomnia's a problem—and it often is for cleaning-yourself-up people—check out the section on exercise. Here's why: Sleep disturbances become a lot less of a problem for people who are committed to doing whatever it takes to handle them. You'll be surprised, for example, at how easy it is to fall asleep once you commit yourself to a serious jogging or aerobics program. And besides, what self-respecting ex-dope fiend or alcoholic would want to waste all those free endorphins?

Body/Mind 201

The second step in recovery involves "re-centering" the mind and emotions to break the habits that contributed to your dependency. This process can involve taking up almost anything from meditation to Mah-Jong, but it ultimately requires breaking habits of the past that have kept you from fully enjoying the present without a chemical crutch.

As you've realized by now, chemicals don't solve problems. What they do is insulate us from problems—which may feel nice for a while, but which rarely resolves anything. By managing problems with chemicals we forget other, more effective ways of dealing with them. Now, you're going to have to teach yourself all over again. And the best—and possibly the most all-encompassing—place to start is learning to manage stress.

Stress

One of the biggest reasons any of us ever had for self-medicating with drugs and alcohol is something we all still have to deal with: simple tension. It's usually one of the biggest pieces of excess baggage that recovering people carry around, and something each of us needs to unpack in one way or another, sooner or later.

The big question for most newly clean-and-sober people is this: How do you start de-stressing when you're an expert at distressing?

For starters, you need to learn to identify tension and beat it to the punch. Then, if you've gotten used to clobbering it with something pharmacological (say, a six-pack or a joint after work), find a new way. You might try something as simple as taking a shower, for example, or learn a meditation technique. Don't know any? Then check out the box "Running From Problems." It describes a stripped-down, no-frills approach to meditation that answers another age-old question about the mind: How do you turn the damn thing off? Just remember—the ability to cool yourself out psycho-emotionally (whether through meditation or not) is like everything else: Practice makes perfect.

New Directions

If you're newly drug-free, we have good news and bad news about your life: It's yours again. Now, all you have to do is make it worth living. How? The details are up to you, but it's probably going to involve change, and it might not be fast or easy. But, it is worth it. Because even though change can look more threatening than the everyday grind (no matter how monotonous and frustrating the everyday grind may seem sometimes), it's part of life. And if you stop and think about it, you may realize that the best, most exciting, most gratifying fun times in your life involved the most change—and often, serious change.

So go out and try something new—aerobics or aikido, web-surfing or white-water rafting—whatever looks like it may help you connect with the future you want to live. If you look hard enough, you'll see alternatives to an unhappy, stuck, chemically-dependent life everywhere.

In case you'd forgotten, you're a unique person who's perfectly designed to go out into the world and discover what you need—and what needs doing. Now all you have to do is go out there and do it.

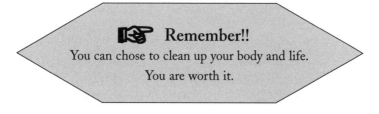

Remember!!
You can chose to clean up your body and life.
You are worth it.

Chapter 34

How To Help A Friend Who Has An Alcohol Problem

Helping A Friend With A Drug Or Alcohol Problem

This chapter provides advice for helping a friend with a drug or alcohol problem. Once you get past the fear of talking with your friend or sibling, you'll need to understand how to approach him or her and know what to say. There is no way to know how your friend might react, but the information in this chapter can help you with the challenge.

My Friend Has A Problem

So you think your friend or sibling has a problem with drugs or alcohol? Maybe he or she seems like a different person since starting to drink or get high. Maybe he's been letting you down because he's using drugs. Or maybe some of the things he does when he is drunk or high are just scary. Whatever it is, the important thing is that you've noticed that your friend might be heading for trouble.

About This Chapter: Text in this chapter is from The National Youth Anti-Drug Media Campaign's "Action Guide: Helping a Friend with a Drug Problem," and "Sample Conversations," 2004. The National Youth Anti-Drug Media Campaign is a program of the White House Office of National Drug Control Policy. For more information visit http://www.freevibe.com.

You can help your friend now—before something really bad happens. Your friend will probably insist that his or her drinking or drug use is not a big deal. This is very common among people with drug or alcohol problems. Don't let your friend's denial keep you from talking with him. If he continues using, he could face serious consequences like getting caught or arrested, losing his drivers' license, getting suspended, or more severely, getting involved in a drug or alcohol-related car crash or becoming addicted.

Should I Help?

If you have a friend or sibling that is experimenting with or regularly using drugs, you are not alone. Many teens are facing the same issue all across the country. Many of us are afraid to discuss serious issues with our friends because we fear being rejected. It is not easy to tell a friend or loved one that they have a problem.

However, what are the alternatives? If you don't discuss a friend's drug or drinking problem with them now, the friendship might change forever. That means no more late night conversations, no more shoulder to cry on, no more laughs, no more holidays together, etc.

No one ever thinks that trying or casually using drugs is going to lead to a life-threatening addiction. That's the reason why substance abuse is so complex—no one thinks they're going to be the one with the problem. Yet, millions of people suffer and die from drug addiction every year.

> ♣ **It's A Fact!!**
> Did you know that 68 percent of teens said they would turn to a friend or brother/sister about a serious problem related to substance abuse? This means that when you talk, your friends will listen—even if you've tried drugs or alcohol yourself.

Getting Past The Fear

It is a critical time for action once you suspect—or know—that your friend has a drug or alcohol problem. This can be a difficult situation to deal with, and sometimes the situation gets worse before it gets better. The most important thing is for you to take action on your friend's behalf the first time that you suspect a problem. Don't make excuses. You can play an important role in your friend's future.

Do you hear yourself saying things like:

If I talk to my friend about his drug problem, he won't like or trust me anymore.

If you aren't going to discuss the problem with your friend, the chances are that no one will. Friendship is all about doing whatever is best for the other person. While it might feel difficult now, think about what may happen down the road if you don't address the issue when you first recognize it.

I won't talk to my friend now because this is his first time using or he only uses or drinks once in a while.

If you don't let your friend know where you stand on drugs and alcohol, you might be enabling them or subconsciously telling them that you don't think it's a problem. You could be the most influential person in your friend or sibling's life. Your words matter. The chances are that your friend will see that you are speaking up out of care and concern, not to be judgmental or critical.

How To Begin

Most of us don't enjoy conflict, particularly with someone we care about. When discussing difficult subjects with a friend or sibling, it is just as important to consider how you say something as it is to decide what to say. Our words are very powerful, especially to our best friends and loved ones. A supportive, caring tone usually goes much farther than the judgmental approach. If you are discussing a serious topic, such as drug and alcohol use, with a close friend you should keep the following points in mind:

- **Privacy.** No one likes their dirty laundry exposed. Discuss important issues in a private place where no one is likely to overhear the details of your conversation.

- **Positive Messages.** Always remember to include some type of positive message before or after expressing an opinion that a friend might perceive as "critical." This will help to remind them that you are expressing yourself out of care and concern. For example, "You are my best friend and one of my favorite people on the planet. But I feel like your drug use is changing the person I know and love." If you're not the type that can express these types of feelings easily, think about sending a postcard that contains a similar message or writing an old-fashioned handwritten note.

- **Research.** Read up on whatever topic you might be discussing with a friend or sibling in need. A little research and specific examples go a long way in discussing tough issues.

- **Solutions.** No one likes it when a person points out a problem but doesn't offer a solution. Even if a solution isn't clear, you can still recommend that your friend talk to a caring adult or health professional.

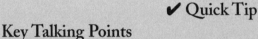

✔ Quick Tip
Key Talking Points

- I don't want anything to happen to you or for you to hurt yourself.

- We all count on you. Your brothers/sisters (if applicable) look up to you/ care about you, as do I. What would they do if you were gone? What would I do if you were gone?

- Look at all the things that you would miss out on. Drugs and alcohol can ruin your future and chances to: keep your drivers' license, graduate, go to college, and get a job.

- What can I do to help you? I am here to support you.

- Are there other problems you want to talk about?

- Are you feeling pressure to use? Let's talk about it.

- I love you and I won't give up on you.

- If you need professional help or you need an adult to talk to, I can help you find someone. I will be here to help you and support you every step of the way.

The point you will have made is that you've come to the table with suggestions and ideas for how to improve the situation.

How Will My Friend React

If a friend drinks alcohol, smokes marijuana, or uses other drugs, there is no way to predict how he or she will act, or what will happen when they are drunk or high. All drugs, including marijuana, can be harmful and addictive. There is no way to know how many drug experiences it takes to become addicted. But drug and alcohol use can lead to abuse, and continued abuse can lead to addiction.

Common sense tells us that helping a friend address a drug or alcohol problem early can help keep it from getting out of control and doing serious harm. This is why it is important to step up and talk with your friend sooner rather than later—you never know what could happen if he or she continues to drink or do drugs—but it can't be good.

The Power Of Friendship

Don't underestimate your own power to influence your friend and explain to him how you see his drug use getting out of hand. Sure, it may have been his choice to start using drugs in the first place, and you may be scared that your friend or sibling will get mad at you and tell you that his choices are none of your business. But if you really think your friend needs help, you have a responsibility to him—and your friendship—to step up and say something. By not talking with your friend about your concerns, you are only sending him the silent message that his drug or alcohol use is no big deal.

The Conversation

If you decide to sit down and talk with your friend or sibling about his or her drinking or drug use, you may not know what to say. You may wonder how she will respond. Will she get defensive? Will she deny she has a problem? Will she get mad at you and tell you to mind your own business? It's likely that she will. People with drug or alcohol problems usually defend their use or make excuses for it. It's hard for people to admit to themselves that they have a drug or alcohol problem.

What To Say

Discussing a friend's drug or alcohol use isn't an easy thing to do. It's very normal to worry about how a friend or sibling will respond to your concerns. If you're at a loss about how to start this type of discussion with someone you care about, we've compiled a list of steps which may help with your approach and delivery.

Make A Plan

Before you engage your friend in a conversation, you'll need to prepare yourself. Go for a walk, sit where you can't be disturbed, and think. Reflect on the facts of the situation. Organize your thoughts. Decide what you want to say to your friend. Focus on a tone that is assertive, but not aggressive. Think about what resources you might need: a parent, a counselor, your faith leader, a school counselor, etc. Once you start the conversation, remain calm and supportive.

Present The Facts

Discuss your concerns and identify some of the changes that you've seen in your friend. For example, you were at a party and saw your friend using drugs or acting in a way that you find inconsistent with their "normal" behavior; their grades have slipped or they're missing classes; your friend has changed from being "the person you

> **☞ Remember!!**
>
> It's ultimately up to your friend to make that change and you can't do that for him. Sometimes, as much as you may try to get your friend to quit or seek help, you just can't seem to make it happen. If this becomes the situation you are in, you should do one of the following:
>
> - Seek support from other friends or trusted adults—your friend is not the only one who needs help in this situation.
>
> - Limit the time you spend with your drug or alcohol-using friend. Remember your friend's use may also be putting you at risk.
>
> - Start thinking about yourself—get out and participate in activities that you enjoy to take your mind off of the situation.

know" to someone who is getting into trouble at home, or school, or in the community; or simply, you have noticed your friend has become quiet and secretive. Tell them you miss them and that you're concerned about them and that's why you want to talk. You may also decide that writing a note to your friend might be an appropriate first step.

Listen

After presenting your side of the story, ask your friend for his/her response to the information you've presented. Listen to your friend. Hear what he/she is saying. Offer your help or ask them if they think they need a professional's help.

Continue The Conversation

Determine a time when you and your friend will follow up about the discussion. Talking to your friend about drugs may be a continuous process—not a one-time event. Let your friend know that you'd like to touch base about the situation again in the near future because you care about them. And, for you, don't be afraid to ask an adult who you can trust for help.

Talking To A Parent Or Supportive Adult

If you decide that your friend's problem is bigger than both of you, it may be time to bring the issue up with your parents, your friend's parents, or another supportive adult (coach, doctor, etc.). Keep in mind that only you know the people and relationships involved. Talking to a counselor about this decision may also be a good idea if you're not sure how your parents or your friend's parents will react.

It's Not Your Fault

Helping a friend with a drug or alcohol problem is hard work and can be a very difficult experience for you as well as your friend. You may feel a great deal of pressure to get your friend to stop drinking or doing drugs. Or you may get discouraged if your efforts to convince your friend to stop using drugs or alcohol don't work. But it is important to know that your friend's drug or alcohol use is not your fault.

Part Seven
Children Of Alcoholics

Chapter 35

Important Facts For Children Of Alcoholics

National Association for Children of Alcoholics believes that no child of an alcoholic should grow up in isolation and without support.

Alcoholism Affects The Entire Family

Living with a non-recovering alcoholic in the family can contribute to stress for all members of the family. Each member may be affected differently. Not all alcoholic families experience or react to this stress in the same way. The level of dysfunction or resiliency of the non-alcoholic spouse is a key factor in the effects of problems impacting children.

- Children raised in alcoholic families have different life experiences than children raised in non-alcoholic families. However, children raised in other types of dysfunctional families may have similar developmental losses and stressors as do children raised in alcoholic families.

- Children living with a non-recovering alcoholic score lower on measures of family cohesion, intellectual-cultural orientation, active-recreational orientation, and independence. They also usually experience higher levels of conflict within the family.

About This Chapter: Text in this chapter is from "Children of Alcoholics: Important Facts," Copyright 1998 National Association for Children of Alcoholics. Reprinted with permission. Reviewed in September, 2004 by Dr. David A. Cooke, MD, Diplomate, American Board of Internal Medicine.

- Many children of alcoholics (COAs) experience other family members as distant and non-communicative.

- Children of alcoholics may be hampered by their inability to grow in developmentally healthy ways.

References

Chafetz, M.E.; Blane, H.T.; Hill, M.F. Children of Alcoholics: Observational child guidance clinic. *Quarterly Journal Studies on Alcoholism.* 32:687-698, 1971.

Filstead, W.; McElfresh, O.; Anderson, C. Comparing the family environment of alcoholic and normal families. *Journal of Alcohol and Drug Education.* 26:24-31, 1981.

Moss, R.H.; Billinop, A.B. Children of alcoholics during the recovery process: Alcoholic and matched control families. *Addictive Behaviors.* 7:115-164, 1982.

Orford, J. Impact of alcoholism on family and home. In Edwards, G. and Grant, M. *Alcoholism: New Knowledge and New Response.* Baltimore, Md.: University Park Press, 1976.

Wilson, C.; Orford, J. Children of Alcoholics: Report of a preliminary study and comments on the literature. *Journal of Studies on Alcohol.* 39: 121-142, 1978.

Windle, Michael. Concepts and Issues in COA Research. *Alcohol Health and Research World.* Vol. 21. No. 3:185-191. 1997.

♣ It's A Fact!!

- In 2002, almost 5 million adults were alcohol-dependent or alcohol-abusing and had at least one child younger than age 18 living in their home.

- Parents dependent on or abusing alcohol in the past year were more likely to have smoked cigarettes or used illicit drugs than parents who were not dependent on or had not abused alcohol.

- Parents with past year alcohol dependence or abuse were more likely to report household turbulence than parents who were not alcohol-dependent or alcohol-abusing.

Source: "Alcohol Dependence or Abuse Among Parents with Children Living in the Home," Substance Abuse and Mental Health Services Administration—Office of Applied Studies (SAMHSA-OAS), February 2004.

Exposure To Alcoholism

Many people report being exposed to alcoholism in their families.

- Seventy-six million Americans, about 43% of the U.S. adult population, have been exposed to alcoholism in the family.

- Almost one in five adult Americans (18%) lived with an alcoholic while growing up.

- Roughly one in eight American adult drinkers is alcoholic or experiences problems due to the use of alcohol. The cost to society is estimated at in excess of $166 billion each year.

- There are an estimated 26.8 million COAs in the United States. Preliminary research suggests that over 11 million are under the age of 18.

References

Cotton, N.S. The familiar incidence of alcoholism: A review. *Journal of Studies on Alcohol*. 40:89-116. 1979.

Eigen, L.; Rowden, D. A Methodology and Current Estimate of the Number of Children of Alcoholics in the United States. *Children of Alcoholics: Selected Readings*, Rockville, MD: National Association for Children of Alcoholics (NACoA), 1996.

"Exposure to Alcoholism in the Family: United States, 1988," a report based on a survey by the National Center for Health Statistics and the National Institute on Alcohol Abuse and Alcoholism, 1991.

Harwood, H.; Fountain, D.; Livermore, G. *The Economic Costs of Alcohol and Drug Abuse in the United States: 1992*. Report prepared for the National Institute on Drug Abuse and the National Institute on Alcohol Abuse and Alcoholism, National Institutes of Health, Department of Health and Human Services. NIH Publication No. 98-4327. Rockville, MD: National Institutes of Health, 1998.

Alcoholism Runs In Families

There is strong, scientific evidence that alcoholism tends to run in families. Children of alcoholics are more at risk for alcoholism and other drug abuse than children of non-alcoholics.

- Genetic factors play a major role in the development of alcoholism. There is an expanding base of literature which strongly supports a heritable basis for alcoholism and a range of family influences that may direct the development of children of alcoholics.

> ♣ **It's A Fact!!**
>
> Children of alcoholics are four times more likely than non-COAs to develop alcoholism.

- Children's perceptions of parental drinking quantity and circumstances appear to influence their own drinking frequency.

- Children's alcohol expectancies reflect recognition of alcohol-related norms and a cognizance of parental drinking patterns by a very early age.

- Alcohol expectancies appear to be one of the mechanisms explaining the relationship between paternal alcoholism and heavy drinking among offspring during college.

- Parental alcoholism and other drug dependencies have an impact upon children's early learning about alcohol and other drugs.

- Family interaction patterns also may influence the COA's risk for alcohol abuse. It has been found that families with an alcoholic parent displayed more negative family interaction during problem-solving discussions than in non-alcoholic families.

- Almost one-third of any sample of alcoholics has at least one parent who also was or is an alcoholic.

- Children of alcoholics are more likely than non-COAs to marry into families in which alcoholism is prevalent.

- Parental alcoholism influences adolescent substance use through several different pathways including stress, negative affect, and decreased parental monitoring. Negative affect and impaired parental monitoring are associated with adolescent's joining in a peer network that supports drug use behavior.

- After drinking alcohol, sons of alcoholics experience more of the physiological changes associated with pleasurable effects compared with sons of non-alcoholics, although only immediately after drinking.

References

Claydon, P. Self-reported alcohol, drug and eating-disorder problems among male and female collegiate children of alcoholics. *Journal of American College Health*. 36:111-116. 1987.

Cotton, N.S. The familiar incidence of alcoholism: A review. *Journal of Studies on Alcohol*. 40:89-116. 1979.

Ellis, Deborah, A.; Zucker, Robert, A.; Fitzgerald, Hiram, E. The Role of Family Influences in Development and Risk. *Alcohol Health and Research World*. Vol. 21, No. 3:218-225. 1997.

Eigen, L.: Rowden, D. A Methodology and Current Estimate of the Number of Children of Alcoholics in the United States. *Children of Alcoholics: Selected Readings*, Rockville, MD: National Association for Children of Alcoholics (NACoA), 1996.

Finn, Peter, R.; Justus, Alicia. Physiological Responses in Sons of Alcoholics. *Alcohol Health and Research World*. Vol. 21, No. 3:227-231. 1997.

Jacob, Theodore; Johnson, Sheri. Parenting Influences on the Development of Alcohol Abuse and Dependence. *Alcohol Health and Research World*. Vol. 21, No. 3:204-209. 1997.

Johnson, S.; Leonard, K.E.; Jacob, T. Drinking, drinking styles and drug use in children of alcoholics, depressives and controls. *Journal of Studies on Alcohol*. 50:427-431. 1989.

Windle, Michael. Concepts and Issues in COA Research. *Alcohol Health and Research World*. Vol. 21, No. 3:185-191. 1997.

Zucker, R.A.; Kincaid, S.B.; Fitzgerald, H.E.; and Bingham, C.R. Alcohol schema acquisition in preschoolers: Differences between children of alcoholics and children of non-alcoholic. *Alcoholism: Clinical and Experimental Research*. 19:1011-1017. 1975.

Alcoholism And Marriage

Alcoholism usually has strong negative effect on marital relationships.

- Separated and divorced men and women were three times as likely as married men and women to say they had been married to an alcoholic or problem drinker.

- Almost two-thirds of separated and divorced women, and almost half of separated or divorced men, under age 46, have been exposed to alcoholism in the family at some time.

✎ Weird Words

Negative Affect: A bad influence or change.

Physiological Changes: Changes to a person's normal physical functions.

Cohesion: Sticking or holding something together.

Hoarding: Keeping something, often secretively, for oneself.

Phobia: A strong fear of something.

Inpatient Admission Rate: The number of people admitted to the hospital during a set time period.

Abstract (Abstraction): Difficult to understand, such as a concept that is not able to be seen with the eyes.

Cognitive: Mental process of thinking and processing information.

Reference

"Exposure to Alcoholism in the Family: United States, 1988," a report based on a survey by the National Center for Health Statistics and the National Institute on Alcohol Abuse and Alcoholism, 1991.

Alcohol And Violence

Alcohol is associated with a substantial proportion of human violence, and perpetrators are often under the influence of alcohol.

> ✤ **It's A Fact!!**
>
> COAs may be more likely to be the targets of physical abuse and to witness family violence.

- Alcohol is a key factor in 68% of murders, 62% of assaults, 54% of murders and attempted murders, 48% of robberies, and 44% of burglaries.

- Studies of family violence frequently document high rates of alcohol and other drug involvement.

- Compared with non-alcoholic families, alcoholic families demonstrate poorer problem-solving abilities, both among the parents and within the family as a whole. These poor communication and problem-solving skills may be mechanisms through which lack of cohesion and increased conflict develop and grow in alcoholic families.

- COAs are more at risk for disruptive behavioral problems and are more likely than non-COAs to be sensation seeking, aggressive, and impulsive.

References

Ninth Special Report to the U.S. Congress on Alcohol and Health, Secretary of Health and Human Services. 1997.

Jacob, Theodore; Johnson, Sheri. Parenting Influences on the Development of Alcohol Abuse and Dependence. *Alcohol Health and Research World*. Vol. 21, No. 3:204-209. 1997.

Sher, Kenneth, J. Psychological Characteristics of Children of Alcoholics. *Alcohol Health and Research World*. Vol. 21, No. 3:247-253. 1997.

Widom, C.S. "Child Abuse and Alcohol Use." Research Monograph 24: *Alcohol and Interpersonal Violence: Fostering Multi-disciplinary Perspectives.* Rockville, Md.: National Institute on Alcohol Abuse and Alcoholism, 1993.

Alcoholism And Child Abuse

Based on clinical observations and preliminary research, a relationship between parental alcoholism and child abuse is indicated in a large proportion of child abuse cases.

- A significant number of children in this country are being raised by addicted parents. With more than one million children confirmed each year as victims of child abuse and neglect by state child protective service

Table 35.1. Percentages of Parents Aged 18 Or Older Reporting Past Year Household Turbulence, by Past Year Alcohol Dependence Or Abuse: 2002

	Past Year Alcohol Dependence Or Abuse	No Past Year Alcohol Dependence Or Abuse
People In Household Often Insult Or Yell At Each Other	40.4	27.3
People In Household Have Serious Arguments	29.8	18.2
Spouse/Partner Hit Or Threaten To Hit One Or More Times	11.8	4.6
Hit Or Threaten To Hit Spouse/ Partner One Or More Times	9.9	3.6

Source: "Alcohol Dependence or Abuse Among Parents with Children Living in the Home," Substance Abuse and Mental Health Services Administration Office of Applied Studies (SAMHSA-OAS), February 2004.

agencies, state welfare records have indicated that substance abuse is one of the top two problems exhibited by families in 81% of the reported cases.

- Studies suggest an increased prevalence of alcoholism among parents who abuse children.

- Existing research suggests alcoholism is more strongly related to child abuse than are other disorders, such as parental depression.

- Although several studies report very high rates of alcoholism among the parents of incest victims, much additional research is needed in this area.

References

Bavolek, S.J.; Henderson, H.L. Child maltreatment and alcohol abuse: Comparisons and perspectives for treatment. In R.T. Potter-Efron and P.S. Potter-Efron. (Eds.) *Aggression, Family Violence and Chemical Dependency*, 165-184. Binghamton: Haworth, 1990.

Famularo, R.; Stone, K.; Barnum, R.; Wharton, R. Alcoholism and severe child maltreatment. *American Journal of Orthopsychiatry*. 56:481-485. 1986.

Hamilton, C.J.; and Collins, J.J., Jr. The role of alcohol in wife beating and child abuse: A review of the literature. In Collins, J.J. (Ed.) *Drinking and crime: Perspectives on the relationship between alcohol consumption and criminal behavior*. 253-287. New York: Guilford, 1985.

Lung, C.T.; Daro, D. *Current trends in child abuse reporting and fatalities*. The results of the 1995 annual fifty state survey. Chicago, IL: National Committee to Prevent Child Abuse. 1976.

Russell, M.; Henderson, C.; Blume, S. *Children of alcoholics: A review of the literature*. New York, NY: Children of Alcoholics Foundation, Inc. 1985.

Depression And Anxiety

Children of alcoholics exhibit symptoms of depression and anxiety more than children of non-alcoholics.

- In general, COAs appear to have lower self-esteem than non-COAs in childhood, adolescence, and young adulthood.

- Children of alcoholics exhibit elevated rates of psychopathology. Anxiety, depression, and externalizing behavior disorders are more common among COAs than among children of non-alcoholics.

Young COAs often show symptoms of depression and anxiety such as crying, bed wetting, not having friends, being afraid to go to school, or having nightmares. Older youth may stay in their rooms for long periods of time and not relate to other children claiming they "have no one to talk to." Teens may show depressive symptoms by being perfectionistic in their endeavors, hoarding, staying by themselves, and being excessively self-conscious. Teenage COAs may begin to develop phobias.

References

Ellis, Deborah, A.; Zucker, Robert, A.; Fitzgerald, Hiram, E. The Role of Family Influences in Development and Risk. *Alcohol Health and Research World*. Vol. 21, No. 3:218-225. 1997.

Johnson, J.; Rolf, J.E. Cognitive functioning in children from alcoholic and non-alcoholic families. *Journal of Addictions*. 83:849-857. 1988.

Sher, K.J. *Children of Alcoholics: A Critical Appraisal of Theory and Research*. Chicago: University of Chicago Press, 1991.

Physical And Mental Health Problems

Children of alcoholics experience greater physical and mental health problems and higher health care costs than children from non-alcoholic families.

- Inpatient admission rates for substance abuse are triple that of other children.

- Inpatient admission rates for mental disorders are almost double that of other children.

- Injuries are more than one and one-half times greater than those of other children.

- The rate of total health care costs for children of alcoholics is 32% greater than children from non-alcoholic families.

References

Children of Alcoholics Foundation. *Children of Alcoholics in the Medical System: Hidden Problems and Hidden Cost.* 1988.

Nixon, Sara Jo; Tivis, Laura J. Neuropsychological Responses in COAs. *Alcohol Health and Research World.* Vol. 21, No. 3:232-235. 1997.

Verbal Ability

Children of alcoholics score lower on tests measuring verbal ability.

- COAs tend to score lower on tests that measure cognitive and verbal skills. Their ability to express themselves may be impaired, which can slow down their school performance, peer relationships, ability to develop and sustain intimate relationships, and hamper performance on job interviews.

- Low verbal scores, however, should not imply that COAs are intellectually impaired.

References

Ervin, C.S.; Little, R.E.; Streissguth, A.P. Alcoholic fathering and its relations to a child's intellectual development: A pilot investigation. *Alcoholism: Clinical and Experimental Research.* 8:363-365. 1980.

Drejer, K.; Theilgaard, A.; Teasdale, T.W. A prospective study of young men at high risk for alcoholism: Neuropsychological assessment. *Alcoholism: Clinical and Experimental Research.* 9:948-502. 1985.

Gabrielli, W.F.; Mednic, S.A. Intellectual performance in children of alcoholics. *Journal of Nervous and Mental Disease.* 171:444-447. 1983.

School Difficulties

Children of alcoholics often have difficulties in school.

- COAs often believe that they will be failures even if they do well academically. They often do not view themselves as successful.

- Children of alcoholics are more likely to be raised by parents with poorer cognitive abilities and in an environment lacking stimulation. A lack of stimulation in the rearing environment may account in part for the pattern of failure found in COAs compared with non-COAs.

- Pre-school aged COAs exhibited poorer language and reasoning skills than did non-COAs, and poorer performance among the COAs was predicted by the lower quality of stimulation present in the home.

- COAs are more likely to be truant, drop out of school, repeat grades, or be referred to a school counselor, or psychologist. This may have little to do with academic ability; rather, COAs may have difficulty bonding with teachers, other students, and school; they may experience anxiety related to performance; or they may be afraid of failure. The actual reasons have yet to be determined.

- There is an increasing body of scientific evidence indicating that risk for later problems, and even alcoholic outcomes is detectable early in the life course and, in some instances, before school entry.

References

Caspi, A.; Moffitt, T.E.; Newman, D.L.; Sylvia, P.A. Behavioral observations at age 3 predict adult psychiatric disorder: Longitudinal evidence from a birth cohort. *Archives of General Psychiatry*. 53:1022-1035. 1996.

Johnson, J.; Rolf, J.E. Cognitive functioning in children from alcoholic and non-alcoholic families. *Journal of Addictions*. 83:849-857. 1988.

Attention Span And Reasoning

Children of alcoholics have greater difficulty with abstraction and conceptual reasoning.

- Abstraction and conceptual reasoning play an important role in problem solving, whether the problems are academic or are situation related to the problems of life. Therefore, children of alcoholics might require very concrete explanations and instructions.

References

Schaefer, K.W.; Parsons, O.A.; Vohman, J.R. Neuropsychological differences between male familial and nonfamilial alcoholics and non-alcoholics. *Alcoholism: Clinical and Experimental Research*. 8:347-351. 1984.

Tarter, R.E.; Hegedus, A.M.; Goldstein, G.; Shelly, C.; Alterman, A.I. Adolescent sons of alcoholics: Neuropsychological and personality characteristics. *Alcoholism: Clinical and Experimental Research*. 8:216-222. 1985.

♣ **It's A Fact!!**

"Children living in homes with alcohol-dependent or abusing parents are at high risk of also becoming alcohol and drug abusers, with the potential of perpetuating the disease when they have their own children," SAMHSA Administrator Charles Curie said. "The good news is children of alcoholic parents can be helped to build on their strengths and develop resilience to overcome their difficulties. We must also reach out to the parents and offer them an opportunity for recovery by encouraging them to enter and remain in substance abuse treatment."

Source: "Five Million Parents Have Alcohol Problems," Press Release, Substance Abuse and Mental Services Administration (SAMHSA), February 11, 2004.

Adult Mentors

Children of alcoholics may benefit from adult efforts which help them to:

- Develop autonomy and independence.

- Develop a strong social orientation and social skills.

- Engage in acts of "required helpfulness."

- Develop a close bond with a caregiver.

- Cope successfully with emotionally hazardous experiences.

- Perceive their experiences constructively, even if those experiences cause pain or suffering, and if early in life they gain other people's positive attention.

- Develop day-to-day coping strategies.

☞ **Remember!!**
Children of alcoholics can overcome their difficult home situation, especially with the help of other adults or support groups like Alateen.

Reference

Werner, E.E. Resilient children. *Young Children*. 40:68-72. 1984.

Protection

Children can be protected from many problems associated with growing up in an alcoholic family.

- If healthy family rituals or traditions, such as vacations, mealtimes, or holidays, are highly valued and maintained, if the active alcoholic is confronted with his or her problem, if there are consistent significant others in the life of the child or children, and if there is moderate to high religious observance, children can be protected from many of the consequences of parental alcoholism.

Reference

Wolin, S.J.; Bennett, L.A.; Noonan, D.L.; et. al. Disrupted family rituals: A factor in the intergenerational transmission of alcoholism. *Journal of Studies on Alcohol*. 41:199-214. 1980.

Alcohol And Pregnancy

Maternal alcohol consumption during any time of pregnancy can cause alcohol related birth defects or alcohol related neurological deficits.

- The rate of drinking during pregnancy appears to be increasing. Prenatal alcohol effects have been detected at moderate levels of alcohol consumption by non-alcoholic women. Even though a mother is not an alcoholic, her child may not be spared the effects of prenatal alcohol exposure.

- Cognitive performance is less affected by alcohol exposure in infants and children whose mothers stopped drinking in early pregnancy, despite the mothers' resumption of alcohol use after giving birth.

- One analysis of 6 year-olds, with demonstrated effects of second-trimester alcohol exposure, had lower academic achievement and problems with reading, spelling, and mathematical skills.

- Approximately 6 percent of the offspring of alcoholic women have Fetal Alcohol Syndrome (FAS); the FAS risk for offspring born after an FAS sibling, is as high as 70 percent.

- Those diagnosed as having Fetal Alcohol Syndrome had IQ scores ranging from 20–105 with a mean of 68. Subjects also demonstrated poor concentration and attention.

- People with FAS demonstrate growth deficits, physical abnormalities, mental retardation, and behavioral difficulties. Secondary effects of FAS among adolescents and adults include mental health problems, disrupted schooling (dropping out or being suspended or expelled), trouble with the law, dependent living as an adult, and problems with employment.

References

Gabrielli, W.F.; Mednic, S.A. Intellectual performance in children of alcoholics. *Journal of Nervous and Mental Disease.* 171:444-447. 1983.

Jacobson, Sandra W. Assessing the Impact of Maternal Drinking During and After Pregnancy. *Alcohol Health and Research World.* Vol. 21, No. 3:199-203. 1997.

Larkby, Cynthia; Day, Nancy. The Effects of Prenatal Alcohol Exposure. *Alcohol Health and Research World.* Vol. 21, No. 3:192-197. 1997.

Chapter 36

Coping With An Alcoholic Parent

Anthony is already in bed when he hears the front door slam. He covers his head with his pillow to drown out the predictable sounds of his parents arguing. Anthony is all too aware that his father has been drinking and his mother is angry.

Many teens like Anthony live with a parent who is an alcoholic, a person physically and emotionally addicted to alcohol. Alcoholism has been around for centuries, yet no one has discovered how to prevent or stop it. Alcoholism continues to cause anguish not only for the person who drinks, but for everyone who is involved with that person.

According to the National Council on Alcoholism and Drug Dependence (NCADD), there are nearly 14 million Americans who are considered problem drinkers (including 8 million who have alcoholism) and 76 million people who are exposed to alcoholism in family settings. Although these numbers show a huge number of problem drinkers, they also show that people who live with alcoholic family members are not alone.

About This Chapter: This information was provided by TeensHealth, one of the largest resources online for medically reviewed health information written for parents, kids, and teens. For more articles like this one, visit www.TeensHealth.org. or www.KidsHealth.org. © 2004 The Nemours Center for Children's Health Media, a division of The Nemours Foundation.

Why Does My Parent Drink?

Alcoholism is a disease. Like any disease, it needs to be treated. Without professional help, an alcoholic will probably continue to drink and may become worse over time.

Just like any other disease, alcoholism is no one's fault. Some people who live with alcoholics blame themselves for their loved one's drinking. But the truth is, that person would drink anyway. If your parent drinks, it won't change

♣ **It's A Fact!!**

Alateen Helps Young People Cope With Alcoholics

Alcoholism is a worldwide issue, causing problems not only for the drinker but for everyone else connected with that person as well. There are more than 20 million alcoholics in the United States and Canada alone, many of them with children troubled by their parents' drinking. Often, these young people have nowhere to turn for help.

This is where Alateen comes in. Alateen is a fellowship of young relatives and friends of alcoholics who come together to discuss their difficulties, encourage one another, and learn how to cope with their problems. These young people are often introduced to Alateen by concerned friends, neighbors, school counselors, or clergy.

Alateen is part of the Al-Anon Family Groups which helps those whose lives have been affected by someone else's drinking. Alateen members learn that compulsive drinking is a disease, an incurable illness which they did not cause, cannot cure, or control.

One of the most important lessons Alateen teaches is how to detach oneself emotionally from the drinker's problems while continuing to love the person.

Like Al-Anon, Alateen is based on the Twelve Steps of Alcoholics Anonymous which members discuss and apply to their own attitudes and relationship

anything if you do better in school, help more around the house, or do any of the other things you may believe your parent wants you to do.

Other people may tell themselves that their parents drink because of some other problem, such as having a rough time at work or being out of work altogether. Parents may be having marital problems, financial problems, or someone may be sick. But even if an alcoholic parent has other problems, nothing you can do will make things better. No one else can help an alcoholic get well.

with others. This can help the Alateen member develop strength to deal with problems maturely and realistically.

Alateen members meet in church halls, school rooms, or other suitable places, often in the same building as an Al-Anon group but in a separate room. What is said there and who attends the meetings is held in the strictest confidence.

With anonymity the watchword, Alateen members share their experiences, strengths, and hopes.

"I used to get so angry all the time. It just made me feel like a crazy person," said one Alateen member. "I'd want to grab somebody and squeeze the life right out of them. Then somebody in one of my Alateen meetings suggested that we try safe ways to express our anger. I didn't even know there were safe ways to be angry. He suggested that when I got real mad at somebody I could try writing their name on the bottom of my shoe. Then, I could spend the whole day walking on them. It works."

The Alateen program has worked for the tens of thousands of youngsters who meet in over 2,300 groups worldwide. Call 888-425-2666 for meeting information or refer to your local telephone directory. Visit the Al-Anon/Alateen web site at http://www.al-anon.alateen.org.

Source: © 2004 Reprinted by permission of Al-Anon Family Group Headquarters.

Why Won't My Parent Stop Drinking?

Denial can play a big role in an alcoholic's life. A person in denial is one who refuses to believe the truth about a situation. A problem drinker may blame another person for the drinking because it is easier than taking responsibility for it. Some alcoholic parents make their kids feel bad by saying things like, "You're driving me crazy!" or "I can't take this anymore." An alcoholic parent may become enraged at the slightest suggestion that drinking is a problem. Those who acknowledge their drinking may show their denial by saying, "I can stop any time I want to," "Everyone drinks to unwind sometimes," or "My drinking is not a problem."

Why Do I Feel So Bad?

If you're like most teens, your life is probably filled with emotional ups and downs, regardless of what's happening at home. Add an alcoholic parent to this tumultuous time and a person's bound to feel overwhelmed. Some of the emotions teens with alcoholic parents report feeling are anger, sadness, embarrassment, loneliness, helplessness, and a lack of self-esteem.

These emotions can be triggered by the added burdens of living with an alcoholic parent. For example, many alcoholics behave unpredictably, and kids growing up with alcoholic parents may spend a lot of energy trying to feel out a parent's mood or guess what he or she wants. One day you might walk on eggshells to avoid an outburst because the dishes aren't done or the lawn mowed; the next day, you may find yourself comforting a parent who promises that things will be better. The pressure to manage these situations in addition to your own life—and maybe take care of younger siblings, too—can leave you exhausted and drained.

Although alcoholism causes similar patterns of damage to many families, each situation is unique. Some alcoholics abuse their children emotionally or physically. Others neglect their children by not providing sufficient nurturing and guidance. Drugs may be involved. Your family may have money troubles. And although each family is different, teens with alcoholic parents almost always report feeling alone, unloved, depressed, or burdened by the secret life they lead at home. Because it's not possible to control the behavior of an alcoholic, what can a person do to feel better?

What Can I Do?

Teenage children of alcoholics are at a higher risk of becoming alcoholics themselves. Acknowledging the problem and reaching out for support can help ensure that your future does not repeat your parent's past.

Acknowledge the problem. An alcoholic parent is never the child's fault. Many children of alcoholics try to hide the problem or find themselves telling lies to cover up for a parent's drinking. Admitting that your parent has a problem—even if he or she won't—is the first step in taking control.

Being aware of how your parent's drinking affects you can help put things in perspective. For example, some teens who live with alcoholic adults become afraid to speak out or show any normal anger or emotion because they worry it may trigger a parent's drinking binge. This can erode self-esteem. Acknowledging feelings of anger or resentment—even if it's just to yourself or a close friend—can help protect against this. Recognizing the emotions that go with the problem can also help you from suppressing your feelings and pretending that everything is okay.

Likewise, realizing that you are not the cause of a parent's drinking problem can help you feel better about yourself.

Find support. It's good to share your feelings with a friend, but it's equally important to talk to an adult you trust. A school counselor, favorite teacher, or coach may be able to help. Some teens turn to their school D.A.R.E. (Drug and Alcohol Resistance Education) officer, whereas others find a sympathetic uncle or aunt.

Because alcoholism is such a widespread problem, several organizations offer confidential support groups and meetings for people living with alcoholics. Al-Anon, an organization designed to help the families and friends of alcoholics, has a group called Alateen that is specifically geared to young people living with adults who have drinking problems. Alateen is not only for children of alcoholics, it can also help teens whose parents may already be in recovery. Another group called Alcoholics Anonymous (AA) also offers a variety of programs and resources for people living with alcoholics.

You're not betraying your parent by seeking help. Keeping "the secret" is part of the disease of alcoholism—and it allows the problems to get worse. As with any disease, it's still possible to love a parent while recognizing that he or she has alcoholism. And it's not disloyal to seek help in dealing with the problems your parent's drinking create for you.

Find a safe environment. If you find yourself avoiding your house as much as possible, or if you're thinking about running away, consider whether you feel in danger at home. If you feel that the situation at home is becoming dangerous, you can call the National Domestic Violence Hotline at 800-799-SAFE. And never hesitate to dial 911 if you think you or another family member is in immediate danger.

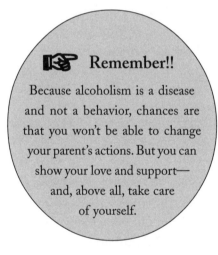

☞ Remember!!

Because alcoholism is a disease and not a behavior, chances are that you won't be able to change your parent's actions. But you can show your love and support— and, above all, take care of yourself.

Chapter 37

Breaking The Family Cycle Of Addiction

A Family History Of Alcoholism

If you are among the millions of people in this country who have a parent, grandparent, or other close relative with alcoholism, you may have wondered what your family's history of alcoholism means for you. Are problems with alcohol a part of your future? Is your risk for becoming an alcoholic greater than for people who do not have a family history of alcoholism? If so, what can you do to lower your risk?

Many scientific studies, including research conducted among twins and children of alcoholics, have shown that genetic factors influence alcoholism. These findings show that children of alcoholics are about four times more likely than the general population to develop alcohol problems. Children of alcoholics also have a higher risk for many other behavioral and emotional problems. But alcoholism is not determined only by the genes you inherit from your parents. In fact, more than one-half of all children of alcoholics do not become alcoholic. Research shows that many factors influence your risk of developing alcoholism. Some factors raise the risk while others lower it.

About This Chapter: Text in this chapter is from "A Family History of Alcoholism," National Institute of Alcohol Abuse and Alcoholism (NIAAA), NIH Publication No. 03–5340, 3/2003. Additional text under its own heading is from "Breaking the Cycle of Addiction," Substance Abuse and Mental Health Services Administration–National Clearinghouse for Alcohol and Drug Information (SAMHSA–NCADI).

✔ Quick Tip
Lower Your Risk For Becoming An Alcoholic

If you are worried that your family's history of alcohol problems or your troubled family life puts you at risk for becoming alcoholic, here is some commonsense advice to help you:

Avoid underage drinking—First, underage drinking is illegal. Second, research shows that the risk for alcoholism is higher among people who begin to drink at an early age, perhaps as a result of both environmental and genetic factors.

Drink moderately as an adult—Even if they do not have a family history of alcoholism, adults who choose to drink alcohol should do so in moderation—no more than one drink a day for most women, and no more than two drinks a day for most men, according to guidelines from the U.S. Department of Agriculture and the U.S. Department of Health and Human Services. Even some adults should not drink at all, including women who are pregnant or who are trying to become pregnant, recovering alcoholics, people who plan to drive or engage in other activities that require attention or skill, people taking certain medications, and people with certain medical conditions.

Adults over 21 with a family history of alcoholism, who have a higher risk for becoming dependent on alcohol, should approach moderate drinking carefully. Maintaining moderate drinking habits may be harder for them than for people without a family history of drinking problems. Once a person moves from moderate to heavier drinking, the risks of social problems (for example, drinking and driving, violence, and trauma) and medical problems (for example, liver disease, brain damage, and cancer) increase greatly.

Talk to a health care professional—Discuss your concerns with a doctor, nurse, nurse practitioner, or other health care provider. They can recommend groups or organizations that could help you avoid alcohol problems. If you are an adult who already has begun to drink, a health care professional can assess your drinking habits to see if you need to cut back on your drinking and advise you about how to do that.

Genes are not the only things children inherit from their parents. How parents act and how they treat each other and their children has an influence on children growing up in the family. These aspects of family life also affect the risk for alcoholism. Researchers believe a person's risk increases if he or she is in a family with the following difficulties:

- An alcoholic parent is depressed or has other psychological problems.

- Both parents abuse alcohol and other drugs.

- The parents' alcohol abuse is severe.

- Conflicts lead to aggression and violence in the family.

The good news is that many children of alcoholics from even the most troubled families do not develop drinking problems. Just as a family history of alcoholism does not guarantee that you will become an alcoholic, neither does growing up in a very troubled household with alcoholic parents. Just because alcoholism tends to run in families does not mean that a child of an alcoholic parent will automatically become an alcoholic too. The risk is higher, but it does not have to happen.

Breaking The Cycle Of Addiction

According to the Substance Abuse and Mental Health Services Administration (SAMHSA), part of the U.S. Department of Health and Human Services, children of alcohol-addicted parents can suffer from physical illness and injury, emotional disturbances, educational deficits, behavior problems, and alcoholism or alcohol abuse later in life. Perhaps most troubling, however, is the fact that children of alcoholics (COAs) are two to four times more likely to become problem drinkers and continue the addictive practices of their parents with similar devastating consequences.[1]

SAMHSA Administrator Charles G. Curie urges every adult to learn about the needs of COAs and the simple actions they can take to help COAs develop into healthy adults. "We know that COAs are at greater risk for substance abuse problems in their own lives. But we also know what to do to help them avoid repeating their family's problems. We can break the generational cycle of alcoholism in families."

That's good news for the millions of children in the United States who live in households in which one or both parents have been actively alcohol dependent in the past. Experts say COAs can be helped, whether or not the alcohol-abusing adults in their families receive treatment. Adult relatives, older siblings, and other adults who have contact with COAs at school, in the community, through faith-based organizations, and through health and social services agencies do not need formal training or special skills to be caring and supportive.

To help a child of an alcoholic, one must take that first step—show care for a child with an alcoholic parent. Since research shows that one in four children lives in a family with alcoholism or alcohol abuse, many adults will not have to look far to find a child to help.

Curie said, "Perhaps the best way adults can help COAs is to provide them with accurate information about alcoholism to help them develop the skills needed to cope with their day-to-day challenges." He added, "Accurate information helps COAs understand that alcoholism is a disease that has nothing to do with them—they are not to blame for the disruptions and other problems happening at home. It clarifies and validates their reality and shows them the choices they can make to be safe and healthy."

According to the National Association for Children of Alcoholics, the life skills that COAs need often are learned outside the family and can be gained through educational support groups and healthy relationships with others, especially adults who show they care about the children. By providing these children with experiences in which they have opportunities to succeed, COAs can learn to respect themselves, which in turn helps them cope with their situations.

Almost every community has resources to help make a difference in the lives of COAs. Services such as educational support groups and counseling are widespread across the country. Free publications, including *It's Not Your Fault* and *You Can Help*, available from SAMHSA's National Clearinghouse for Alcohol and Drug Information, offer important insights and resources for adults who want to help.

Reference

1. Johnson, S; Leonard, K.E.; Jacob, T. (1989). Drinking, drinking styles, and drug use in children of alcoholics, depressives, and controls. *Journal of Studies on Alcohol.* 50:427-431.

☞ Remember!!

The family cycle of alcoholism can be broken. Start by learning coping skills that help you with problems, and decide that you will not drink alcohol before you are 21.

For Additional Information About Breaking The Cycle Of Alcoholism

Al-Anon Family Group Headquarters, Inc.
1600 Corporate Landing Parkway
Virginia Beach, VA 23454
Toll-Free: 888-425-2666
Phone: 757-563-1600
Fax: 613-723-0151
Website: http://www.al-anon.alateen.org
E-mail: WSO@al-anon.org

National Association for Children of Alcoholics
11426 Rockville Pike, Suite 100
Rockville, MD 20852
Toll-Free: 888-554-2627
Phone: 301-468-0985
Fax: 301-468-0987
Website: http://www.childrenofalcoholics.org
E-mail: nacoa@nacoa.org

National Institute on Alcohol Abuse and Alcoholism
5635 Fishers Lane, MSC 9304
Bethesda, MD 20892
Phone: 301-435-0714
Website: http://www.niaaa.nih.gov

Substance Abuse and Mental Health Services Administration (SAMHSA)
5600 Fishers Lane
Rockville, MD 20857
Phone: 301-443-4795
Fax: 301-443-0284
Website: http://www.samhsa.gov

Part Eight

If You Need More Information

Chapter 38

Additional Reading About Alcohol Use And Abuse

Alcohol 101: Overview/Teens
By Margaret O. Hyde, John F. Setaro
Published by 21st Century,
October 1, 1999
ISBN: 0761312749

Alcohol (Teen Decisions)
By William Dudley
Published by Greenhaven Press;
September 1, 2000
ISBN: 073770490X

Alcohol Drug Dangers
By Lawrence, Ph.D. Clayton
Published by Enslow Publishers,
May 1, 1999
ISBN: 0766011593

The Big Deal About Alcohol: What Teens Need to Know About Drinking (Issues in Focus)
By Marilyn McClellan
Published by Enslow Publishers,
June 22, 2004
ISBN: 0766021637

For Teenagers Living With a Parent Who Abuses Alcohol/ Drugs
By Edith Hornik-Beer
Published by Backinprint.com;
Authors Guild Backinprint.
January 1, 2001
ISBN: 059515994X

About This Chapter: The books and web pages in this chapter were selected from a wide variety of sources deemed accurate. Inclusion does not constitute endorsement. To make topics readily apparent, they are listed alphabetically by title within each category.

Life Strategies for Teens
By Jay McGraw
Published by Fireside,
December 4, 2000
ISBN: 074321546X

Real Teens, Real Stories, Real Lives
By T. Suzanne Eller
Published by Chariot Victor Pub.,
November 30, 2002
ISBN: 1589195000

Tackling Tough Choices: Discussion-Starting Skits for Teens (Acting It Out Series)
By Doris Anita Anderson
Published by Resource Publications
(CA), August 1, 2001
ISBN: 0893905186

Teen Alcoholics (Other America)
By Gail Stewart
Published by Lucent Books,
January 1, 2000
ISBN: 1560066067

Teen Alcoholism (Contemporary Issues Companion)
By Laura K. Egendorf, Bonnie
Szumski, Scott Barbour, Brenda
Stalcup
Published by Greenhaven Press,
April 1, 2001
ISBN: 0737706821

Teen Alcoholism (Teen Issues)
By Barbara Sheen
Published by Lucent Books,
January 1, 2004
ISBN: 1590185013

Teens and Alcohol (Current Controversies)
By James D. Torr
Published by Greenhaven Press,
December 1, 2001
ISBN: 073770859X

Teens & Alcohol (Gallup Youth Survey: Major Issues and Trends)
By Gail Snyder
Published by Mason Crest Publishers, April 1, 2004
ISBN: 1590847237

Teens and Drunk Driving (Teen Issues)
By Nathan Aaseng
Published by Lucent Books,
January 1, 2000
ISBN: 1560065184

Websites And Web Page Documents

Addiction Science Made Easy (series)
Addiction Technology Transfer Center
http://www.nattc.org/asme.html

Alcohol/Alcoholism Topics
Do It Now Foundation
http://www.doitnow.org/pages/alcohol.html

Alcohol Alert Series
National Institute on Alcohol Abuse and Alcoholism
http://www.niaaa.nih.gov/publications/alalerts.htm

Alcohol and Teen Drinking
Focus Adolescent Services
http://www.focusas.com/Alcohol.html

Alcohol Cost Calculator for Kids
Ensuring Solutions to Alcohol Problems
http://www.alcoholcostcalculator.org/kids/index2.html

Alcohol-Online Tests
Substance Abuse and Mental Health Services Administration
http://getfit.samhsa.gov/Alcohol/Tests/default.aspx?position=2

Alcohol Policies Project
Center for Science in the Public Interest
http://www.cspinet.org/booze

Alcohol Prevention Research Information
Pacific Institute for Research and Evaluation
http://www.pire.org/categories/Alcohol.asp

Alcohol Screening Day
Screening for Mental Health, Inc.
http://www.nationalalcoholscreeningday.org/alcohol.asp

Campaign for Alcohol-Free Sports TV
Center for Science in the Public Interest
http://cspinet.org/booze/CAFST

Frequently Asked Questions
Ensuring Solutions to Alcohol Problems
http://www.ensuringsolutions.org/pages/faq.html

MADD Youth in Action
Mother Against Drunk Driving (MADD)
http://www.youthinaction.org

National Alcohol and Drug Addiction Recovery Month
Substance Abuse and Mental Health Services Administration
http://www.recoverymonth.gov

Substance Abuse in Your Family
Children of Alcoholics Foundation
http://www.coaf.org/family/familymain.htm

Students Examining the Culture of College Drinking
National Institute on Alcohol Abuse and Alcoholism
http://www.collegedrinkingprevention.gov/Students

Substance Abuse Treatment Facility Locator
Substance Abuse and Mental Health Services Administration
http://www.findtreatment.samhsa.gov

Tips for Teens on Alcohol
National Clearinghouse for Alcohol and Drug Information
http://www.health.org/govpubs/ph323

Too Smart to Start Youth Pages
Substance Abuse and Mental Health Services Administration
http://www.toosmarttostart.samhsa.gov/youth.html

Zero Tolerance Means Zero Chances: Underage Drinking Prevention Program
National Highway Traffic Safety Administration
http://www.nhtsa.dot.gov/people/injury/alcohol/zero

Chapter 39

Support Groups For Alcoholics And Children Of Alcoholics

Adult Children of Alcoholics World Services Organization, Inc.

P.O. Box 3216
Torrance, CA 90510-3216
Phone: 310-534-1815 (message only)
Website: http://adultchildren.org
E-mail: info@adultchildren.org

Alcoholics Anonymous

General Service Office
P.O. Box 459
New York, NY 10163
Phone: 212-870-3400
Website: http://www.alcoholics-anonymous.org

Alcoholics Victorious

Association of Gospel Rescue Missions
1045 Swift St.
Kansas City, MO 64116-4127
Toll-Free: 800-624-5156
Phone: 816-471-8020
Fax: 816-471-3718
Website: http://alcoholicsvictorious.org
E-mail: info@alcoholicsvictorious.org

About This Chapter: Information in this chapter was compiled from sources deemed accurate. All information was updated and verified in September 2004.

Al-Anon/Alateen Family Groups

1600 Corporate Landing Parkway
Virginia Beach, VA 23454
Toll-Free: 888-425-2666
Phone: 757-563-1600
Fax: 613-723-0151
Website: http://www.al-anon
.alateen.org
E-mail: WSO@al-anon.org

Calix Society

Association of Catholic Alcoholics
2555 Hazelwood Ave.
St. Paul, MN 55109
Toll-Free: 800-398-0524
Phone: 651-773-3117
Fax: 651-777-3069
Website: http://
www.calixsociety.org
E-mail: calix@usfamily.net

Chemically Dependent Anonymous

P.O. Box 423
Severna Park, MD 21146-0423
Toll-Free: 888-232-4673
Website: http://www.cdaweb.org

Double Trouble in Recovery, Inc.

Sanity and Sobriety Recovery
P.O. Box 245055
Brooklyn, NY 11224
Phone: 718-373-2684
Website: http://
www.doubletroubleinrecovery.org
E-mail: information@doubletrouble
inrecovery.org

Dual Recovery Anonymous

P.O. Box 8107
Prairie Village, KS 66208
Toll-Free: 877-883-2332
Fax: 615-297-9346
Website: http://draonline.org
E-mail: draws@draonline.org

Families Anonymous

P.O. Box 3475
Culver City, CA 90231-3475
Toll-Free: 800-736-9805
Fax: 310-815-9682
Website: http://
www.FamiliesAnonymous.org
E-mail: famanon@Families
Anonymous.org

JACS (Jewish Alcoholics, Chemically Dependent Persons, and Significant Others)
850 Seventh Ave.
New York, NY 10019
Phone: 212-397-4197
Fax: 212-399-3525
Website: http://www.jacsweb.org
E-mail: jacs@jacsweb.org

LifeRing Secular Recovery
1440 Broadway, Suite 312
Oakland, CA 94612-2029
Phone: 510-763-0779
Website: http://
www.unhooked.com
E-mail: service@lifering.org

Men for Sobriety
P.O. Box 618
Quakertown, PA 18951-0618
Phone: 215-536-8026
Fax: 215-538-9026
E-mail: NewLife@nni.com

Moderation Management Network, Inc.
22 West 27th St.
New York, NY
Phone: 212-871-0974
Fax: 212-213-6582
Website: http://moderation.org
E-mail: mm@moderation.org

Overcomers Outreach, Inc.
P.O. Box 2208
Oakland, CA 93644
Toll-Free: 800-310-3001
Phone: 714-491-3000
Fax: 714-491-3004
Website: http://
www.overcomersoutreach.org
E-mail: info@overcomers
outreach.org

Secular Organizations for Sobriety (Save Ourselves)
4773 Hollywood Blvd.
Hollywood, CA 90027
Phone: 323-666-4295
Fax: 323-666-4271
Website: http://www.cfiwest.org/
sos
E-mail: sos@cfiwest.org

Substance Abuse Treatment Facility Locator
Substance Abuse and Mental
Health Services Administration
(SAMHSA)
5600 Fishers Lane
Rockville, MD 20857
Website: http://www.findtreatment
.samhsa.gov

Women For Sobriety, Inc.

P.O. Box 618
Quakertown, PA 18951-0618
Toll-Free: 800-333-1606
Phone: 215-536-8026
Fax: 215-538-9026
Website: http://
www.womenforsobriety.org/
body.html
E-mail: NewLife@nni.com

Chapter 40

Organizations Providing Information About Alcohol And Alcoholism

Federal Agencies

Centers for Disease Control and Prevention (CDC)
1600 Clifton Road
Atlanta, GA 30333
Toll-Free: 800-311-3435
Phone: 404-639-3311
Website: http://www.cdc.gov

Juvenile Justice Clearinghouse
National Criminal Justice Reference Service
P.O. Box 6000
Rockville, MD 20849
Toll-Free: 800-851-3420
Phone: 301-519-5500
Fax: 301-519-5212
Toll-Free TTY: 877-712-9279
TTY: 301-947-8374
Website: http://virlib.ncjrs.org/
JuvenileJustice.asp
E-mail: askncjrs@ncjrs.org (General questions)

About This Chapter: The list of organizations in this chapter was compiled from many sources deemed accurate. Inclusion does not constitute endorsement. All contact information was verified in August 2004.

National Health Information Center

P.O. Box 1133
Washington, DC 20013
Toll-Free: 800-336-4797
Phone: 301-565-4167
Website: http://www.health.gov/nhic
E-mail: info@nhic.org

National Highway and Traffic Safety Administration (NHTSA)

400 Seventh St., S.W.
NAO-10
Washington, DC 20590
Toll-Free: 800-424-9393
Toll-Free TDD: 800-424-9153
Phone: 202-366-7800
Website: http://www.nhtsa.dot.gov
E-mail: custservice@nhtsa.dot.gov

National Institute on Alcohol Abuse and Alcoholism

5635 Fishers Lane, MSC 9304
Bethesda, MD 20892
Phone: 301-435-0714
Websites: http://
www.niaaa.nih.gov; and http://
www.collegedrinkingprevention.gov

National Institutes of Health

9000 Rockville Pike
Bethesda, MD 20892
Phone: 301-496-4000
Website: http://www.nih.gov
E-mail: NIHinfo@OD.nih.gov

National Youth Anti-Drug Media Campaign

White House Office of National
Drug Control Policy
Drug Policy Information Clearing-
house
P.O. Box 6000
Rockville, MD 20849-6000
Toll-Free: 800-666-3332
Fax: 301-519-6212
Website: http://freevibe.com
E-mail: ondcp@nqrs.org

Safe and Drug-Free Schools

400 Maryland Avenue S.W.
Washington, DC 20202
Toll-Free: 800-624-0100
Phone: 202-260-3954
Website: http://www.ed.gov/
offices/OESE/SDFS
E-mail: safeschl@ed.gov

Substance Abuse and Mental Health Services Administration (SAMHSA)

5600 Fishers Lane
Rockville, MD 20857
Phone: 301-443-4795
Fax: 301-443-0284
Website: http://www.samhsa.gov/
index.aspx

SAMHSA's Center for Substance Abuse Prevention (CSAP)

5600 Fishers Lane
Rockwall II Building, Suite 800
Rockville, MD 20857
Toll-Free: 800-729-6686
Drug-Free Workplace Toll-Free
Help Line: 800-967-5752
Phone: 301-443-0365
Website: http://
prevention.samhsa.gov
E-mail: info@samhsa.gov

SAMHSA's National Clearinghouse for Alcohol and Drug Information

http://www.health.org

Private Organizations, Civic Groups, And Religious Organizations

Al-Anon/Alateen Family Groups

1600 Corporate Landing Parkway
Virginia Beach, VA 23454
Toll-Free: 888-425-2666
Phone: 757-563-1600
Fax: 613-723-0151
Website: http://www.al-anon
.alateen.org
E-mail: WSO@al-anon.org

Alcoholics Anonymous

General Service Office
P.O. Box 459
New York, NY 10163
Phone: 212-870-3400
Website: http://www.alcoholics-
anonymous.org

BACCHUS Peer Education Network and GAMMA

P.O. Box 100043
Denver, CO 80250
Phone: 303-871-0901
Fax: 303-871-0907
Website: http://www.bacchusgamma.org
E-mail: admin@bacchusgamma.org

Center on Alcohol Advertising

Trauma Foundation
San Francisco General Hospital
Bldg. 1, Room 300
San Francisco, CA 94110
Phone: 415-821-8209
Fax: 415-821-8202
Website: http://www.tf.org/tf/
index.html
E-mail: tf@tf.org

Do It Now Foundation
Box 27568
Tempe, AZ 85285-7568
Phone: 480-736-0599
Fax: 480-736-0771
Website: http://www.doitnow.org/
pages/nowhome2.html
E-mail: email@doitnow

FACE® Truth and Clarity on Alcohol
105 W. Fourth St.
Clare, MI 48617
Toll-Free: 888-822-3223
Fax: 989-386-3532
Website: http://
www.faceproject.org/
whatsnewpage.html
E-mail: faceproject@factproject.org

Higher Education Center for Alcohol and Other Drug Prevention
Education Development Center, Inc.
55 Chapel Street
Newton, MA 02158
Toll-Free: 800-676-1730
Phone: 617-618-2285
Website: http://www.edc.org/hec
E-mail: HigherEdCtr@edc.org

Join Together
One Appleton St., 4th Floor
Boston, MA 02116-5223
Phone: 617-437-1500
Fax: 617-437-9394
Website: http://
wwwjointogether.org/home
E-mail: info@jointogether.org

Mothers Against Drunk Driving (MADD)
National Headquarters
511 E. John Carpenter Freeway,
Suite 700
Irving, TX 75062
Toll-Free: 800-438-6233
Phone: 214-744-6233
Fax: 972-869-2206
Website: http://www.madd.org

National Center on Addiction and Substance Abuse at Columbia University
633 Third Ave., 19th Floor
New York, NY 10017-6706
Phone: 212-841-5200
Website: http://
www.casacolumbia.org/absolutenm/
templates/
article.asp?articleid=287&zoneid=32

National Council on Alcoholism and Drug Dependence, Inc.
20 Exchange Place, Suite 2902
New York, NY 10005-3201
Toll-Free: 800-622-2255
Phone: 212-269-7797
Fax: 212-269-7510
Website: http://www.ncadd.org
E-mail: national@ncadd.org

National Safety Council
1121 Spring Lake Drive
Itasca, IL 60143
Toll-Free: 800-621-7619
Phone: 630-285-1121
Fax: 630-284-1315
Website: http://www.nsc.org
E-mail: info@nsc.org

Red Ribbon Works
617 East McBee Avenue
P.O. Box 10203
Greenville, SC 29603
Phone: 864-467-4099
Fax: 864-467-4102
Website: http://www.redribbon
works.org

Students Against Destructive Decisions (SADD)
Box 800
Marlboro, MA 01752
Toll-Free: 877-SADD-INC (723-3462)
Fax: 508-481-5759
Website: http://
www.saddonline.com

Resources For Children Of Alcoholics

Adult Children of Alcoholics
P.O. Box 3216
Torrance, CA 90510
Phone: 310-534-1815 Message
Only
Website: http://
www.adultchildren.org
E-mail: info@adultchildren.org

Al-Anon/Alateen Family Groups
1600 Corporate Landing Parkway
Virginia Beach, VA 23454
Toll-Free: 888-425-2666
Phone: 757-563-1600
Fax: 613-723-0151
Website: http://www.al-anon
.alateen.org
E-mail: WSO@al-anon.org

**National Association for
Children of Alcoholics**
11426 Rockville Pike, Suite 100
Rockville, MD 20852
Toll-Free: 888-55-4COAS (2627)
Phone: 301-468-0985
Fax: 301468-0987
Website: http://
www.childrenofalcoholics.org
E-mail: nacoa@nacoa.org

Resources About Alcohol-Related Birth Defects

The Arc of the United States
1010 Wayne Ave., Suite 650
Silver Spring, MD 20910
Phone: 301-565-3842
Fax: 301-565-5342
Website: http://www.thearc.org
E-mail: Info@TheArc

**National Organization on
Fetal Alcohol Syndrome
(NOFAS)**
900 17th Street, N.W.
Suite 910
Washington, DC 20006
Toll-Free: 800-66NOFAS (66327)
Phone: 202-785-4585
Fax: 202-466-6456
Website: http://www.nofas.org
E-mail: information@nofas.org

**National Center on Birth
Defects and Developmental
Disabilities (NCBDDD)**
Fetal Alcohol Syndrome Prevention
Section
Centers for Disease Control and
Prevention
4770 Buford Highway N.E.
MSF-49
Atlanta, GA 30341-3724
Phone: 770-488-7370
Fax: 770-488-7361
Website: http://www.cdc.gov/
ncbddd

MADD Youth Alcohol Use Prevention Programs

Protecting You Protecting Me (PYPM)

Junior and senior high school students teach MADD's classroom-based alcohol use and safety prevention curriculum to elementary students in grades 1–5. Both the teen peer helpers and children learn about the risks of under-age alcohol use, adolescent brain development, and vehicle safety skills.

Multimedia Shows

MADD produces multi-media school assembly programs for elementary, middle, and high school students that use the latest DVD technology to incorporate current movie, music video, and television segments into a powerful prevention message. Showcased on three 15'x45' screens and using stories of youth who have made good and bad decisions about alcohol, the shows illustrate the lasting consequences of alcohol use and emphasize the importance of making healthy choices.

Youth In Action (YIA)

Youth In Action is MADD's community-based program that engages high school students in the prevention of underage drinking. This service-oriented leadership program trains students on how to implement projects designed to limit youth access to alcohol. Instead of targeting students with their message, YIA teams partner with law enforcement and adults to help create a community environment where underage drinking is not considered a rite of passage. Activities include making sure store clerks check IDs, finding out if adults will buy beer for minors, and talking to police officers about the importance of enforcing underage drinking laws.

Power Camps

MADD's summer youth leadership power camps provide an opportunity designed to help high school students develop advocacy skills, interact with other teen leaders, and learn about environmental change to make a difference in their schools and communities.

AlcoholEdu for High School

In partnership with online education provider Outside the Classroom, MADD co-created AlcoholEdu for High School, a science-based, non-opinionated online course that teaches youth about alcohol, its effects on the body, and its place in high school culture. It provides the facts youth need to determine the role alcohol may or may not play in their life. It also helps youth understand the secondary effects of high-risk drinking to help them keep themselves, their friends, and community safe.

UMADD

A UMADD chapter is a university, campus-based, student chapter comprised of student leaders concerned about underage drinking, high-risk (binge) drinking, and impaired driving. UMADD chapters are dedicated to finding solutions to these problems by involving both the campus and community. Students are encouraged to advocate for change on campus and in their towns as they encounter misperceptions and challenges through educational, systemic, and community policy change.

Mothers Against Drunk Driving (MADD)

National Headquarters
511 E. John Carpenter Freeway, Suite 700
Irving, TX 75062
Toll-Free: 800-438-6233
Phone: 214-744-6233
Fax: 972-869-2206
Website: http://www.madd.org

Index

Index

Page numbers that appear in *Italics* refer to illustrations. Page numbers that have a small 'n' after the page number refer to information shown as Notes at the beginning of each chapter. Page numbers that appear in **Bold** refer to information contained in boxes on that page (except Notes information at the beginning of each chapter).